WEAPON OF CHOICE

MATTHEW FORD

Weapon of Choice

*Small Arms and the Culture
of Military Innovation*

HURST & COMPANY, LONDON

First published in the United Kingdom in 2017 by
C. Hurst & Co. (Publishers) Ltd.,
41 Great Russell Street, London, WC1B 3PL
© Matthew Ford, 2017
All rights reserved.
Printed in India

A Cataloguing-in-Publication data record for this book
is available from the British Library.

ISBN: 9781849046503 *hardback*

This book is printed using paper from registered sustainable
and managed sources.

www.hurstpublishers.com

CONTENTS

ACKNOWLEDGEMENTS

I would like to offer my sincere thanks to everyone I have worked with in academia, at the Royal Armouries and at the UK's Ministry of Defence.

In particular, the following people have generously offered their time and expertise, for which I am extremely grateful: David Vassallo, David Parker, Pete Warden, Roy Brenton and Ian Passingham. I thank John Starling for helping me navigate and access the Ezell Archive at Cranfield University. I thoroughly enjoyed long discussions on small arms matters with David Benest, Tony Thornburn, Alex Watts and William F. Owen. I am particularly grateful to Major-general Colin Shortis, who helped me understand the decision-making on the adoption of SA80. Dr Dick Cave and Bob Evans have been instrumental in the latter parts of my research efforts, and I would like to thank them for encouraging me to work on more recent issues on small arms.

I would also like to thank a number of former RSAF employees and apprentices, including: Frank Vowles, Geoff Ellis, Paul Ellis, Ken Wilkes, Malcolm Slater, John Henshaw and Ray Tuthill. Each of them has been very generous with their time, helping me to understand what it was like to work at Enfield and offering me invaluable insights into the problems of large-scale small arms manufacturing.

In the early days of my research, there were a number of people who were crucial to making this project possible. All connected to the Royal Armouries, these people made research fun while keeping me true to my salt. I would particularly like to thank the last custodian of the MOD Pattern Room and now editor of *Jane's Infantry Weapons*, Richard Jones. Apart from making me lug boxes of weapons from place to place while the National Firearms Centre was being set up, Richard gave me the benefit of his exhaustive firearms' knowledge. Writing about small arms is made complicated by the unwillingness of commentators to cite primary sources and the use of the Internet to propagate all sorts of myths. Richard helped me navigate my way through the pitfalls and kept me on the straight and narrow.

Apart from Richard, Jonathan Ferguson, curator of firearms at the National Firearms Centre, has regularly made time for lively and sometimes heated discussion. I would also like to thank my fellow honorary historical consultant colleagues at the Royal Armouries, Professor David Williams and David Penn. Both have generously given their time and offered detailed and invaluable observations. I would also like to thank the librarians at the Royal Armouries and especially Philip Abbot and Stuart Ivinson as well as a fellow regular reader in the library, Stuart Taylor. All of these people helped me stay focused on my research. Thanks go to them all.

A number of academic colleagues have also given their time to help me bring this project to fruition. To start, I would like to thank my PhD supervisor, Dr John Stone. Given the subject matter, most academics would not have been so generous, but John created an intellectual space that allowed me to take guns seriously. I am very grateful to him for this. Apart from John, I would also like to thank: Professor Anthony King, Professor John Buckley, Assistant Professor Matthew Barlow and Drs Tim Gale, Phillip Blood, Glenn Flint, Jeff Michaels, Andrew Hargreaves and Patrick Rose. I should also thank two very smart students, Jeremy Levett and Alexander Gould, who found a couple of things I did not have time to identify. Thanks also go to my colleagues at the University of Hull and the University of Sussex. I'd especially like to single out Dr Anna Stavrianakis and Professor Jan Selby for taking the time to read and comment on my manuscript.

Lastly, I'd like to thank my family and especially my mum, Gillie, and my daughter, Sarah; but most importantly, my wife Dr Sally Drayton.

Sally made this project. This book is dedicated to her.

LIST OF ABBREVIATIONS

ABC	America–Britain–Canada
A/CEAD	Assistant Chief Engineer Armament Design
ADE	Armament Design Establishment
BAR	Browning Automatic Rifle
BAOR	British Army of the Rhine
BBC	Britain–Belgium–Canada
BJSM	British Joint Services Mission
BSA	Birmingham Small Arms Company
CEAD	Chief Engineer Armament Design
CGS	Chief of the General Staff
CIGS	Chief of the Imperial General Staff
CISA	Chief Inspector of Small Arms
CS(M)	Controller Supplies (Munitions)
DCIGS	Deputy Chief of the Imperial General Staff
DGofA	Director General of Artillery
DInf	Director of Infantry
DMT	Director of Military Training
DofA (SA)	Director of Artillery (Small Arms)
DoD	Department of Defense
DWD	Director of Weapons and Development
EM-1	Experimental Model No. 1
EM-2	Experimental Model No. 2
FAL	Fusil Automatique Léger
FARELF	Far East Land Forces
FN	Fabrique Nationale d'Armes de Guerre: Belgian manufacturer
GPMG	General Purpose Machine Gun

LIST OF ABBREVIATIONS

GSR	General Staff Requirement
H&K	Heckler & Koch: German manufacturer
IGO	Inspector Government Ordnance
IRA	Irish Republican Army
IW	Individual Weapon
IFV	Infantry Fighting Vehicle
LMG	Light Machine Gun
LSW	Light Support Weapon
MCV	Mechanised Combat Vehicle
MG	Machine Gun
MGO	Master General of Ordnance
MMG	Medium Machine Gun
MOD	Ministry of Defence
NATO	North Atlantic Treaty Organisation
OWPC	Organisation and Weapons Policy Committee
RSAF	Royal Small Arms Factory
SA80	Section Small Arms Post 1980
SAA	Small Arms Ammunition
SAG	Small Arms Group
SSK	Sociology of Scientific Knowledge
SLEM	Self-Loading Experimental Model
SLR	Self-Loading Rifle
SMG	Sub-Machine Gun
SMLE	Short Magazine Lee–Enfield
SST	Social Shaping of Technology
STANAG	NATO standardisation agreements
VCIGS	Vice Chief of the Imperial General Staff

GLOSSARY OF TERMS

Arme Blanche	Cavalry armed with a cutting weapon like a sword rather than a firearm.
Bolt	A cylindrical sliding bar for closing the breech of a weapon. Typically the bolt is hollow so that, when the rifle is cocked, a striker (sometimes also known as a firing pin) contained within the mechanism is held under tension by a mainspring away from the firing chamber. Upon pressing the trigger, the tension on the mainspring is released, allowing the striker to move towards the firing chamber where it strikes the rear of the ammunition.
Bore	The internal diameter of the barrel. See also calibre.
Bullpup Rifle	A weapon that has been shortened by the removal of the butt and the repositioning of the trigger house mechanism forward of the magazine. Typically, the barrel of a bullpup design is comparable to that of a conventionally configured rifle.
Calibre	The nominal internal diameter of the bore of the barrel.
Clip	A holder that contains a number of cartridges for the magazine of a rifle. On loading, the clip and cartridges are inserted into the magazine and the clip drops out of the bottom when the magazine is empty.
Engagement Range	The range at which combatants come into shooting contact with the enemy.
Handiness	A term used by designers to refer to how ergonomic a weapon might be.

Kinetic Energy	Kinetic Energy is the energy possessed by a body by virtue of its being in motion. It is calculated by multiplying half the body's mass by the square of its velocity.
Momentum	Momentum is the force possessed by a body by virtue of its being in motion. It is defined as mass multiplied by velocity.
Muzzle Velocity	The velocity of the projectile at the muzzle of the gun.
Optical Sight	A sight that provides optical magnification, sometimes also known as a telescopic sight
Rifling	Spiral grooving inside the barrel of the weapon used to make the projectile spin around its axis. This has the effect of making the projectile more stable in flight. Rifling is usually measured in terms of one turn in a certain distance e.g. one turn in 22 inches (a one in 22 turn).
Rounds per minute	The number of firing cycles undertaken by an automated fire and feed weapon.

INTRODUCTION

FROM MY COLD, DEAD HANDS

... it didn't quite cross my mind that, you know, we had small guns and they had big guns. A gun is a gun.

Abdul Hajji, Kenyan businessman[1]

At 12.30 p.m. on Saturday, 21 September 2013, four gunmen from the Somali militant group al-Shabaab launched an attack on the Westgate Mall in Nairobi, Kenya. The attackers entered the building from two directions, the main entrance and the ramp of the mall's car park, before herding the shoppers around the complex, indiscriminately firing AK-47 Kalashnikov rifles and throwing hand grenades to kill sixty-seven people and injure a further 175. With the Kenyan security services failing to isolate the building or organise and coordinate a response, police officers and citizens like Abdul Hajji made a number of successful attempts to rescue groups of shoppers.

Eventually securing an outer perimeter, the Kenyan Army's first attempt to resolve the situation by force resulted in a number of soldiers being shot and to the conclusion that the attackers had 'an arsenal in there'.[2] The Kenyans continued to attack the four defenders at regular intervals, but over the course of three days their efforts proved unsuccessful. When they eventually cornered the terrorists in a part of the mall, the security forces decided to use some kind of explosive device to kill the al-Shabaab gunmen without further recourse to close quarter battle.

The Islamist militants that launched this attack had tried to avoid killing Muslims. Despite this, the subsequent killing spree resulted in the deaths of people from all races and religions. Guns had been a great equaliser, empowering the terrorists to produce mass terror but at the same time fortifying those civilians who intervened to rescue the trapped shoppers. While the AK-47 might have come to symbolise the plight of those trying to upend the international system, it was the pistol in the hands of Kenyans like Abdul Hajji that echoed the call of Charlton Heston and the American National Rifle Association to protect freedom and defend the safety of the ordinary citizen.

Although rare, these scenarios increasingly frame the preparations of those working in counter-terrorism and the military. The Unmanned Aerial Vehicle—the iconic weapon of the Global War on Terror—captures the headlines. But terror attacks in Paris and Brussels and battles with the Islamic State in Syria and Iraq are intimately associated with access to light weapons and small arms. Widely available and cheap, small arms thus retain a utility that many commentators might assume has been lost given the widespread attention typically paid to more advanced technology.

For those soldiers charged with delivering victory on the ground, this reality is well understood. A gun is not just a gun. The battlefield challenges that combatants will face are varied. Countering terror attacks requires different tactics and weapons from those used when fighting a conventional army. In such circumstances, guns may be similar in form and function, but their utility and effectiveness has to be understood in relation to the context of their use. This book shows that soldiers, engineers, scientists, bureaucrats, alliance partners and industry recognise this as they design and manufacture equipment for various roles and purposes. Making these different perspectives fully transparent, however, requires a broader investigation into the sociological factors that intimately frame design and selection.

What emerges out of this investigation is the way that even the simplest of technologies is deeply contested. Indeed, given the degree to which the perspectives of each of these groups differ, in many respects it is more appropriate to think of technical artefacts as social constructs. The advantage of this approach is that the layers of meaning embodied by small arms are revealed. Guns aren't just weapons; they are also status symbols. Industry shapes fashions in weapon design, framing soldier preferences. Lethality is subject to a number of interpretations, and ballistic science has not determined weapon selection. Bureaucrats are not always the bumbling incompetents they are typically described as being, and despite its status as a superpower, the United States has not always had its way in NATO discussions on technology. Above all else, what this book shows is how small arms reflect and contain the power relations within and between the military and its partners in the military–industrial complex.

Explaining how small arms come into existence, what shapes their design and why different weapons are selected thus constitutes the spine of this book. Starting with the Anglo-American debates of the Second World War, small arms innovation is placed into a post-1945 context where transatlantic disagreements were intimately linked to NATO's emerging defence–industrial policy and its ability to generate credible conventional forces. The American experience of developing small arms can only be properly contextualised in reference to British and subsequently NATO design choices. An exploration of how the perspectives of all those involved in small arms development map together will lead to a comprehensive analysis of military innovation from the battlefield to the back office.

This book offers a new perspective on the military's attitudes towards change by showing how one of the simplest weapons in the inventory gets into the hands of soldiers. However, it also establishes a coordinate from which we can compare and contrast the way mundane weapons like small arms are developed with the way that more sophisticated weapons come into service. In contrast to other books on military–technical change, this sociologically informed investigation shows how the balance of power between soldiers, civil servants and industry has shifted in favour of industry, predominantly in the UK but also in the United States. The result is that industry now finds it easier to treat the military as consumers, constructing their needs and getting them interested in buying equipment that may otherwise be unnecessary. They do this by playing with what might be described as soldier status anxiety in the hope of upselling equipment. Government policy has played into this. This book prompts us to think through how such policies frame technology choice and what the implications may be in terms of democratic accountability and strategic choice.

Thinking about small arms

There are a number of ways to interpret and understand small arms. These range from a concern for technical and engineering detail to the gendered and cultural significance of the firearm.[3] Some studies explore the technological trajectory of small arms.[4] Others try to explain why firearms emerged in one part of the world before some other.[5] In the United States, access to small arms is a constitutional right but also a source of great social concern following a number of horrific attacks by psychologically disturbed individuals.[6] On the libertarian right, the question is what would happen if Westgate Mall took place in the United States. For the liberal left, gun ownership has already led to a number of Westgate Malls.

Identifying what is politically, culturally and organisationally significant out of the intricate technical detail on small arms is crucial for understanding how these weapons have evolved since the Second World War. Finding ways to sift through the details and develop a meaningful story is hard. After all, any one gun appears to do much the same as any other. Guns are broadly similar in form. Weapons in similar classes weigh similar amounts and are apparently designed to work in similar ways. In these circumstances, the challenge is to identify what is relevant here and what is not. From the lay perspective, it is difficult to tell. From a strictly engineering point of view, however, identifying these specificities is critical. If everything works according to the design specifications set out by the engineer, then the firearms user can expect combustion to occur within inches of their face. Precise tolerances can mean the difference between life and death: not just for the target but also for the person operating the weapon.

As far as engineers are concerned, then, the broader cultural context that frames technical choice is not as important as the calculations that go into constructing the gun. For centuries, engineers and gunsmiths have sought to find technically viable responses to difficult combat and battlefield problems.[7] In its narrowest sense, this has resulted in engineers trying to find the technical means to get a projectile to hit a target at a certain range with a reasonable chance of achieving a desired effect. Looked at this way, gun design is simply a matter of defining the target type, the range to target, the handling preferences of the weapon and then identifying the technological solution that addresses these considerations.[8] In this context, the engineering is a question of tensile strengths, recoil energies and muzzle velocities. In the popular imagination, the result of these efforts ought to be the best possible weapon given the parameters that have been set.

This mode of thinking fits with a form of analysis that looks at the evolution of small arms as a process of ironing out technical difficulties before reaching an ideal form of weapon. In small arms terms, the exemplar of this appears to be the assault rifle. Thus for those that are interested in the nuts and bolts of contemporary firearms, the conventional story usually starts with a discussion of the Sturmgewehr 44.[9] The Sturmgewehr 44 (StG44) was a creation of the Nazi war machine during the Second World War. Combining some of the features of a rifle and a sub-machine gun, the concepts that under-pinned the StG44 went on to frame the imagination of Russian and American engineers, and according to many, they led, almost inevitably, to the produc-tion of the AK-47 and the M16.[10] Neither the AK-47 nor the M16 necessarily had the range or lethality of a large calibre rifle like the Second World War M-1 Garand, but the volume of fire these assault rifles produced allowed the infantryman to put into practice more flexible tactics.

With the adoption of the assault rifle, soldiers finally had a technology able to meet the challenges of modern battle. Industrialisation, barbed wire and the availability of firepower-intensive weapons had created a stalemate on the battlefield.[11] To survive and overcome the enemy in this increasingly lethal environment, a new system of tactics needed to be developed. This new system of tactics first emerged during the First World War. Involving the careful use of firepower so as to keep the defenders' heads down, the attackers could then move from cover to cover before making a final rush on an enemy position. When combined with artillery, Stephen Biddle describes these fire and move-ment tactics as the 'Modern System'.[12] Difficult to implement, this system depended on a set of cultural, social and political variables that, according to Biddle, were typically only available in societies that valued 'extensive inde-pendent decision making'.[13] Unsurprisingly, then, there was a strong relation-ship between mastering this modern system and modes of governance that valued democracy.

Working within this line of reasoning, the introduction of the assault rifle was simply a case of optimising technologies so as to further enable a Modern System of tactics first identified during the First World War. Achieving this goal was dependent on developing the necessary technological knowhow and, just as crucially, forms of society that could produce independent decision-makers. For just as the technology made modern tactics possible, so society made it possible to field soldiers capable of using that equipment.

For many, this is a convincing story. As you will see in this book, however, the idea that the emergence of new infantry weapons was simply a case of technology catching up with social values and a recognised system of tactics does not do justice to the process of developing the assault rifle. Although these weapons were the product of deeply social, even cultural processes, a country's social structure and mode of government did not inevitably result in the development of certain types of equipment. The United States was arguably most likely to adopt infantry weapons suitable for fire and move-ment. And yet the StG44 emerged out of Nazi Germany and the AK-47 from

Communist Russia. After the Second World War, British engineers pioneered the development of the assault rifle even as Americans resisted the change. The British may have opted to adopt a self-loading rifle in 1957, but this was only because the Americans refused to accept the logic of an assault rifle.

The ambivalence of the Americans regarding the development of an assault rifle can be explained in a number of ways. One of the most powerful forms of analysis links the rifle to national identity and martial prowess.[14] Reflecting the fighting spirit of the American soldier and their commitment to overcome the enemy, the rifle resonated with a national identity framed by the Minutemen of the Revolution and the pioneers of the 'First West'.[15] Unlike other societies that sought to control access to firearms, the United States enshrined the right to bear arms in the Second Amendment. The rifle was a 'distinctively American' weapon, symbolising a country that valued freedom and individual spirit.[16]

Tying the values of freedom and individualism to a particular rifle would make giving up certain types of weapon much harder. The exigencies of the Second World War and the confrontation with Communists during the Cold War would nevertheless make the transference of allegiance from the 1906 Springfield to the M-1 Garand to the M16 that much easier. While the AK-47 formed the technological vanguard around which communist ideology might be advanced, the M16 represented American ambitions to defend Western democracy.[17] Lightweight and built from aluminium and modern plastics, the M16 took on the Communists in Vietnam and continues to go head to head, in various forms, with insurgents wielding the AK-47.

Just as the rifle can be viewed as a symbol of national struggle, it can also frame and mark military identity.[18] In this respect, the interest in identifying the firearms used by the US Navy SEAL team responsible for the killing of Osama Bin Laden testifies to the enduring place of small arms in the popular imagination of Americans.[19] It does not, however, represent a fascination with the gory details of how one of America's most wanted terrorists was eventually killed. It instead serves to connect American citizens to their armed forces, reminding them that older, more intimate expressions of combat and killing still retain their fascination and place in the warrior code, irrespective of the fetish for remote war.

At its deepest and most critical levels, investigating small arms can tell us something about the politics of life itself. Thus, for Michael Shapiro, the technical details of a weapon, 'its ballistics and delivery system', offer insights into 'the state's approach to valuing, excluding, and sustaining versus eliminating forms of life'.[20] By examining the development of weapons like the assault rifle, we begin to learn something deeper about whether society is prepared to provide the necessary resources for its armed forces. At the same time, the balance of investments in various technologies tells us something about whether society expects its armed forces to fight at close quarters or prefers remote war; whether it respects the Geneva Conventions or doesn't. As a result, technology becomes the framing device for determining not just the limits of the battlefield/bureaucracy but also the imaginations of those who seek to control and manage it.[21]

Of all the approaches that might have relevance to the study of firearms, however, this book focuses on what small arms development tells us about military innovation. In the first instance, I will explain why different assault rifles were adopted by different NATO powers. This will show that there was more going on in weapon development than just responding to battlefield demands. I will then examine what changes in small arms tell us about the distribution of power among the different social groups within NATO's military–industrial complexes. This will show how the power of soldiers, engineers, scientists, bureaucrats, alliance partners and industrialists has changed relative to each other since the Second World War. In the process, this will reveal how small arms are socially constructed. Lastly, I will ask what a detailed investigation into small arms tells us about theories of military innovation.

Research design

My goal is to investigate small arms development and use this to evaluate processes of military innovation. To do so, I trace the discussions of certain types of weapons between different users, experts and professions. The book works chronologically from 1900 to the present day, but it is also organised thematically around the innovation lifecycle from battlefield to industrialist. This analysis is made possible by drawing on previously untapped archival sources from the United Kingdom, Canada and the United States, as well as interviews with a large number of soldiers, officers and industrialists. The archives include: the National Archive, London; the Royal Armouries Archive, Leeds; the Royal Artillery Museum, Woolwich; the Zuckerman Archive, University of East Anglia; the Churchill Archives, Churchill College, Cambridge; the Cherwell Papers, Nuffield College, Oxford; the Liddell Hart Centre for Military Archives, King's College London; the Library and Archives Canada; the Laurier Centre for Military, Strategic and Disarmament

Studies, Ontario; the Army Heritage and Education Center, Carlisle Barracks, United States; and the NATO archives in Brussels.

The organising principle underpinning the structure of my argument is found in the work of Keith Grint and Steve Woolgar, who advance what they describe as an 'Anti-essentialist theory of technology' in their book *The Machine at Work*.[22] Typical theories of technology locate some design property within the artefact itself. Consequently, the capacity of a technology is defined by its physical characteristics. What such an approach implies is that an interpretation of an artefact must bear some relationship to the artefact's inherent design characteristics in order to be valid. By taking an anti-essentialist approach, however, the way different representations of a technology are constructed by different social groups involved in the design, production and use of an artefact can be exposed for examination. Such an approach is not based on the assumption that a technology has an essential capacity, because that is precisely what is being argued over by all those engaged in its creation and use. That is not to claim that machines do not have effects. Rather it is to observe that the process of defining what those effects are is a decidedly social process where different actors must persuade, cajole or ignore the interpretations of other social groups as they insist on the truth of their perspective. As an approach, Grint and Woolgar invoke us to think through the different interpretations of a weapon's capability and ask 'who are we to believe, and why?'[23]

For the purposes of this study, the anti-essentialism of *The Machine at Work* offers a useful heuristic—rather than a rigidly applied method—for examining how representations of small arms emerge from the considerations of different social groups as they seek to assert themselves and their values. Such an approach serves as a useful point of contrast with existing approaches to military innovation, which take as settled the essential properties of a technology and as a result close down further empirical investigations prematurely. Chapter 1 thus starts by examining the literature on military innovation, exposing the strengths and weaknesses of existing ways of thinking while introducing the core concepts found in the Social Shaping of Technology (SST) literature. SST literature then forms the theoretical basis for developing each of the chapters in the book as the argument progresses from front line to back office. Later chapters explore the perspectives, values and concerns of those actors engaged in the various stages of the innovation cycle. Lastly, to further help readers orientate themselves, each chapter makes limited use of a selection of ideas drawn from the social sciences with a view to deepening the analysis and further exposing the tensions in the process of innovation.

Chapter 2 focuses on the user and their perspectives on battle. Equipment, tactics and techniques are being designed to solve a particular military problem. In order to help navigate through the different user perspectives on firearms, I break down military discussion of these weapons into a matrix of factors that reappear throughout the book: marksmanship, firepower, willpower and stopping power. By doing this, I can more clearly show that there are arguments going on within the user community about weapons and tactics, and at the same time help readers get to grips with the complex and contested nature of small arms development.

As we move away from the battlefield, other voices start to become influential. Chapter 3, for example, introduces engineers into the innovation cycle. Although engineers are typically overlooked in existing approaches to military innovation, new technologies would not be possible without them. That is not to say engineers don't produce different types of challenges. Chapter 4 therefore considers the way scientists are recruited into the innovation cycle to settle the theoretical problems created by engineering solutions. Lethality is a concept employed to determine whether British or American small arms were more deadly, but this chapter will show that the term is a highly contested and falls between a range of scientific, medical and engineering disciplines. The problem of defining lethality could not be resolved from within the scientific community. Consequently, as we see in Chapter 5, the question of what defined lethality was answered through bureaucratic rather than scientific processes. Chapter 6 explores the way that the United States tried to use its power to determine how the science of lethality would apply to future small arms innovations within NATO. What this chapter also shows, however, is that apparently insignificant actors can out-game dominant actors, realigning the network of alliance partners so as to deliver socio-technical change in unexpected ways. Chapter 7 finally introduces industry into the picture and explores how soldiers are turned into consumers. Drawing on the British Army's experience of privatisation under the Thatcher government, this chapter shows how industry manipulates soldier status anxiety in ways that encourage the purchase of weapons that other expert communities—including other soldiers from within the Army itself—would otherwise not recommend. This indicates that soldiers are subject to the whims of fashion. Chapter 8 draws these points together, explores what the book says about military innovation studies and argues that socio-technical change is driven as much by fashion as it is by military effectiveness.

Before we can authoritatively comment on whether any of this makes a contribution to discussions of military innovation, Chapter 1 explains the existing literature in the field. This chapter forms the framework for evaluating what small arms tell us about the military–industrial complex's attitude towards change.

1

TECHNOLOGY AND CULTURE

GUNS AND INNOVATION

Let us not hear of generals who conquer without bloodshed. If a bloody slaughter is a horrible sight, then that is a ground for paying more respect to war ...

Carl von Clausewitz, *On War*[1]

This book examines the twentieth century development of small arms in order to assess the nature of Western military innovation. Small arms are not ordinarily associated with revolutionary changes to the battlefield. In existence for centuries, these weapons are mature and appear to have improved only incrementally. As such, they are unlikely technologies for investigating the trajectory of military–technical change. Although cheap and unsophisticated, they are the weapons that have helped to unhinge Western strategy in Iraq, Afghanistan and elsewhere. Small arms thus constitute something of a paradox for those interested in innovation, technology and war: spectacular, hi-tech weapons like the drone may well capture the headlines but it is the infantry and their mundane rifles that are invariably left to secure the battlefield.

This is a particularly acute observation given that the prevailing assumption for many writers working on technology and change is that victory in war belongs to the masters of military innovation.[2] If armed forces fail to act on this single insight, then defeat in battle is all but certain. Those countries that develop superior technologies, technologies that help them to stay one step ahead of their adversaries, survive. Those that do not master the challenge eventually submit to the militarily stronger. To study military innovation is, therefore, to investigate the sources of state power and by implication to develop a deeper appreciation for the way the international system is ordered.

The irony of contemporary warfare, however, is the way in which a tenacious adversary has exploited terrain in such a way as to offset the huge advantages conferred by advanced technology.[3] Nowhere has this been more obvious than on the battlefields of Iraq and Afghanistan. Even as unmanned Predator drones loitered above, riflemen struggled to avoid roadside bombs below. High technologies have framed, enabled and captured the military imagination, offering the possibility of clean and decisive outcomes, just as the grimy infantryman has learnt to understand the truth of Clausewitz's observation about bloodshed and war. For it is the infantryman who has had to muddle through, finding unsophisticated solutions to the intractable military problems of counterinsurgency.[4]

Such observations are far from novel.[5] During the Cold War, even as the US Department of Defense (DoD) was perfecting the application of advanced technologies to deter the Soviet Union, US armed forces were fighting a difficult and ultimately unsuccessful counterinsurgency in Vietnam. The jungles and the desire to field a modern weapon that might counter the advantages of the AK-47 produced the conditions in which the M16 rifle could successfully be introduced into US service.[6] The underlying ideas for the M16, however, had been inspired by Anglo-American debates about small arms in the period immediately after the Second World War. These debates were not just about whether the M-1 Garand was to be replaced by the M-14 automatic rifle, but about which country would provide small arms to the whole of the NATO alliance.

Small arms were the trailblazer for NATO standardisation in general. If an agreement could not be reached over simple and mature technologies like small arms, then what hope was there for standardisation on more complex technologies? The resulting agreements, deeply political in nature, were fashioned by interventions from a number of different constituencies including Winston Churchill and would go on to frame Anglo-American and NATO defence–industrial policy. Understanding what shaped the way in which these and later agreements were reached offers an insight into the values of different NATO partners.

In this context, studying how the simplest and cheapest of technologies has evolved over time also offers us a yardstick for thinking about how more advanced technology change occurs. I do this by asking us to reflect on the way a number of different actors interlock and frame the technical problems associated with understanding the battlefield; interpreting user requirements, optimising killing, managing bureaucratic processes and working with alliance and industrial partners. As this book shows, making the innovation cycle explicit in this way helps to generate further and more challenging insights into the mechanics of power across the military–industrial complex. It also allows us to draw wider conclusions about the politics of military innovation, how technologies have spread in practice and why the West likes buying hi-tech equipment.[7]

Military innovation

Generating military power in ways that produce war-winning results is a subject that is of great interest to planners at the very heart of governments. It is no surprise, then, that the core literatures on military innovation were initially inspired by and paid for by government. Centred in the United States, Andrew Marshall, the director of the Office of Net Assessment (ONA), played a vital role in the emergence of this new literature.[8] Having started his career at RAND, Marshall went on to help establish the ONA within the US DoD in 1973.[9] Stimulated by failure in Vietnam and the conventional threat from the Warsaw Pact, the ONA was concerned with 'estimating the likely performance of one's armed forces against one's potential enemy' as part of a defence planning process.[10] The goal was to optimise investment decisions so as to increase the chances of success in war. By the mid-1970s, with the US military still struggling to recover from the shock of Vietnam, the US Department of Defense adopted what has become known as an Offset Strategy.[11] Stimulated by the ONA's analysis, this led to a new range of technologies that we now take for granted: intelligence, surveillance and reconnaissance (ISR) platforms like Unmanned Aerial Vehicles; improved battle management capabilities; tactical exploitation of space for ISR purposes; precision strike munitions like cruise missiles; and stealth technology.[12]

The problem facing the US DoD was deciding when to back a technology. Innovations took time to implement. Optimising investment was dependent on identifying which innovations were most likely to produce successful outcomes in the future. This meant linking innovation to some measure of battlefield performance. Read in this way, three conditions had to be met for a change to count as military innovation. First, innovation had to change the manner in which military formations functioned in the field. Secondly, an innovation had to be significant in scope and impact. Lastly, an innovation needed to result in greater military effectiveness.[13]

In the early 1970s, the challenge facing the ONA was the poor state of the existing analytical techniques for describing the nature of military effectiveness. Previous approaches had centred on comparing existing quantities of similar types of equipment or trying to work out what future equipment purchases might do to the balance of capability.[14] As far as Marshall was concerned, however, developing a more robust approach to modelling military change would involve understanding the decision-making processes within a particular country.[15] Validating the resultant models would depend on identifying historical examples of successful and not so successful change from a range of different countries across a set period of time. Marshall later sponsored a number of historians, led by Allan Millett and Williamson Murray, to identify the nature of military effectiveness in seven countries from 1914 through the inter-war period to 1945.[16]

Taking their cue from their ONA sponsors, Millett and Murray defined military effectiveness as 'the process by which armed forces convert resources into fighting power'. Maximum power would only come from the efficient use of the political will and physical resources available. Fighting power could be judged by the 'ability to destroy the enemy while limiting the damage that he can inflict in return'.[17] To explain effectiveness properly meant developing case studies that considered the 'non-quantifiable organisational attitudes, behaviours, and relationships that span a military organisation's full activities at the political, strategic, operational and tactical levels'.[18]

From the beginning, then, the analytical study of effectiveness was multi-dimensional and framed by material considerations to do with the harnessing of resources and identifying human factors that might help or hinder the process of fielding military capability. The challenge was to understand how effectiveness worked across the whole of the military organisation from top to bottom, such that tactical, operational and strategic activities could be harmonised towards realising one goal. Because the ONA was interested in projects that would have a significant impact, they were not prepared to invest in projects that produced incremental change. This almost inevitably skewed the focus of this emerging field of scholarship towards analysing change that Adam Grissom would later characterise as top-down innovation.[19] Only changes that harnessed the full potential of the military organisation could produce fundamental change, and only those with command or budgetary responsibilities could sanction this scale of activity.

That is not to say that academics agreed on how top-down innovation worked.[20] For some, the interaction between civilian and military authorities would provide the impulse for innovation.[21] Political classes looking to deliver coherent defence and security strategies could harness maverick officers to deliver new war-winning solutions to military problems. Alternatively, change might be produced out of the limited availability of resources combined with inter-service rivalry. In this model, different services would look to maintain their budget authority and control over their traditional missions. This fight produced the conditions for greater innovation.[22] The final model associated with this top-down approach to change focused on competition between branches of the same service providing the stimulus for innovation.[23] Here the focus was on aligning the thinking of leaders, mid-level officers and the institutional resources to ensure that innovation was entrenched and secure.

Military innovation studies has, then, traditionally viewed socio-technical change as a top-down process set and led by senior officers or civilians. More recently, however, scholars have turned this top-down approach on its head and pointed out that there are also processes of bottom-up innovation.[24] Scholars such as Theo Farrell, Terry Terriff and James Russell, for instance, have emphasised what they describe as military–technical adaptation in the face of the enemy.[25] In many respects, adaptation scholarship was born out of the decade-long counterinsurgency campaigns in Iraq and Afghanistan,[26] for this kind of change was stimulated by the demands of battle itself. As such, whereas innovation involved developing 'new technologies, tactics, strategies and structures ... adaptation involves adjusting existing military means and methods.'[27]

Although incremental in nature, Farrell et al. insisted that enough of this type of change could lead to comprehensive innovation. However, they did not consider it 'feasible or fruitful to draw too fine a distinction between adaptation and innovation.'[28] In particular, they disagreed with the criterion that innovative change had to be significant. From our point of view, the implication of these analytical niceties is that incremental and small-scale innovations, innovations that might occur across a whole range of dimensions from the strategic to the tactical, are worth studying.

The possibility that innovations might be stimulated by specific local conditions and lead to change in different parts of the organisation nonetheless takes military innovation studies in a new direction. Military planners, like Andrew Marshall, were looking to optimise investment decisions so as to maximise the potential for military effectiveness into the future. However, local innovations that occur in different parts of the organisation may lead to contradictions or inefficiencies. When looked at this way, adaptation by itself cannot produce the kind of future war-winning results that analysts like Marshall hoped to generate. For that to happen, adaptations would need to be nurtured and reproduced across the whole of the organisation. Such an approach to organisational change is clearly possible. Analytically speaking, however, adaptation is perfectly consistent with tactical success and strategic failure, a criticism that has been levelled at Western Coalition forces in Iraq and Afghanistan during the decade-long counterinsurgency of the early twenty-first century.[29]

There is a tension, therefore, between the traditional interpretations of military innovation and the more recent scholarship on adaptation. This is indicative of a deeper tension between military planners pressing to introduce wide-ranging innovative capabilities and the immediate demands of the armed forces.[30] In the past, historians and scholars of military innovation have typically explained this in terms of the inherently conservative nature of the armed forces.[31] Thus the slow take-up of the machine gun or the desire to maintain the lance and sword over the magazine rifle has been the product of highly regimented, hierarchical organisation structures.[32] More recently, a literature has developed that has sought to explain resistance to change as a product of a military culture that is not conducive to accepting new systems, techniques or technologies.

In many respects, the cultural explanations are compelling. It cannot be denied that technologies and techniques, organisational processes and routines are deeply cultural. Thomas Mahnken convincingly shows how US military intelligence possessed a great deal of technical intelligence about foreign innovations but continued to read this material in ways that mirrored their cultural predispositions.[33] Elizabeth Kier uses culture to explain the different doctrines of British and French armies, showing how the French preference for methodical engagements reflected a deeper attitude towards citizen soldiers and the Nation in Arms.[34] Cultural norms defined as 'intersubjective beliefs about the social and natural world' clearly have a role to play in defining 'actors, their situations, and the possibilities of action'.[35]

There are, however, two philosophical questions that emerge out of the turn to culture. The first relates to the place of technological artefacts themselves. Should technologies be understood as different from culture or simply as materialisations of culture? To understand the various meanings and interpretations of the rifle, we must place it within its cultural contexts. But the rifle is clearly more than an idea. Do we also need to think of it as an object with certain intrinsic capabilities, or are these capabilities themselves culturally defined?

The second question is concerned with whether culture constitutes the context for innovation or whether culture actually causes change to happen. Culture by itself lacks agency. Culture does not have the capacity to act. Soldiers, engineers and scientists need to act to cause change to happen. And yet the choices they make are clearly framed by the 'repertoire or "tool kit" of habits, skills, and styles' they possess.[36]

Bearing in mind the way these questions were deeply embedded into the literature on military effectiveness, it is no surprise that scholars who have sought cultural explanations for military innovation have generally sought to elide these philosophical matters. After all, the formula for effectiveness used by Millett and Murray took as its starting point the idea that military success would result from combining material resources and human factors. This binary set of concepts reflected the need of policymakers to use innovation for military-strategic purposes. As Dima Adamsky notes in his study of military culture and innovation, however, emerging technologies and culture are 'not independent of each other but interact in the context of organizational and strategic environments'.[37] Analytical explanations of innovation that can trace their roots back to reifications of the concepts of culture and technology are in danger, therefore, of producing tautological arguments. When seeking to explain innovation, the question at stake is not how to explain culture as cause, but to explore what various innovation practices say about the cultural tool kits that have incubated them.

Over the last thirty years, a number of approaches rooted in science and technology studies have emerged that have provided scholars with a route through the conundrum created by these two philosophical questions.[38] Supplementing other modes of study found in economics, political science or business studies, the literatures associated with the Social Shaping of Technology (SST) offer a way of thinking about innovation that avoids the reification of technology and culture and the latent determinisms that typically creep into an analysis of weapons.[39] Based on the ideas associated with social constructivism, SST refocuses attention on how design is the result of human choice and not simply resource limitations. This is achieved by locating the development of a technology and technique within a variety of social contexts. These social contexts can be defined in relation to those actors and social groups who have an interest in using, developing and sustaining these technologies.[40]

As a result, it becomes clearer that there is more than one culture framing innovation. Users, engineers, scientists, bureaucrats, politicians, alliance partners and industry all have perspectives on an emerging technology. In trying to define how these perspectives overlap in relation to new equipment, we need to understand the path dependency of the ideas, beliefs and values of each of these social groups. Taking an approach derived from the sociology of knowledge, SST treats each set of beliefs impartially. This makes visible the process by which a belief becomes acceptable or not to all of the groups concerned.[41] This in turn informs the choices that are made about selecting the features of a technology. This goes on until the technology has reached a stage where it is ready for testing with users, engineers or scientists, and can then go through another round of changes if necessary before being introduced.

This process is not neutral but reflects the power relations that exist between the social groups concerned. As such, the technology is a metaphor for the political machinations of the various groups involved in its design. Where agreement about a final iteration of a technology can be reached, SST scholars describe this as a closure mechanism.[42] This closure mechanism is a social process in which one of two things might happen. First, agreement might be reached between the social groups who have a self-declared interest in the technology on the final form of the equipment. Second, the technology or the problems it has been designed to solve may be re-described in such a way as to remove the need for disagreement between the various parties.

An approach to military–technical change based on the Social Shaping of Technology cuts across the top-down and bottom-up ways of thinking about innovation in a number of ways. By putting the technology at the centre of the discussion and mapping its longitudinal trajectory through stages of development, it becomes easier to see how a particular system reorders military organisations over time, throwing into relief the politics of the socio-technical system in micro-detail. Such an approach highlights the role of different expert communities without privileging any one of them. Instead, SST shows how different groups shape arguments and create appropriate conditions for delivering innovative change. This has the virtue of broadening debates over military culture and models that suggest the changes occur simply on the basis of either a top-down or bottom-up stimuli. In effect, by methodically working around the philosophical questions about culture, SST opens up a space to look at innovation debates as both a process of consensus-building and as asynchronous and contradictory.[43]

Industry and experts, knowledge and power

Civil–military relations and inter-service and intra-service rivalries have been extensively discussed in the innovation literature. However, the existing approaches to military innovation continue to make assumptions about the place of the bureaucracy as a mechanism for mediating and implementing change. In particular, they do not call out the possibility that expert communities within and beyond the bureaucracy may have a role to play in shaping military–technical change. By omitting these possibilities, forces that exist outside the bottom-up or top-down matrix of military innovation cannot be readily accounted for.

This contrasts with a number of studies by authors working on military–industrial policy and its associated complexes. At one end of this spectrum are those who are conscious that arms manufacturers can use their financial power to manipulate democratic decision-making.[44] At the other, the goal has been to optimise weapon procurement as part of a democratic process. Traditional scholarship on the military–industrial complex has, therefore, sought to test the extent to which private industry shapes procurement or whether the military have determined the predominant form of industry within society.[45] More recently, this scholarship has investigated specific companies, the emergence of private military contractors and the effects these organisations have had on wider security and society,[46] thereby highlighting the way extended communities play a role in military–technical change.

From our point of view, some of the most interesting scholars working in this area include Mary Kaldor, who has sought to explain how military equipment has a tendency to become unnecessarily complex in the absence of war.[47] Citing the development of the M-1 Abrams Tank and the F-111 bomber, Kaldor argues that these weapons were the product of an overly conservative military establishment working with a highly dynamic arms industry. Whereas the military preferred to stick with existing systems, industry constantly sought to keep and win new customers. This dynamic led to the perfection of technologies for their own sakes, producing what she describes as a baroque arsenal. While these weapons might sustain a relationship between the military and industry, the equipment that came out of this process did not address the actual security environment. Moreover, by consuming limited financial resources, alternative approaches to security were made impossible. Not only did the increased complexity of these weapons create the conditions for their failure on the battlefield, but they also distorted the economies of Western countries in undemocratic ways.

Working in the same vein as Kaldor, Tom McNaugher observes that a highly bureaucratised approach to development and a preference for 'gold-plated' weapons is counterproductive from a cost/performance perspective.[48] McNaugher argues that, for political and bureaucratic reasons, industrial partners 'underbid for development contracts' and 'thus retain the need to "get well" during production'.[49] This in turn tilts the development cycle in ways that may not lead to the most appropriate technology given the need to recoup development costs in sales. In particular, McNaugher notes that a lot of effort is put into squeezing out the last 10 per cent of performance from an innovation, but that this does not make sense if this consumes 30 per cent of the total budget.[50]

Similarly, in a study preceding his work on adaptation, Theo Farrell had observed that innovations might take on trajectories that could not be explained either as a result of warfighting or because of top-down decisions. The B-1 Bomber, for instance, had been cancelled by President Ford, but the US Air Force team responsible for innovation within the DoD continued with limited research into an updated B-2 programme.[51] Ronald Reagan's election heralded an opportunity for the US Air Force to breathe new life into this strategic bomber research programme. This led to the creation of proto-type strategic bombers. By the time the weapon was available for service, however, the Soviet Union had collapsed and the original rationale for the B-2 was no longer relevant. At this point, a new reason for acquiring the weapon had to be invented to justify its procurement. The First Gulf War helped the US Air Force construct such a battlefield requirement. Even as the acquisition process had become detached from the strategic rationale of the weapon, Congressional support ensured the survival of the programme despite the prevailing demand for a 1990s peace-dividend.

Developing the idea that there are several constituencies engaged in weapon design, Eric Prokosch and David Edgerton have the virtue of broadening the discussion away from focusing on industry and the military.[52] Prokosch, for example, details how engineering and scientific challenges framed weapon design for a range of different American munitions. By contrast, David Edgerton observes the way that research and development in the UK was fundamentally shaped by continued British government investment. From our point of view, both authors helpfully demonstrate that thinking about innovation needs to escape from the limitations created by a top-down or bottom-up framework.

By way of contrast with the more critical perspectives advanced by Kaldor, McNaugher and others, Peter Dombrowski, Eugene Gholz and Michael

O'Hanlon offer approaches aimed at solving innovation bottlenecks within the military industrial complex.[53] In *Buying Military Transformation*, which was written immediately after al-Qaeda's 9/11 attacks, Dombrowski and Gholz argue that only by unleashing the creative capacity of the free-market will the military acquire transformative innovations from industry. According to the two authors, this requires a relaxing of the regulatory framework as existing Congressional oversight hampers innovation and undermines the process by which industry gains the trust of the military.

Dombrowski and Gholz are confident that industry itself will not abuse military relationships for their own profit. In such circumstances, however, the only means to guarantee that industry does not try to oversell a solution is by applying the kinds of analytical techniques outlined by Michael O'Hanlon in his book *The Science of War*. Developing his argument in relation to a number of advanced technologies, O'Hanlon claims that the systematic application of operational analysis makes it possible to optimise innovations within budgetary constraints and still meet military needs. The underlying and policy-relevant argument in O'Hanlon's book is that mathematical modelling should be used to arbitrate between different solutions. Although not directly concerned with innovation per se, the ideas behind *The Science of War* nevertheless point towards the increasing importance of analysts, scientists and consultants working on the interface between industry, the military and government. While assumed to be impartial and objective, these groups themselves have interests that have not been accounted for in the literature on military innovation.

The possibility that new weapons could be acquired for a number of reasons that were not simply concerned with military necessity, but might have something to do with defence industrial policy, points to the need to think again about innovation in the armed forces. Weapon technologies need more than industrialists if they are to move from concept to reality. In the first instance, engineers have to design and test equipment. Scientists may be necessary to evaluate the performance of certain materials. Project managers and civilian analysts have a role to play in making sure that programmes work to budget, are delivered on time and efficiencies appropriately identified. On top of this, there are of course the preferences of alliance partners and private industry, both of which may have their own programmes of innovation under way.

The engagement between these different groups, organisations and professions is indicative of the complexity of weapon design. In the twentieth century, however, the involvement of these different communities can also be traced back to a process of professionalisation in the bureaucracy. According to one sociologist, even though public sector bureaucratisation can be viewed as distinct from its equivalent in private sector businesses, both groups have similar ambitions. Key among these is the desire of emerging professions within bureaucracies to gain control of their own work and declare evaluations that have been undertaken by those outside the profession as illegitimate.[54] To sustain this kind of autonomy, a process of socialisation occurs in which certain types of knowledge are produced and used to secure the profession from scrutiny. This is important for an emerging profession in the private sector, but is even more so in a public sector where the absence of a free market for services makes this process key to generating social status.[55]

The control and production of certain kinds of knowledge is a marker of professional status. Where a number of emerging professions are working on similar issues, a typical constructivist approach will look to show how these different kinds of knowledge overlay. In technology or innovation terms, professional knowledge might materialise in the form of an artefact, a new technique or process. Some of those working in the field of SST would observe that these emergent technologies are not just constructed between groups, but also reflect the relative power of different groups.[56] That is to say that knowledge is used to tilt the terms of a debate in an attempt to impose the perspective of one group over that of another. As Stephen Lukes would observe, the result is that one group might have to accept a solution it did not believe to be appropriate or have its choices framed in such a way as to exclude options that it may otherwise have preferred.[57]

If a social group can produce knowledge to advance their perspectives, then different groups can do the same to resist these efforts. Instead of reading this as simply a conservative culture resisting change, innovation may well represent a fight for access to resources or professional status. As such, the process is not necessarily about consensus-building.[58] Equally, for those working in the SST, it remains possible to produce innovations within the organisation in ways that do not involve any consensus whatsoever.

In this situation, an innovation may come into existence, but each social group that is party to the change feels no compulsion to accept the perspective of any of the other groups involved in its design. The contradictions of this position remain hidden within an artefact until the different interpretations are revealed in the struggle for power among those groups that have an interest in the technology. This does not mean that all interpretations are equally good. Rather, different groups will use their power to try and dictate the meaning of the artefact. According to this line of reasoning, then, power works through knowledge, such that 'truth isn't outside power ... [instead,] each society has its regime of truth, its "general politics" of truth'.[59]

Conclusion

Top-down and bottom-up approaches to military innovation have long been the dominant modes of investigation into military–technical change. In many respects, these analyses mirrored the dominant challenges facing the military at particular moments in time. Top-down approaches reflected the needs of the US military following defeat in Vietnam. With the support of Andrew Marshall and the ONA, the US military was eager to develop war-winning technology that could defeat the Soviet Union on the plains of West Germany. For US policymakers, the focus was on directing innovation towards solutions that could revolutionise the battlefield.

By contrast, bottom-up approaches have been strongly influenced by the tactical and operational considerations of counterinsurgencies in Iraq and Afghanistan. Less ambitious in nature than the analyses that emerged out of the 1970s and 1980s, the bottom-up mode of analysis has relevance to a study of small arms technology. Bottom-up approaches do, however, raise questions about what might produce resistance to change. Recent attempts to answer this question have invoked discussions of culture. Arguing that innovation is as much a cultural as a managerial, financial and resource-bounded issue has much to offer.

As a mode of investigation, however, the turn to culture is in danger of running into two deeply philosophical questions. These philosophical questions can be navigated by drawing on an alternative mode of sociological analysis known as the Social Shaping of Technology. SST recognises that there are multiple groups involved in technology design. These groups potentially see innovation in different ways. SST offers a method for helping us to understand how these views map together in such a way as to ensure that a technology reaches a degree of design stability. Invoking the idea of power relations and closure mechanisms, SST's inherent constructivism aims to show how a group's subjective interpretations become recognised social facts.

Producing social facts about emerging technologies creates an opportunity for different professional groups to either gain autonomy or assert their status. There is every incentive, then, to construct knowledge in order to shape innovation outcomes. As such, the idea that power might frame knowledge-production is a significant additional variable that studies in military innovation have yet to consider. With maybe only 120 different components to consider, an investigation into small arms makes it easier to trace the argument that different communities of soldiers, engineers, scientists, bureaucrats, alliance partners and industrialists use. In the process we can see how these various communities use knowledge to realise professional advantages. Following the development of the rifle is, therefore, a way to learn something about what a particular piece of equipment will do as well as the political preferences of those involved in its design and selection. By investigating the mundane, however, we also have an opportunity to develop a vista on the way more complex military technology is produced and in the process take a more critical perspective towards the existing literature on military innovation.

As we work through the various perspectives on the rifle, it will become clear that there have been all sorts of influences on weapon design and selection. Soldiers did not dictate what weapons would be developed and used despite their status as combatants. Engineers could not impose their technologies on bureaucrats. Scientists could not agree on the science of lethality and did not arbitrate between lesser and more efficient modes of killing. Strong alliance partners could not simply decide what technology weaker countries would select. Users did not always know best, and industrialists have not always provided the most innovative of technologies. No one social group at either the top or the bottom of the organisation could claim to have determined technological outcomes. This is the weakness of existing top-down and bottom-up approaches to military innovation.

2

BATTLEFIELD DEMANDS

THE VIEWS OF THE INFANTRY

The awful fact was that, with the short life expectancy of the infantry subaltern, few can have survived long enough to gain the experience and develop the battlefield instinct that would enable them to 'read the battle'.

Lieutenant Sydney Jary MC, 18 Platoon, 4th Battalion Somerset Light Infantry on the Normandy Campaign 1944[1]

Except for one or two of them, the men in Alpha Company were quietly, flippantly desperate for a rear job.

Tim O'Brien, G.I., Vietnam, 1969[2]

The ability to convey an experience of battle to others depends on the soldier's ability to survive in combat. In this respect, and contrary to the assertion of Professor Joanna Bourke, 'looking after number one' has typically been the first impulse of those facing extreme danger.[3] In such circumstances, soldiers have developed all sorts of strategies to help them increase their prospects of survival, from tripping over during the last 100-metre dash to an enemy position, to falling asleep during a heavy bombardment. Soldiers might slink off and desert their posts, undermine or disobey their commanders or they might act collectively and mutiny.[4] At the most extreme end of this spectrum, during the Vietnam War there were a number of examples of soldiers fragging, using a fragmentation grenade to kill their officers, a consideration that shaped the design of hand grenade selected by the US Marine Corps.[5]

Without a sense of collective allegiance, individual soldiers might strive to enhance their personal chance of survival while undermining the ability of the commander to deliver the military objective. Aware of this tendency, military authorities have throughout history developed a whole series of techniques to ensure that soldiers put the collective good of their unit in front of their own individual safety. Principal among these is the use of close surveillance to monitor the behaviour of the lower ranks, followed by coercive punishment to guarantee soldier compliance with orders. Codified in and backed by military law, these mechanisms would offer commanders the explicit means through which social control and military effectiveness might be maintained. At the same time, military authorities have also recognised the value of cultivating a strong sense of corporate and group identity among their men.[6] In contrast to the more coercive approach, here the ambition has been to inculcate cohesion for the sake of one's comrades or for God, Corps and Country.

The manner through which military authorities could assert control over the rank and file did not, however, rely purely on social engineering. Weapons themselves have embedded the social relations that framed soldier behaviour on the battlefield.[7] Small arms in particular have offered a means through which the soldier might achieve survival—by killing the enemy—and at the same time realise wider military objectives. Thus, for the soldier, 'the rifle is a good friend ...' Handled with care, 'It can save your life.'[8] In one technology, then, military authorities could unify the infantryman's desire to stay alive with the commander's ambition to achieve success in battle. Consequently, the rifle is deeply symbolic of the bargain between those who lead and those who follow, signifying the paternalistic relationship that usually exists in Western militaries between officers and men, governments and the armed forces.

From an engineer's perspective, the challenge has been to underpin this bargain with a sufficiently robust weapon that will keep the soldier alive and help the commander achieve their military objective. In this context, the central problem for the engineer is to identify, isolate and then control for the range of variables that shape the soldier's effectiveness with their weapon. Typically, this has involved a weapon engineer drawing connections between the characteristics of a firearm and soldier performance so that choices can be made to balance competing features such as weapon reliability, weight, ergonomics, ammunition-consumption and training. While this may sound like a purely technical exercise, making these trade-offs in a manner that proves to be acceptable to the infantry depends on more than effective quantitative data collection and soldiers honestly reporting their battlefield experiences. For, as

I will show in this chapter, developing a coherent and effective weapon is greatly complicated by the way in which different constituencies within armies first think about and describe the battlefield problems they face and then use their power to carve out their particular interpretation of battle.

When set in this more subjective context, mapping a weapon's design features to user arguments over how to think about the battlefield can be especially complex. To help the reader navigate these complexities, this chapter considers the matrix of choices that have framed the technical response of the engineer responsible for designing weapons. At the same time, the chapter establishes the privileged place of the soldier in the design and selection of weapons even as opinions about what constitutes the best weapon are contested within the user community itself.

Drawing the reader through a chronological series of Anglo-American rifle debates that have historically shaped weapon design, I explore a matrix of ideas that have framed the debate about small arms over the past 100 years. The starting place for this exercise lies with the way that the infantry have thought about marksmanship and firepower. The subsequent sections discuss the way engineers have responded to marksmanship and firepower and thought about a soldier's will to use their weapons as balanced against their demands for ammunition-stopping power. Encapsulating the range of design challenges facing the engineer, the argument I develop shows that competing interpretations of the battlefield shape weapon design from the bottom-up. More fundamentally, however, I show that powerful constituencies within the military itself can determine how battle will be understood, shaping debates irrespective of the evidence.

Marksmanship or firepower?

The underlying reason for debate on weapons and tactics has long been recognised by strategists, soldiers, military historians and psychologists who have noted how the chaos and complexity of combat leads to uncertainty and misunderstanding.[9] As the late military historian Richard Holmes has observed, however, making sense of combat is something of a social process. Resolving the divide between rational meaning and personal experience involves discussion and reflection among the combatants. Thus, while interviewing soldiers returning from the Falklands, Holmes watched 'the way in which a carapace of accepted fact hardened almost before my eyes' as soldiers discussed the events of battle.[10] This in turn was shaped by what Emile

Simpson describes as a military frame of reference that lent battle 'a rational meaning to events'.[11] When it comes to weapon development, however, a military frame of reference has to relate to wider perspectives among those professionals who have to design, develop and build a new technology or technique. In these circumstances, the process of designing a technology thus offers another vehicle for making sense of battle and resolving the divide between rational meaning and personal experience.

The most common starting point for many commentators who discuss the evolution of small unit tactics is the assumption that the technical capability of a contemporary infantry platoon has essentially remained unchanged since the First World War. Indeed, when contextualised this way, the only factor that has significantly changed in that time is weapon reliability, for the 'rifle, bayonet, pistol and portable light machine gun' of the early twentieth century remains 'broadly equivalent' with compatible weaponry from the early twenty-first century.[12] If this is the case, and all guns have been created equal over time, then how might an infantryman decide what rifle they would like to use?

While the assumption that there has been no revolution in infantry weapons might appear true at first glance, a detailed analysis of changes in tactics and technology does not lend support to the claim. For even when weapon systems are broadly comparable—have reached certain NATO set standards, for example—allied armed forces continue to resist using common small arms. The British Army has consistently turned down the opportunity to introduce the M16 and its variants into general service. Similarly, the French have preferred their own weapon, the FAMAS (Fusil d'Assaut de la Manufacture d'Armes de Saint-Étienne), to anything produced by other NATO powers. In the early 1980s, the German Army refused to adopt a 5.56mm light machine gun (LMG) instead of their heavier, larger 7.62mm calibre MG-3.[13] More fundamentally, the NATO alliance only agreed to use the same ammunition types in 1979, and even now different armies use different calibre weapon systems in what otherwise might be described as similar tactical roles. Previously, France, the United States, Portugal, Greece and Turkey used a variety of ammunition types in general and limited service. Bearing in mind that even apparently tiny changes in ammunition calibre have significant ramifications in terms of engagement ranges, soldier burden, maintenance and logistics—and therefore directly impinge on tactics—this kind of technical detail cannot easily be overlooked. Indeed, ultimately it suggests that there is more to small arms selection than straightforward criteria of perceived combat effectiveness.

If there is more to weapon selection than reliability, then what else frames choice? Francis Fukuyama makes some cogent observations about this when describing the challenges facing bureaucratic decision-making. Writing specifically in the context of developing the capacity of the state to make effective policy, Fukuyama argues that, 'While some labor assignment problems are susceptible to mathematical optimization, others are not because they involve trade-offs between goals whose relative utility is indeterminate or politically determined.'[14] Thus, for Fukuyama, optimising choices on the basis of the evidence can sometimes only take bureaucratic discussions so far. If, for example, two options are equally viable, equally consistent and produce similar results, then ultimately the choice over which approach to take cannot be based on the internal logic of the stated position. In these situations, the only way to explain how a decision was reached is by reference to the political preferences of the actors involved in the decision-making process. As I elaborate over the course of this book, this does not reflect the nature of every bureaucratic decision, but as a thought experiment it does provide some coordinates for thinking about and analysing the process of technology selection. In particular, it offers useful guidance for thinking through the protracted and opaque Anglo-American debates that framed the relative merits of small arms acquisition.

Since at least the First World War, most commentators note that fire and movement has been the mainstay of small unit infantry tactics. That is to say at least one soldier advances toward, or closes with, the enemy while another uses their firearm to prevent the enemy from shooting. The roots of this tactical schema emerged during the eighteenth and nineteenth centuries, and the tactic was normally pioneered by light riflemen equipped with rifles rather than the line infantry, who were generally armed with smoothbore muskets. A rifle took longer to load than a musket since the rifling of the weapon made it harder for soldiers to ram the bullet down into the barrel. This required riflemen to work in pairs so that one could defend the other who was reloading. The lengthier range of the weapon made riflemen ideal for skirmishing or screening the main advance of troops or targeting officers and NCOs who were orchestrating the enemy's movements. The downside of these arrangements was that a rifle regiment's inability to deliver concentrated firepower or form a bayonet square made them vulnerable to cavalry shock charge.[15] This again meant that a rifleman had to have higher levels of individual motivation and initiative than his line counterpart if he were to act effectively and avoid disaster in the face of a cavalry attack. Thus the physical and tactical differences of employing a rifle on the battlefield meant that specific training and doctrine was required over and above that necessary for the line infantry equipped with muskets.

These tactical differences had a wider cultural impact on the British Army of the nineteenth century. The Rifle Regiments took a particularly progressive attitude towards discipline on the basis that riflemen would have to disperse and use cover to avoid enemy counter-fire and thus use their weapon independently without orders from commanders who might be out of shouting range.[16] In this respect, the weapon was the physical representation of the bargain between the regiment's officers and men. While this philosophy was respected, it was nonetheless an attitude that caused a great degree of suspicion and some antagonism with the rest of the line infantry. For the rifle in effect challenged the contemporary social norms on how discipline should be employed to maintain social order and the hierarchical relationship between officers and men. With the Army famously described by the Duke of Wellington as being 'composed of the scum of the earth', such a progressive approach did not sit well with those line infantry regiments that preferred to instil a more traditional system of discipline and drill.[17] This was mainly because it was not certain that officers could trust their men to do the right thing at the moment of decision. Instead, officers needed to adopt a paternal attitude towards their men, treating soldiers like children and expecting them to obey orders on the battlefield in the same way as they drilled them on the parade ground. One of the most obvious areas where this manifested itself was in relation to corporal punishment. For while the British light infantry had avoided making excessive use of flogging since Sir John Moore's time 100 years earlier, the rest of the British Army only abolished it in 1881.[18] The Rifle Regiments were, therefore, considerably more radical in their attitude and approach to officer–man relations and weapon selection than the line infantry regiments.

Other armies in Europe and the United States faced similar challenges, but their technical and organisational responses to them were different. This reflected the differing social conditions that influenced the relationship between officers and men in these countries. In France, for example, revolution, followed by restoration, republic and empire split military opinion on who ought to be recruited into the Army, for how long and under what conditions.[19] Could the average citizen be trusted with their weapon? Should the rank and file meet certain criteria, or should certain regiments be created more equal than others? Balanced against these civil–military considerations, the threat of German invasion demanded that troops be armed with weapons that could match their potential adversary. However, it is no coincidence that interest in magazine rifles typically started in naval quarters where access to firepower-intensive weapons could be limited to a small number of the ship's crew.[20] Only when the naval service had demonstrated the reliability of the magazine rifle over that of manually operated machine guns and technical features had been designed to prevent the weapon's misuse did armies come to the conclusion that these firearms were safe for wide distribution to soldiers.[21]

The British Army's decision to adopt the kinds of small unit tactics that had been pioneered by the Rifle Regiments in the lead up to, and in more systematic ways during, the First World War consequently drove considerable cultural and attitudinal change among those officers and men recruited before 1914.[22] However, the take-up of fire and movement tactics, even by the time of the 100 Days Campaign during the last few months of the First World War, was far from universal.[23] Indeed, it could be argued that certain constituencies within the British Army were so powerful that only by forging a completely separate Machine Gun Corps could the professionalism and training of specialist troops be properly realised and the employment of various configuration of machine gun within the line infantry be more effectively orchestrated.[24]

The central technological challenge posed by fire and movement during the First World War was principally one of soldier burden and the ability to generate sufficient quantities of fire to permit troop movement in front of an enemy position. Sustained-fire machine guns like the .303 belt-fed, water-cooled Vickers (18.1kg/39lbs 9oz) were too heavy and cumbersome to disassemble and set-up in a quick-moving infantry assault. Instead, light machine guns were used, but as they ranged from 20lbs (9kg) for the French Chauchat (technically a machine rifle) to 28lbs (13kg) for the British Lewis, movement could still be difficult, especially given the demands to carry large quantities of ammunition.[25] At the same time, while they were significantly lighter at around 8–9lbs (4kgs), magazine rifles could not produce the rapidity of fire necessary for winning in close quarters in a trench. In this situation, the bayonet might still have its utility, offering troops the means to defend themselves at the point where quick recharging of an expended magazine was not possible.

The technical response to the challenge of fire and movement had already been identified in the period between 1900 and 1914, when a large number of automatic firearms had been evaluated both in Britain and among other powers. For a variety of reasons, however, the move to adopt automatic weapons foundered. In France, for instance, an auto-loading rifle—the A6 Meunier—was successfully tested for adoption by the Army in 1913, but it was not introduced into service because of its cost and because war with Germany was considered too imminent for such a major refit.[26]

In Britain, by contrast, officers demanded limitations to the technical capabilities of automatic weapons. Automatic capability had to be tempered such that the weapon could continue to be used like a bolt-operated rifle, weigh less than 9.5lbs (4.3kg) and hit targets out to 800 yards.[27] Given the complexities of automatic fire and potential for stoppages, demanding a single-shot capability was a sure way of ensuring that soldiers would always have the ability to fire their weapon. However, as the development of the American M-14 (5.1kg/11lbs 2oz) rifle showed, this was a technical specification that proved to be difficult to deliver after the Second World War. It can be surmised, then, that automatic rifles were not necessarily of interest to the British Army before the beginning of the First World War, as it was unwilling to compromise on the technical specification simply in order to acquire a rifle with greater firepower.

There were, however, a number of sound technical and organisational reasons why the Army might want to slow down the introduction of a new rifle so soon after it had brought the .303 Short Magazine Lee–Enfield (SMLE) into service in 1903.[28] This was not about the naturally conservative nature of the officer class but rather the nature of the bargains that had been struck within the Army as it pertained to the SMLE.[29] In this respect, the argument over a shorter version of the existing Lee–Enfield rifle emerged out of the British Army's failings on the North West Frontier during the Tirah Campaign of 1897–8. Fighting on the North West Frontier categorically demonstrated the weakness of British marksmanship, skill at arms and drill in the face of highly effective Pashtun shooting.[30] The result was a move to bring Colonel Ian Hamilton, an Indian Army officer, to the British Army's School of Musketry at Hythe.[31]

Given the line infantry's antipathy to the Rifle Regiments, it is probably no surprise that the move to embrace technologies that encouraged independent initiative and marksmanship actually developed outside the British Army proper. For it was only with the support of the Indian Army's commander-in-chief, General Frederick Roberts, that Hamilton could work to improve individual marksmanship in the Indian Army, a feat that led one paper to conclude that the real British school of musketry 'is at Simla and not Hythe'.[32] As a result of these successes, Hamilton eventually came to the attention of the Adjutant General Sir Evelyn Wood, who appointed him commandant of the School of Musketry in 1898. Not only did this appointment offer Hamilton the chance to improve British Army musketry skill but it also offered those Indian Army officers with a different experience of warfare an opportunity to reinvigorate discussion about future small arms. For Hamilton's position at Hythe automatically ensured that he would directly oversee those committees responsible for considering new small arms, thus putting him in the driving seat for deciding on the British Army's future weapon.

Before Hamilton's appointment, the idea for a 'handier' infantry rifle—technical parlance for an easier to handle rifle—had been suppressed. Indeed, in December 1895, Colonel N. Lockyer, chief inspector of small arms, had suggested that carbines ought to be issued to all arms of the Army, including the infantry.[33] Carbines had shorter barrels than rifles, struggled to hit targets at range and were usually issued to artillery and horse-mounted infantry. However, they were lighter and shorter and consequently easier to handle and quickly bring to bear on a moving target. Instead of firing by line and volley, the handiness of the weapon would facilitate the initiative of the soldier. The danger was that the soldier would fire off their ammunition too quickly and neither hit their intended target nor realise the commander's objective. Making the Lee-Enfield lighter and shorter so that it would be suitable for snap shooting, or shooting quickly at fleeting targets, therefore made it appear that infantrymen would be issued with inferior weapons more appropriate to the other branches of the Army. In these circumstances, Lord Wolseley—the commander-in-chief—resisted the suggestion.[34] However, new cordite propellants made it easier to generate sufficient muzzle velocity for bullets to hit targets at greater distances from shorter rifle barrels. The technology existed to reduce the number and varieties of firearms issued to the various branches of the Army and at the same time make it easier for soldiers of all branches to engage in independent fire.

Nonetheless, resistance to the idea of a new, shortened rifle only changed following British defeats by Boers in what became known as Black Week in December 1899. This led to the appointment of Lord Roberts to command troops in South Africa who insisted on the kinds of tactical skirmishing and marksmanship that he and Ian Hamilton had championed in the Indian Army. Subsequently becoming commander-in-chief, Roberts pioneered the introduction of the SMLE—a version of the weapon having been considered by Hamilton before the Boer War—and was determined to improve soldier marksmanship. At the same time, sceptical of the battlefield value of the *arme blanche*, Roberts also decided to remove the lance from service in 1903.[35] Despite this attack on their functional capability, however, Lord Roberts found that he could rely on the commitment of the cavalry for the implementation of a new magazine rifle. Why was this?

In the immediate aftermath of the Boer War, what is clear is that cavalry officers feared they would soon be replaced by the mounted infantry, a horse-mounted soldier whose utility had been demonstrated on the South African veld.[36] Given this possibility, cavalry officers were determined to find a way to retain a central role for their branch in the face of those critics who argued that the horse and sword were no longer relevant in the firepower-intensive battlefield of the future.[37] For the cavalry, adopting the SMLE would demonstrate a willingness to embrace fire action and at the same time ensure that their branch retained a unique role on the battlefield. Not only could they argue that they were suitable for undertaking shock action, reconnaissance and flank protection but they could also claim that their inherent mobility enabled them to play a crucial role, either in the vanguard of a meeting engagement, or as an emergency stop-gap in defence.[38]

The nature of the bargain that had been struck on the SMLE thus allowed the Treasury, the cavalry and the commander-in-chief to agree to a technical solution that met a number of potentially conflicting perspectives. The Treasury could reduce the financial implication of changes in small arms technology by taking carbines out of the inventory. The cavalry could retain the sword while demonstrating they were still relevant in future battle, and Lord Roberts would have a weapon that reflected his belief in marksmanship and soldiers using their initiative. That is not to say, however, that everyone was satisfied, for there remained a number of constituencies within the Army who were unconvinced about the SMLE and in particular were concerned by the ability of the weapon to stop an enemy dead. Nonetheless, for the time being, the SMLE allowed the various branches of the Army to continue to think about the battlefield and tactics in ways that suited them.

Related but different concerns dominated the equivalent discussions in the US Army both before and after the First World War. Here the central issue related to the US Army's attachment to .30'06 ammunition and its capacity to stop dead an enemy at extended ranges. Symbolic of this was the process by which the .30'06 M-1 Garand came into service.[39] Designed by John Garand, introduced in 1936 and described as the 'the greatest battle implement ever devised' by General George S. Patton, the Garand was the standard US rifle of the Second World War.[40] The underpinning bargain that framed the introduction of the M-1 was the belief that a new infantry weapon had to match the Army's traditional values of long-range, accurate shooting with the need to increase the infantryman's rate of fire. If this could successfully be accomplished, then it would be possible to mask the fact that, when it came to infantry tactics, there were two distinct camps within the inter-war Army, each with different views on how to engage with the enemy.

The first group included mainly higher echelon officers whose non-tactical experience of the First World War resulted in their continuing belief in marksmanship traditions. General Pershing, for instance, came away from the First World War convinced that good rifle shooting was essential to American successes, while other American officers concluded that, 'The Automatic weapon is not the natural weapon of an American.'[41] Although it ran counter to the experience of those French troops who had been asked to train the Americans,[42] for US officers the 'cult of the rifle' was all-important: the soldier must be skilled in the use of deliberate aimed fire in order to hit targets at extended ranges over 500 yards. In this situation, the only way to guarantee that the infantry could do this was if they were equipped with the M1903 Springfield Rifle and the .30'06 ammunition it fired. Anything less than this would prevent the US infantry from reaching this benchmark level of attainment.

The second group, in contrast, were more likely to have seen combat and had a closer appreciation of the battlefield. To this group, the First World War suggested that there were potential benefits that could be derived from increasing the rate of fire.[43] Having failed to collect enough sound data in a systematic manner, it was difficult to prove this to be the case. However, the European nations' increased interest in automatic firearms and the acceptance of the Browning Automatic Rifle (BAR) into American service in 1919 underlined a tacit acceptance of the benefits of greater firepower.[44]

Nevertheless, achieving the ambitions of both sides in this debate was technically challenging. This was because the qualities required of a rifle that needed to shoot to long ranges with maximum accuracy were different from those where an increase in firepower was deemed necessary. High rates of fire invariably meant increased stress on the weapon. Changing the characteristics of the ammunition or increasing the weight of the rifle could alleviate this. However, this resulted in either a compromise on long-range capabilities or making the weapon impossible to carry and use. The inter-war technical dilemma the US Army consequently presented to the Ordnance Department was therefore extremely difficult to resolve.

The first attempt at finding an answer lay with the efforts of the designer John Pedersen, who was contracted to the Ordnance Department in 1928. Pedersen pointed out that by reducing the size of bullet to .276" it would be possible to develop a semiautomatic rifle of a reasonable weight and still maintain some of the range capabilities of the .30'06 round. Unfortunately for

Pedersen, this was not a view that was well received by the Ordnance Committee, whose members included representatives from the combat commands, technical services and other liaison staff and whose responsibilities included setting specifications and overseeing research and development.[45] The reason the committee objected to the reduction in calibre was that in their opinion smaller bullets brought into question both the lethality of the round and the extent to which it could be deflected by cross winds. With insufficient independently documented data to support this view, it was decided that trials would be organised, undertaken by a special Caliber Board, to establish the lethality of Pedersen's round against the standard .30'06. This board, which became known as the Pig Board because the ammunition was tested on anaesthetised pigs, reported in 1929 that the Pedersen .276″ was extremely lethal at 300 yards, just as lethal as the .30'06 at 600 yards and only slightly less lethal at 1,000 yards.[46]

Despite the board's findings, however, the chief of the infantry was not so easily convinced, arguing that pigs were insufficiently like humans to establish ammunition lethality.[47] This objection led the Ordnance Committee to organise another set of trials which would be conducted on goats. In 1931, this so-called Goat Board tested Pedersen's .276″ semiautomatic rifle alongside two semiautomatic rifles by John Garand, one of which was chambered to .276″ and the other to .30'06. Unluckily for those who advocated a larger calibre, Garand's .30'06 weapon suffered a cracked bolt at the trials and left the Caliber Board reassured that their earlier conclusions concerning bullet size were correct.[48] Accordingly, and with Congressional funding for further trials in doubt, the Goat Board recommended the .276″ round for service and Garand's semiautomatic weapon to fire it. The report went to the Ordnance Committee which agreed with the board's findings, and it was then sent on to the War Department which still needed to give its final approval.[49]

Unfortunately for those on the Ordnance Committee who believed that a small calibre round could resolve the firepower question, their recommendation still did not meet with the approval of the Army's chief of the infantry. For those in the infantry still wedded to marksmanship, the .276″ was rejected on the basis that it was important to guarantee the inter-changeability of ammunition between rifles and Medium Machine Guns (MMG).[50] Effectively, the chief of infantry was insisting that an infantryman use a high-powered cartridge that was more relevant to the needs of an MMG than it was to the design of a rifle. For an MMG, weight and recoil considerations were of less significance, as these weapons needed to be more robust in order to deal with their role of providing longer-range sustained fire.

In contrast, for the firepower enthusiasts, these issues were of critical importance in the design of an automatic rifle for general issue to the infantry. The insistence on one class of ammunition for both an MMG and rifle meant limiting the chance of increasing the firepower that the ordinary rifleman could generate. For the chief of infantry, however, two issues were at stake; one with a tactical dimension and the other logistical. The tactical issue was that inter-changeability guaranteed that, in case of emergency, a squad would have the ability to swap Small Arms Ammunition (SAA) intended for machine guns and use it in their rifles. The logistical issue concerned the fact that it was easier for one type of ordnance to be shipped to front line units in bulk than it was for two. An infantry company that needed .30'06 ammunition for its LMGs and BARs and .276″ for its semiautomatic rifles clearly had huge implications for logisticians who at that time were primarily interested in simplifying the supply chain, not increasing its complexity.

Animosity to the .276″ did not end there, however. Even the chief of the Ordnance Department moved to distance himself from the Caliber Board's reports by arguing that changing calibre would mean replacing the tooling for both the .30'06 round and the various weapons that fired it.[51] With such a significant voice pointing out the financial consequences, logisticians arguing that a change would complicate the supply chain, and the chief of infantry unhappy about lethality and inter-changeability, senior Army commanders started to question the wisdom of the Caliber Board's findings. In particular, they were concerned that a move to a new type of ammunition would not be well received by a Congress more worried about the Great Depression. Indeed, with a perfectly sound system already in existence, any spending on a new rifle was likely to lead to increased Congressional scrutiny, which could undermine the administrative functions of the War Department.[52] With an eye on the political situation facing the Army, it could come as no surprise that the chief of staff, General MacArthur, decided to overrule the Caliber Board, stating, 'To make this change will introduce an element of chaos, confusion, and uncertainty which, magnified under war conditions, would more than counteract the beneficial effect of any semiautomatic rifle.'[53] MacArthur rejected the evidence offered by the Caliber Boards, stopped further research into .276″ and instructed that more effort be made to find a solution using the existing .30'06 ammunition.

For those who favoured marksmanship, MacArthur's decision appeared to resolve the debate in their favour. However, the firepower advocates were saved by the fact that John Garand had also been working on another firearm chambered to fire the .30'06 round.[54] When Garand revealed that this new self-loading weapon was only slightly heavier than the existing service rifle but did not involve a change of calibre, the US Army seemed to have found a technical solution to the firepower problem that the marksmanship advocates could not refute. Consequently, in 1936, Garand's rifle replaced the Springfield as the service weapon of the US Army.

Both the SMLE and the Garand reflected a number of different interpretations of the battlefield within one weapon. With regard to the SMLE, a number of technical contrivances made it easier for use by both the cavalry and the infantry such that both branches of the Army could retain distinct battlefield roles. The infantry had a handier weapon that encouraged marksmanship and initiative. The cavalry could supplement their main reconnaissance and screening roles with a rifle that gave them an equivalent capability to the infantry. Consequently, they could claim a unique position on the battlefield that sceptics found hard to challenge despite the battlefield evidence that suggested the irrelevance of the *arme blanche*.

By contrast, the Garand bridged a firepower/marksmanship divide in part by balancing the marksman's belief in .30'06 ammunition with the firepower enthusiasts' desire for an automatic weapon. While the weapon was limited to semiautomatic fire—that is, firing a single shot every time the trigger was pulled, automatically and without having to manually re-cock the weapon— there was little chance of alienating either the firepower or marksmanship constituency within the Army. As became clear from the development of the M-14 and M16 in the 1950s, however, any move to adopt a fully automatic weapon would produce a further round of debates about the importance of marksmanship.

Before the Second World War, then, the technological bargains of the British and American Armies proved difficult to unpick, despite the increasing viability of technologies that might have revolutionised infantry firepower. In this respect, fully automatic rifles would not enter into service in either the US or British Armies because ordnance officials typically responsible for policing the existing bargain refused to countenance alternative technical requirements. Thus the SMLE and its main iteration, the No. 4 Rifle, remained in service with the British Army from 1903 until 1957 even after viable semiautomatic rifles had been evaluated in 1932 and during the Second World War.[55] In the pre-war case, financial constraints could of course be used to excuse this decision. It is more accurate to say, however, that the switch over to a new rifle was not considered sufficiently important given the range of other technical choices confronting the British Army at that time.

The idea that the selection of a new rifle had more to do with organisational preferences than the availability of finance is reflected in the discussions that were being held during the Second World War on whether the infantry section ought to be armed with some kind of automatic rifle. Once the war had started, the financial constraints were removed and a range of automatic weapons were developed including the very rapid and ultimately successful Sten machine carbine or sub-machine gun (SMG).[56] However, as I will show, any ambition to adopt a fully automatic rifle had to be put aside in the face of fierce opposition both from Field Marshall Montgomery, who had a fundamentally different conception of battle from those who advocated tactical reforms in the infantry, and by frontline commands themselves.

By contrast, in the American Army it was easier to revere the M-1 Garand's performance during the Second World War than it was to implement engineering solutions that might more accurately reflect the battlefield problems being faced by GIs. Thus, in many respects, British and American attitudes towards changing the firepower capability of their infantrymen were different but curiously aligned. Unlike the Germans, who were willing to quickly develop and adopt compromise weapons like the Sturmgewehr 44 assault rifle, the Allies stood doggedly to their pre-war choices, only considering alternatives after 1945.[57]

Willpower or stopping-power?

Until 1939, the debates were primarily focused on the relative importance of marksmanship over firepower. This pitched different tactical conceptions of the battlefield against each other. For the marksmanship camp, the question was associated with the infantry's skill at arms and inculcating soldiers into a particular British or American martial culture. For the firepower enthusiasts, the issue was to build a weapon that reflected the tactical imperative of fire and movement. In some respects, maintaining the First World War-era convention of distributing LMGs like the US BAR or the British Bren gun to the infantry platoon alleviated the immediate problem. Nonetheless, the real test of these different perspectives on battle would be the Second World War itself. It would be easy to claim that this would produce a fight between conservatives and modernisers within each army. It is, however, more accurate to say that the arguments over weapon systems reflected the relative gains that might be realised from changing technologies, bearing in mind the strategic constraints and operational preferences of those involved in decision-making.

These preferences were in turn linked to the way that various arguments were presented by different powerful groups within the respective armies.

Comparisons between the fighting performance of the German, British and American infantry during the Second World War have not been particularly flattering. According to some commentators, German fighting performance, 'man for man and unit for unit', was 20 to 30 per cent more effective than either its British or American counterparts.[58] Max Hastings and Carlo D'Este reinforce this message in their account of the Normandy Campaign but go further and suggest that British performance was even worse than that of the Americans.[59] If these accounts are to be believed, there was, and had been for several years during the course of the war, a *prima facie* case for undertaking wide-ranging change in the organisation, tactical prowess and types of equipment for British and American infantry.

To suggest that this possibility had not been grasped by a number of officers within the respective armies would, however, be a gross misrepresentation of the facts. Indeed, when it came to the British Army, a more accurate representation of the challenges can be summed up in the efforts to introduce tactical, technical and bureaucratic changes so that any shortcomings in the fighting performance of the infantry might be more readily addressed. From a tactical training perspective, key among the new developments was the creation of Battle Schools and the School of Infantry. With the objective of transforming a conscript Army into an effective fighting force, the first Battle Schools started to appear in the summer of 1941 and were attached to 47th Division located in the Home Army's Southern Command. Established by Major Lionel Wigram, a Territorial Army officer and former lawyer, the school taught Battle Drill and soon came to the attention of General Sir Bernard Paget, general officer commanding Southern Command. Upon his appointment to command all Home Forces in late 1941, General Paget expanded the Battle School programme and created the School of Infantry in 1942.[60]

The creation of a School of Infantry produced the circumstances for further bureaucratic changes at the War Office, and in early 1943 led to the establishment of the director of infantry (DInf). Charged with 'giving the infantry a voice on a par with the other teeth arms', the DInf set about drawing together the various administrative levers that had been considering tactical and technical matters relating to the infantry and providing them with a focus and direction.[61] Thus in early 1943, the new DInf, Major-general T.N.F. Wilson, working alongside colleagues from Military Intelligence, the Ministry of Supply and representatives from the Field Armies, established a Standing Committee on Infantry

Weapon Development. Tactical considerations were integral to the objectives of this new Committee, which aimed at forecasting 'our own Infantry tactics in relation to the enemy's in order to assess the battle conditions under which weapons may be required'.[62] The upshot of these changes in training and bureaucracy was a growing determination to ensure that the infantry had the best possible equipment it could have given that infantry 'casualties on the battlefield are higher than those of any other service'.[63]

With regard to the tactics that would be employed to use these firearms, Wigram had developed an approach in response to the needs of his Division following the defeat at Dunkirk and the significant increase in Army personnel through conscription. Rapidly rising to the rank of lieutenant colonel, it was not until Wigram went out to join the Army in Sicily in 1943 that he finally got to see first-hand whether soldiers in the field were properly implementing the ideas that were being taught in Battle Schools.[64] The drills taught at these schools involved combining fire and movement so as to achieve tactical success and were not dissimilar to those being applied by the British Army in the final year of the First World War.[65] Thus, for instance, if an infantry section were split down into a Bren LMG group and a manoeuvre group, the Bren would lay down covering fire to keep the enemy's head down while the rest of the troops worked their way forward to attack at close quarters. The goal of this tactic, which formed the basis for virtually all of the minor tactics being taught at the Infantry Schools, was to get the infantryman to think tactically using the drill as a starting point for more creative approaches to battlefield problems when directly in front of the enemy.

At the same time, through the Standing Committee on Infantry Weapon Development, the DInf put considerable effort into ensuring that 'all the available infantry weapons [were] brought to bear on the enemy, not only in the initial advance, but also up to the last possible moment so that the infantry [could] literally be shot into close quarters'.[66] The DInf firmly believed that there needed to be 'a balance between firepower, assault power and manoeuvrability'.[67] If this was the goal, then the infantry had to have the right mix of weapons so that they could increase their battle tempo and deliver more effective fire and movement in the attack. Since the beginning of the war, the infantry section had supplemented their 8.8lb (4kg) SMLEs and 22lb (10.15kg—Mark III and IV were lighter) Bren guns with the 6lbs 6oz (3kg) Sten (MkII) Machine Carbine.[68] While the LMG could lay down covering fire, its weight, lack of handiness and the requirement for large quantities of ammunition meant that moving the weapon forwards after the initial attack had started would be difficult and require significant manpower.[69] Unable to fire automatically, the SMLE and No. 4 Rifle hampered the manoeuvre group's ability to generate firepower in the final phases of the assault.

According to analysis undertaken by operational researchers attached to the School of Infantry, however, one solution to this problem was to equip the entire infantry section with the Sten machine carbine.[70] The Sten could generate high quantities of fire, could strike targets at similar ranges to the Bren and, given the potential volume of rounds that could be fired, could compensate for poor marksmanship and increase the likelihood of hitting the enemy.[71] If the operational researchers were to be believed, it would appear that the infantry could solve its problem of fire and movement straight away without having to introduce a new weapon. This would obviate the need to introduce a completely new weapon which would require retooling manufacturing capability, adapting the logistics infrastructure and developing new training and maintenance regimes. By adopting the Sten, however, changes in infantry section armament would provide an immediate solution to the limitation imposed by existing equipment. This would in turn give time for the small arms community in the UK to develop and put into production a weapon that would be specially built to balance firepower, assault power and manoeuvre.[72]

Unfortunately, however, the Field Armies were not interested in either revising the infantry section's weapons mix, new infantry weapons, or in the tactics that had worked at the end of the First World War and were now being taught in the Battle Schools. This became abundantly clear when Wigram went to the Mediterranean during 1943. What Wigram found when he arrived in Sicily was that fire and movement was in reality 'Guts and Movement'.[73] Wigram described the infantry battle in some detail, outlining how in practice a number of steps unfold the result of which was three or four 'gutful men under the Platoon Commander' dash 'straight in to the enemy position without any covering fire and always succeed in taking the position'.[74] Effectively, then, the courageous few did most of the dangerous work and were consequently more likely to become casualties. The twelve or so 'sheep' would follow if well led, but as many as six might abandon their position and run away.

Wigram had ample opportunity to see the effectiveness of the infantry in battle because he was afforded the opportunity to command every unit from a section to a battalion and eventually led the 5th Buffs (Royal East Kent Regiment) while attached to 36 Brigade during the Sicilian campaign. In Wigram's subsequent report to the Directorate of Military Training, a report he produced in the hope of refining the Battle Drill being taught in the UK, he offered a close analysis of the infantry's fighting prowess. This document ultimately found its way to Montgomery (at the time still commanding 8th Army), who called Wigram to his HQ in Bari and demoted him to major on the basis that he was publicly criticising his senior commanders, and made it clear that he would not command a battalion again.[75] On top of this, the Directorate of Military Training at the War Office prevented the Wigram report from being circulated as part of the *Current Reports from Overseas* pamphlet and, as a result, his evidence could not be examined by other commands.[76] Military authorities were happy to identify shortfalls in performance so long as the right man following the right process had identified them.

One might argue that Montgomery's reaction was testament to the lack of a learning culture in the British Army. However, since taking command of 8th Army, Montgomery had been instituting his own organisational changes associated with the higher level of command in an effort to improve the overall cohesion and effectiveness of divisional engagements through a stronger command culture. Encapsulated in his December 1942 pamphlet, 'Some Brief Notes on the Conduct of Battle for Senior Commanders', Montgomery was virtually at the point where his efforts were coming to fruition.[77] Moreover, by October 1943, it was starting to become clear that Britain's manpower reserves were in decline.[78] In these circumstances, it did not make sense to risk manpower in an effort to improve the immediate tactical capability of the infantry when alternative operational and technological solutions to the battlefield problem—in particular artillery but latterly also airpower—were less likely to undermine Britain's ability to keep an Army in the field.[79]

Challenges to Montgomery's authority and the success of his operational schemes were therefore unwelcome. It did not matter that Wigram's analysis was based on sound principles and derived from battlefield investigations. The suggestions he made as a junior-ranked former Territorial Army officer to a very senior regular Army officer were badly timed and unhelpful. The possibility that his views might also have powerful support from the director of infantry was even less helpful. By convention, the DInf had no authority to realise changes in the organisation of frontline commands.[80] Consequently, what the DInf believed to be appropriate was irrelevant. Montgomery could choose how to shape the battle and it was his preference to deliver changes at an operational level in an effort to overcome any tactical and material shortcomings that might exist in the British Army.[81] Anything that might unpick this goal was not acceptable. After all, the 8th Army was achieving battlefield success. Wigram had to go and his ideas put back in their place. After so many defeats and setbacks, why undermine Montgomery's winning formula?

If the willpower to produce greater quantities of infantry fire was lacking at the senior levels of the British Army, then related challenges were apparently facing troops in the firing line. The calculation that Montgomery had made was that a conscript army built out of a limited supply of quality manpower could not be needlessly wasted at the altar of advanced infantry tactics. Non-professional armies might learn how to survive and thrive in small unit encounters, but the battle needed to be prepared properly. For Montgomery, this was best achieved at the operational level where different branches of the military could be coordinated to deliver multiple blows to an enemy in advance of a wider assault.[82] Like the First World War, Montgomery's preference was to use artillery to suppress the enemy, thereby giving the infantry the time to occupy and hold ground. For the purposes of this argument, it does not matter whether Wigram or Montgomery was right. The main observation to be drawn from this is that delivering organisational change did not, of and by itself, depend on the battlefield evidence. What counted in this situation was a powerful figure in the command structure who could discount any evidence that did not fit with his tactical and operational preferences.

In many respects, the US Army took a comparable approach to that of the British. Recognising the advantages that could be derived from combining arms at the operational level, Americans sought to orchestrate the timely delivery of multiple blows to an enemy.[83] Whether the focus on operational technique compensated for the poor fighting prowess of American GIs is now contested. At the time, however, a debate about the ability of US infantry mirrored the prevailing perspective within British command circles. Michael D. Doubler has since shown that GIs were considerably more ingenious at tactical innovations and small unit engagements than was initially thought. Nevertheless, field research by US Army Historian S.L.A. Marshall fuelled the idea that American conscripts were not up to the challenge of advanced small unit tactics.

Marshall's findings, which were eventually published in a book called *Men Against Fire*, caused a great deal of controversy at the time and the veracity of his work has since been challenged by a number of historians who contend that he had little evidence for his observations.[84] In the years immediately after the war, however, Marshall's arguments proved to be extremely persuasive. On the basis of interviewing American GIs as they came off the firing line in both the Pacific and European theatres, Marshall claimed that on average no more than 25 per cent of front line troops actively used their personal weapon even in the most severe of engagements.[85] This could be explained by the fact that the US infantryman came from a civilised society where the taking of life was prohibited and unacceptable.

According to Marshall, such sentiments were particularly acute for those GIs armed with a rifle. Soldiers who fought as individuals were more inclined to a temperament that prohibited the taking of life.[86] Marshall observed that most of the active firers used heavy weapons, were in small groups together and used several firearms in such a way that 'if the machine gun went out, they picked up a rifle; when they ran out of rifle ammunition, they used grenades'.[87] The firing behaviour of these soldiers was reinforced by working in teams or by servicing a crewed weapon that did not require them to think about the effects of their work on their enemy combatants. They consequently kept up their rate of fire, which Marshall believed to be important because 'Fire wins wars, and it wins the skirmishes of which war is composed. Toss the willing firers out of an action and there can be no victory.'[88] In effect, Marshall argued that the real problem of small arms usage was not necessarily the need for accurate, long-range shooting, but rather with building up the volume of fire.

At its heart, then, *Men Against Fire* demanded that military authorities pay more attention to getting the soldier to pull the trigger reflexively. This called into question the whole method of psychometric testing used to identify potential infantrymen.[89] This in turn led to the suggestion that social context was more important in framing soldier firing behaviour than individual psychology. Consequently, in the years immediately after the Second World War, a number of studies were commissioned that sought to establish why, for example, the German Army kept on fighting even when defeat was inevitable.[90] With a greater focus on the idea of small unit cohesion, the results of these findings not only shaped the emerging field of military sociology, but also had a great impact on tactical training and shooter behaviours.

One way of inculcating a stronger sense of small unit cohesion was obviously through more effective training. The other was by increasing the professional attitudes and skills of soldiers that were being accepted in the infantry. But while training and professionalisation formed part of the solution to the problem of achieving fire superiority, the other conclusion that could be drawn was the adoption of technologies that could encourage the soldier to pull the trigger. In many respects, the German Sturmgewehr 44 Assault Rifle seemed to offer a potential solution to the engineering challenge of generating fire. Using a 7.92 x 33mm *Kurz* round, the smaller calibre ammunition—when compared with a standard Mauser infantry rifle 7.92 x 57mm round—had less recoil, making it easier to control those automatic weapons designed to fire it. However, to the

US military establishment, the Stg 44 ammunition compromised on range and would therefore undermine the ability to reproduce the marksmanship skills traditionally taught to the average soldier. The German weapon was, therefore, a way to water down the professionalism of the infantry when whatever replaced the M-1 Garand needed to embrace the culture and doctrine that inspired it. Long-range marksmanship remained the priority as far as the War Department was concerned and could not be sacrificed. Generating greater volumes of fire, while important, was a secondary concern.

Thus the initial post-War American response to Marshall's controversial findings was to limit the technical options that might be considered in the future. Having won a major world war, the War Department was not ready to sacrifice shooting skills that, at least on the surface, seemed to have provided the key to victory. Accordingly, while the Infantry School implemented a new training regimen to teach 'the fundamentals of precision firing ... from many unconventional positions', the Army was not willing to forego 'the accuracy and functioning associated with a purely semiautomatic rifle' for the sake of increased firepower.[91]

Part of the reason for the fixation on .30'06 SAA was the way it embodied the marksmanship traditions of the infantry. At the same time, there was a general belief in the stopping power of large calibre rounds. Popularised and discussed in detail by Major General Julian Hatcher, former chief of the Small Arms Division at the US Ordnance Department, the inter-war notion of stopping power was derived from early work by Major Louis LaGarde (of whom we will hear more in Chapter 4).[92] By 1945, however, there were plenty of facts available to the Americans to indicate that this notion of stopping power did not adequately explain wounding and that the M-1 Garand had achieved its reputation, 'in spite of, rather than because of, the rifle doctrine that inspired it'.[93]

Indeed, the Second World War evidence directly undermined several strands of the arguments developed before the war in favour of the .30'06 round. Surgical studies of US casualties during the Bougainville campaign suggested that the Pig Board's 1929 findings regarding round lethality were broadly correct: smaller calibre rounds could be equally as effective as larger rounds.[94] At the same time, battlefield conditions appeared to be even less conducive to marksmanship than they had appeared to be before the First World War. Studies showed that small arms fire accounted for the smallest number of casualties as a proportion of the overall casualty rate during the Second World War. Indeed, close examination of medical reports from the

European and Pacific theatres showed that small arms fire accounted respectively for 25 and 33 per cent of all casualties inflicted. It was possible to argue, therefore, that there was even less reason for the infantry to be issued with a rifle based on marksmanship principles when other weapons in the inventory were more successfully employed on long-range targets. Secondly, SAA interchangeability was not considered by US field commanders to be a significant problem, as the limited tactical advantage provided was, towards the end of the war, negated by the large quantities of ammunition being sent to the front lines pre-loaded in clips or belts and ready for use. If the supply chain had been adapted to cope with the quantities of ammunition required, then it could potentially allow for even more ammunition variants to be distributed, facilitating further weapon specialisation in the infantry squad.

While marksmanship might have appealed to military authorities trying to produce professional infantry, a big round was also—and in many respects continues to be—more reassuring to the soldier, offering them the security and certainty that an enemy, once shot, would not get up again and return fire. However, willpower and stopping power were flipsides of the same problem. Increasing the stopping power of a bullet had traditionally involved increasing the size of the bullet and the propellant needed to get the round to hit the target. More propellant meant more recoil, which meant either more weapon weight to soak up the energies produced or entailed the soldier having to accept more recoil energy directly into the shoulder. As recoil could produce severe bruising injuries, many soldiers flinched when firing their weapons. Consequently, ordnance officials have repeatedly been asked to produce training ammunition with reduced range and recoil so as to facilitate soldier training.[95]

The language of stopping power as it relates to the science of weapon lethality will be explored in considerable detail in Chapter 4. It is important to note here, however, that the question of stopping power had been a repeated feature of soldier commentary on weapons since at least the 1880s as armies switched away from large calibre .450-type rounds to smaller .30 ones. In the nineteenth century, the concern was whether a small round below .30 would actually be sufficient to stop a charging cavalry horse. When the British Army was considering replacing the Martini-Henry .450 round with a .303 in the mid-1880s, for instance, a number of commanders wanted reassurances on the ammunition lethality before they could come to agreement about replacing the Martini–Henry.[96] Equally, on the North West Frontier, soldiers were unimpressed by the stopping power of the .303 Mark II ammunition in the Lee–Metford and Lee–Enfield. Consequently, a new hollow-point round named after the Dum Dum arsenal in India was created which was used during the Boer War and subsequently prohibited by the 1899 Hague Convention. Yet the illegality of hollow-point rounds did not prevent further debates on the most effective way to stop an enemy. On the contrary, even during the War in Iraq in 2006, 20 per cent of American soldiers interviewed were critical of the stopping power of their M4 Carbine.[97] Equally, a number of American and British commentators are critical of existing ammunition lethality, suggesting that it is unequal to the task facing contemporary soldiers.[98] Thus the ongoing debate about stopping power continues to frame discussion about current small arms and infantry capability.[99]

Conclusion

In terms of military innovation, it is clear that when looked at from the bottom up, soldier perspectives on their weapons and tactics was subject to a great deal of debate. Fire and movement was one way of defeating the Axis powers. This would have benefited from a number of technological innovations that the Allies could have introduced during the war. However, senior officers within the British and American Armies preferred to develop a number of operational techniques to overwhelm the enemy without having to resort to close quarter battle. In this respect, the user's perspective of the battlefield problem was subject to the will of powerful senior officers within the Army itself who could favour one type of solution irrespective of the evidence. This reflected the relative professional status of the infantry compared with the other technical arms of the Army.

In terms of marksmanship and firepower, senior officers in both the British and the American Armies tended to believe that aimed, deliberate fire against targets at range was an important skill for infantrymen to develop, irrespective of the battlefield conditions. If the First World War produced the right circumstances for introducing light machine guns into service, even sometimes in the face of institutional opposition, then the Second World War offered the circumstances to further test the enthusiasm for firepower. This did not, however, lead military authorities in either the UK or the United States to acquire fully automatic rifles for individual soldiers while still fighting the Axis powers.

In this respect, there were a number of reasons for not doing so, mainly framed by the preference for precision marksmanship but also because the infantryman and his rifle was not necessarily considered to be the main vehicle for delivering victory. Rather, combined arms and mastering operational techniques that perfected the coordination of blows by different elements of the army were, in the opinion of both British and American officers, more likely to create the conditions for defeating the enemy. Trying to deliver more effective small arms to the infantry was a distraction, as perfecting fire and movement could further affect the limited availability of suitable manpower. After the war, this belief was reinforced by Marshall, who claimed that the average citizen soldier was unlikely to use their weapon and was, therefore, more vulnerable to enemy action.

In technical terms, this meant the British Army retained the magazine-fed, bolt-action rifle throughout the Second World War and up to 1957. In the US Army, it meant retaining the Garand and an ethos that valued a self-loading rifle geared for hitting targets at range. The technologies may have been different, but in both instances, the impulse was the same: to inculcate appropriate martial and professional skills in the infantry. Lacking firepower, however, Anglo-American conscript armies did not have the means for decisively realising the commander's intent. This in turn reinforced the dominant narratives within command circles that preferred operational technique to tactical prowess.

That is not to say that there were no infantry firepower advocates within the military and technical establishments of both armies. Their ability to produce the right kinds of evidence that could effectively persuade other parts of the military of the validity of their views was, however, limited by their positions within their respected organisations. Unable to dictate the terms of a discussion, these people found themselves fighting to develop the evidential base for delivering wider tactical and technical change.

In this respect, *Men Against Fire* helped to propel a debate within engineering circles that had already started several decades earlier. By challenging the dominant American narrative on small arms in the years between 1900 and 1945, Marshall reframed the earlier competing interpretations of battle away from marksmanship and stopping power towards firepower and willpower. This did not guarantee Marshall's ideas would be taken up. On the contrary, small arms designers continued to search for ways to bring the engineering possibilities produced out of this vision of the battlefield into mainstream discussion.

In Britain, however, the challenge lay in identifying the sort of evidence that would sustain a debate centred on tactical flexibility and firepower. This had emerged from within the War Office and Ministry of Supply during the Second World War. Consequently, British analysts and engineers had already grasped the problem and identified potential solutions to it even before *Men Against Fire* had been published. In the next chapter, I will show how Anglo-

American technicians engineered the battlefield evidence so as to make sense of the users' requirements, in the hope that they could make their technological visions real. In the process, I will say something about the changing power relationships between civilians and the military after 1945.

3

ENGINEERING THE BATTLEFIELD

DEFINING THE REQUIREMENT

How many educated people know anything about productive industry ...? What is a machine-tool? I once asked a literary party; and they looked shifty. Unless one knows, industrial production is as mysterious as witch-doctoring.

C.P. Snow, *The Two Cultures*[1]

If we accepted majority opinion on scientific matters, it would still be axiomatic that the Sun revolves around the Earth

Report by Major-general E. Clarke, director general of artillery, June 1942[2]

It is extremely difficult to establish the causal links between military activity and battlefield outcome. Getting it wrong significantly complicates the design of weapons. Not only can it divert research and development towards sub-optimal technologies, it can also complicate industrial production and its associated supply chains. Ultimately, a failure to identify the relationship between cause and effect accurately can cost lives and potentially lead to defeat. It is important, therefore, to get inside the science of this causal conundrum. Unfortunately, however, for the analysts charged with this responsibility, this involves identifying and logging the minutiae of battlefield events in intimate detail. Having done this, it is then extremely important to think carefully about how to interpret the evidence. As Major-general Clarke, director general of artillery, implies in the quote above, it is particularly important to carefully interrogate evidence offered by those on the frontlines.

In December 1941, for example, British tank crews observed that German 'thermit armoured piercing shells' were proving to be particularly effective at destroying their tanks. Greatly concerned by this turn of events, tank commanders made an immediate and urgent request to the War Office for British units to be issued with similar ammunition. Tank crews had decided that the fires in their tanks were the result of this more effective German incendiary ammunition and they wanted to even up the odds.

In the subsequent investigation by weapons technical staff from the Ministry of Supply, the true cause of the problem was identified. German 'thermit' ammunition was a myth. British tank crews were not being outgunned. The underlying reason for the increased incidence of tank destruction was the susceptibility of ammunition racks in British tanks to internal splintering. These splinters ignited the ammunition held in the racks and caused British tanks to 'brew up'.

Only by critically reviewing the claims being made by tank crews and comparing this with their own technical trials could Weapons Technical Staff identify the chain of causality effectively. Tank crews had drawn the wrong conclusions, conclusions which if followed unthinkingly would have forced British industrial capacity to be recalibrated for a new type of ammunition. Early intervention by analysts and engineers prevented this and refocused research and design effort on armour protection. In June 1942, it was this experience that led Major-general Clarke, director-general of artillery, to conclude that the majority of user opinion within the Army was much like majority opinion on scientific matters: not to be trusted.

This did not mean that users should not be consulted. What this 1941 experience did suggest, however, was that user opinions needed to be treated with some considerable care. This became abundantly clear following the defeat of Axis forces in North Africa in May 1943. With the conclusion of the campaign, a small cadre of British Army officers attached to the Ministry of Supply undertook a survey of the victorious 1st and 8th Armies—subsequently identified as 18 Army Group—to record the infantry's experiences with their weapons. This survey team, known as the Weapons Technical Staff Field Forces (WTSFF), offered the user community a unique opportunity to critique the entire portfolio of infantry weapons and shape the supply and development of future iterations of their equipment: from the anti-tank gun to the hand grenade, the pistol to the bayonet.

Having tabulated 15,000 replies to their questionnaire, however, it might have come as something of a surprise to the WTSFF survey team to find that battalion commanders' knowledge of the weapons available to them needed 'to be put right' and that 'little value should be attached to the opinion of one battalion or lower formation'. The report went on to observe that soldiers' 'opinions on quite elementary points are frequently conflicting, if not directly contradictory, as between different units and formations' and that 'it would appear that many battalion commanders are not really qualified to comment usefully on their weapons'.[3]

On one level, the survey established the need to change a number of technical matters pertaining to the way weapons were issued, maintained and used. More fundamentally, however, the report's authors came to the conclusion that unless the user understood the technology that was available to them, their comments were not particularly useful. Remarkably, then, and despite protestations to the contrary, the infantry themselves were not in a position to offer credible or authoritative opinions on small arms. Despite their privileged position on the battlefield, engineers concluded that infantrymen simply did not know what was best for them.

Taken as a one-off, the results of this questionnaire might easily be dismissed. The WTSFF's findings do, however, mirror a wider pattern of poor 'weapon mindedness' among Anglo-American infantrymen that can be traced back to before the First World War. Surveys of small arms use during the Boer War, for example, revealed an equally troubling set of contradictory perspectives.[4] Similarly, in 1953, a British study revealed that in Malaya, 'the poor performance of the Sten and Owen, compared even with the rifle, is largely attributable to the firers. More emphasis should be laid on training ...'[5] In 1967, during the Vietnam War, the average frequency of soldiers zeroing their M16 was every 4.96 months, with 10 per cent of those surveyed never zeroing their weapon at all.[6] That is to say that 10 per cent of GIs had not adjusted their sights to match the ballistic characteristics of the ammunition and the peculiarities of their specific weapon and as such could not be relied upon to hit a target they were ostensibly aiming at.

While it would be easy to argue that these were isolated moments that reflected the citizen conscript nature of the armies concerned, similar problems have been noted among professional soldiers. Thus, in the early 1970s, both a new recruit and an average soldier in the professional British Army were still some way short of the envisaged level of skill even after having completed their allotted ten hours training with a rifle.[7] Equally, in the United States, it was not clear in the mid-1980s whether soldier effectiveness with the M16 would be sufficient to win an opening engagement, in part because the training criteria were 'only marginally linked with combat-referenced criteria'.[8]

Nor was this a problem confined to a Cold War in which nuclear weapons might obviate the need for the infantry and their personal weapons. In 2002, for example, as part of Operation JACANA (Britain's early involvement in Afghanistan) a number of newspapers reported that SA80 rifles given to the Royal Marines Commandos did not work.[9] However, a later investigation by the Ministry of Defence concluded that the SA80s were being poorly maintained and that the Marines themselves did not know how to use their weapons.[10] While such a perspective inflamed the opinion of many in the forces, the MOD's findings were subsequently proven to be accurate. Further testing in the deserts of Oman had shown that the SA80A2 averaged 95 per cent reliability in sandy conditions when properly maintained and operated.[11] By 2008, the British Army had launched Project Odysseus to address the problem of weapon mindedness after it was established that only 59 per cent of the Army (including combat arms) would potentially pass their Annual Personal Weapon Test.

It would be too easy, then, to privilege the experience of the soldier and dismiss the WTSFF's conclusions. A more accurate reflection would accept that the soldier's ability to use their firearm with confidence, knowing the basics of marksmanship—so that they can get the best out of the weapon while adjusting for specific conditions—is a recurring issue that needs to be managed through training and education. More complex weapons make greater demands of the average soldier. For the Army, this poses a number of organisational and ongoing challenges associated with the provision of shooting ranges, time for shooting practice and sufficient quantities of ammunition to allow soldiers to bring themselves up to proficiency. These practicalities in turn have an impact on soldier recruitment profiles.

For the engineer, however, this poses some even more complex challenges relating to optimising weapon design. In the first instance, they must deal with the challenges created by a user community whose level of technical understanding is not always as great as is sometimes assumed. In the second, they must also choose whether to optimise for the most efficient shooter or make allowances for those with poor skills. Elite troops will probably have a different response to this question when compared with the majority of the infantry. Civil servants and those responsible for finance will view the call for more money for training ammunition sceptically. Commanders, especially those working in a counterinsurgency context, will want to know that soldiers are not causing collateral deaths through poor marksmanship.

Invariably, the result of these different expectation levels is that more and more requirements are added into the design specification. As far as the engineer is concerned, however, the different expectation levels of these different groups within the Army and its associated bureaucracy can be a boon for developing new technologies. Knowing that there are a lot of soldiers who do not really understand how to get the best out of their weapon, the engineer can reframe the user's thinking on small arms. In the process, they can create an opportunity to produce a new technology that not only balances marksmanship, firepower, willpower and stopping power, but might also be cheap and easy to produce.[12]

In this regard, the engineer's challenge is twofold. In the first place, they must develop a technology that works within the laws of physics. Just as importantly, however, the engineer must reconfigure the user's thinking in such a way as to avoid the suggestion that engineers know better than users. As engineers typically lack combat experience, this second imperative can sometimes be more difficult than simply developing a weapon system that works.

Yet in the years immediately after the Second World War, convincing users that it was possible to develop a rifle that more accurately reflected the challenges of the contemporary battlefield was precisely what British and latterly American engineers sought to do. Surveys like the one conducted by the WTSFF in May 1943 made it clear to those involved in the design and development of equipment that experience of battle did not qualify soldiers to offer an especially useful insight on weapon design. Consequently, if engineers were going to make a contribution towards solving battlefield problems and thus winning wars, then they, not the soldiers, would need to more objectively and consistently define both the user's requirements and the underlying nature of battle.

This chapter is, therefore, mainly concerned with exploring the way that engineers sought to reframe and make sense of user experiences of battle. Centred on the British perspective, the chapter shows how Britain's engineers tried to introduce an innovative design of assault rifle into the British Army. The arguments they developed in turn had a range of impacts on American engineers who were themselves going through a series of discussions on how to update rifle technology. In terms of military innovation, this represented neither top-down nor bottom-up innovation. Instead, we might describe the efforts of these engineers as middle-out innovation.

Set against a backdrop of post-war cooperation between transatlantic partners, rifle design offered a test case for establishing where power within the emerging North Atlantic Treaty Organisation would lie. If British engineers were successful at having their weapons adopted, then the whole of NATO would have to adopt British engineering standards. This brought with it the possibility of more direct influence over future weapon development and, in the process, held out the possibility that British small arms designers might avoid redundancy in any future financial retrenchment. Small arms thus represented a fight for power among Anglo-American engineers that would continue to have significant impact on NATO armed forces right up to the recent wars in Iraq and Afghanistan.

Defining the user requirements

In their failure to show how engineers make sense of and shape the organisational and technical challenges they are presented with, conventional approaches to military innovation tend to suggest that technologies evolve according to a utility or optimisation calculus. While such calculations may sometimes have accorded with the process of technological innovation, by themselves such analyses do not offer a sufficient explanation for the role of engineers in solving battlefield problems. In effect, then, what falls out of an analysis that exclusively discusses the battlefield, the soldier and the politico-military establishment is the role and agency of the engineer—the middleman who translates ideas and negotiates possibilities between user, civil servant and senior officers.

Conventional discussions do not consider the relative power and status of the engineer and therefore have little to say about how a successful engineer works to reinterpret and introduce different factors into the process of military–technical change. This somewhat theoretical perspective might sound detached from the specific process of small arms design. However, the literature on Science and Technology Studies offers us some coordinates that allow us to orientate our thinking on how designers and engineers understand and delimit socio-technical problems.[13] From this burgeoning literature, two ideas will help us to develop appropriate insights on the role of the engineer in small arms design.

The first is the idea that to be successful, an engineer must take on a number of roles that allow them to solve a technological problem. The underlying assumption here is the notion that there are social and technical aspects associated with researching, designing and developing a new technology. These domains demand different qualities from the engineer, allowing them to discuss and translate ideas between different constituencies that range from project and programme managers to finance teams, scientists, industrialists, soldiers, senior civilian and military personnel and of course those technologists who actually have to build effective prototype technologies. In the language of Science and Technology Studies, 'new technology requires the combining of different kinds of knowledge, stemming from different kinds of technological specialities and different social fields'.[14] As such, to be successful, the engineer needs to have as many heterogeneous qualities as the technological problem itself.

The second idea found in the STS literature that has application in this context is the notion of configuring users.[15] Here the central concern is in how to refashion the user problem in a manner that engineers believe they can work with. In the process, they reinterpret user expectations in such a way that the users believe they are getting the best possible solution. In this respect, engineers have to construct arguments that constrain the way users define their needs and interpret a particular technology. The engineer's challenge is to delimit the possibilities available to the user to such an extent as to make it possible to actually build a weapon. Thus, the testing phase of a technology becomes a central location for establishing how powerful the engineer is at asserting their particular technological interpretation over that of the user. The weapon consequently becomes a point of contestation, allowing users to resist the ambitions of the engineer and instead assert their own preferences. Viewed this way, weapons become a metaphor for investigating the power of different expert communities within the military–technical bureaucracy: whether engineers or users might be considered more or less powerful relative to each other.[16]

In the context of post-Second World War small arms debates, the ability of British engineers to assert their own power relative to that of the War Office or the infantry demanded they address existing plans that had already been put in place. Powerful constituencies like former field commanders, officers who had come to settled perspectives on small arms, would have to be taken into account before it would be possible to advance alternative suggestions. For British and American engineers, this meant dealing with the nexus of issues associated with marksmanship, firepower, willpower and stopping power. However, the transatlantic responses to these impulses were different. American ordnance officials were unwilling to challenge the pre-eminence of the .30 calibre found in the M-1 Garand. As a result, American post-war small arms would be bound by an ammunition type that engineers would find difficult to work with in their efforts to design a new automatic rifle.

By contrast, British engineers were willing to have a go at challenging the considered views of senior officers, but faced opposition from within the War Office and eventually from American ordnance officials, opposition that would need to be countered before a new proposal could get off the ground. Both the General Staff at the War Office and commanders in the field were all committed to the importance of marksmanship over firepower, just as Britain's industrial infrastructure was geared towards maintaining it. Set against this backdrop, it is remarkable that British engineers should attempt to reframe military thinking and deliver a new fully automatic firearm at a time when the Army itself was unwilling to contemplate radical changes to its small arms. As historians have been critical of British tactical prowess, it is even more remarkable that the initial impulse to develop an assault weapon should emerge in the UK and not in the United States.

In the first instance, the post-war development of infantry weapons in Britain was left to the Small Arms Group (SAG) of the Armament Design Establishment (ADE).[17] This group had emerged out of the wartime Armament Design Department. Administratively a part of the Ministry of Supply, the wartime section was commanded by Assistant Chief Engineer Armament Design (A/CEAD) Colonel R. Shepard and was located in the Drill hall at Cheshunt. At its height it could boast as many as 170 design staff. Many of these designers had escaped occupied Europe, and some, including the Belgian engineers who would go back to Liège after the war and set up the arms manufacturer Fabrique Nationale d'Armes de Guerre (FN), went on to become key to small arms development across NATO.[18]

Answerable to the director general of artillery, the ADE emerged after the end of the Second World War with a much greater range of facilities and capabilities than it had had before 1939. In particular, according to Commander Mitchell, the chief engineer armament design (CEAD), the SAG was now 'capable of dealing with complete design and the Department was determined that it should not be allowed to return to its pre-war condition.'[19] Yet even before fighting in Europe came to a close, the engineers who had escaped from various occupied countries started to disperse back to their home countries, making it hard to maintain capability. Furthermore, by 1945 it was clear that Britain faced a potential financial crisis, which the newly elected Labour Government was anxiously looking to avoid. One of the most obvious places for the Treasury to seek to cut costs was in the realm of defence and especially research and development.[20] There was, therefore, a very strong possibility that the Ordnance Departments would be pared back to pre-war levels.[21]

During the war, the SAG had been engaged in developing a number of firearms including the Sten sub-machine gun and various experimental automatic and semiautomatic rifles. These included Self-Loading Experimental Models 1 & 2 (SLEM 1&2) brought from Belgium. Chambered to fire rimless 7.92 x 57mm German ammunition—the same ammunition used in Royal Armour Corps Besa tank machine guns—these weapons could have provided the UK with a near instant semiautomatic weapon while Britain was still fighting.[22] In the early years, however, British manufacturing capability was stretched to its limits in trying to replace what had been lost at Dunkirk and keep up with the demand created through conscription.[23] Consequently, the War Office believed it to be impracticable to replace the SMLE and No. 4 Rifle, especially given the need to rapidly field a sub-machine gun comparable to the German MP40.

Thus, at the beginning of the war, the focus was on designing and manufacturing the Sten machine carbine or SMG.[24] Although the Sten ultimately proved to be a very successful innovation, the earlier versions had been very poorly put together and 237,732 Mk. Is and Mk. IIs, or 16 per cent of the total, were withdrawn from service.[25] This shook the confidence of many in the infantry and shaped the views of those on the General Staff who were concerned with ensuring soldiers had sufficient quantities of reliable equipment. Contextualised in this way, it is no surprise that while Britain was committed to fighting alongside and dependent on equipment provided by the United States, General Staff policy would be to standardise on American calibres wherever possible.[26] Consequently, as of March 1943, the British Army was set to adopt—depending on future US small arms policy—the .30'06 calibre round and M-1 Garand rifle once the war against the Axis powers was over.[27] By January 1944, after lobbying by the director of infantry, this policy was relaxed to allow experimental work conducted by the ADE on 7.92 x 57mm ammunition to continue. However, it was also explicitly stated that all future research efforts would be directed towards developing a round that was compatible with US preferences.[28]

While the SAG could design and build weapons, any real influence on the director of infantry could only be asserted with the help of the director of artillery (small arms), Brigadier J.A. Barlow. Barlow was deputy head of the Weapons Technical Staff at the Ministry of Supply during the war and was responsible for feeding back user requests to the War Office Committee on Infantry Weapon Development. As a rare two-time winner of the King's Prize at Bisley, Barlow was recognised as a keen marksman, having been a member of the Army Eight shooting team sixteen times and its captain between 1925 and 1946. Apart from his involvement in the Army shooting team, Barlow also shot for Britain at the 1948 and 1952 Olympics.[29]

Before the war, while assistant superintendent at the Design Department at Hythe, Barlow had given evidence to the Special Meeting of the Small Arms Committee investigating the inefficiencies of British small arms development. Consequently, Barlow knew very well how far Britain's design establishments had come since 1937.[30] It was Barlow who would make the case for a new weapon designed by the ADE and it was Barlow who would persuade the director of infantry that an alternative to an American calibre was the best solution to the problem of infantry combat. On top of this, however, it was also Barlow's evidence, while he was part of the WTSFF, which would shape the way the director of infantry understood the infantry's technical problems during and immediately after the Second World War.

The challenge facing Britain's engineers was twofold. In the first instance, they had to unpick existing Army policy on standardising US calibres. At the same time, they had to develop a new weapon system which might fit the gap they had created by undermining the Army's policy on US ammunition. Of the two challenges, the issue that needed most urgent resolution concerned the design of new small arms ammunition. Without a change of calibre, it would not be possible to resolve the marksmanship, firepower, willpower, stopping-power conundrum and deliver the tactical flexibility they believed the infantry actually needed. At the same time, however, engineers could not allow the General Staff to choose an existing type of rimless ammunition, or else their own ambitions for a new type of firearm would be dashed before they had even got it off the drawing board.

According to the engineers, there were several reasons why the US .30'06 round and M-1 Garand rifle were inappropriate for British service. First, they argued that the M-1's use of an eight-round clip mechanism made the rifle hard to reload. Secondly, they pointed out that the adoption of .30'06 ammunition would result in having two distinct cartridges in an infantry battalion at the same time: one for the .30'06 Garand and one for the .303 Bren LMG and Vickers MMG. This would complicate logistics and make it harder to swap ammunition between weapon systems in an emergency and when unit reserves were low. Thirdly, the ADE was aware that the Americans were redesigning their existing cartridge so nothing would be gained from prematurely converting to a round that would become outdated. Fourthly, the .30'06 round was longer than the .303 cartridge. Consequently, it would be both difficult and extremely costly to change the length of the firing chamber in existing British firearms so as to make room for the longer American cartridge.[31] Lastly, the ADE argued that changing to an American calibre would compromise existing Army tactics and organisational practices. They wrote,

> It can be said in general that American weapons are technically efficient. Since, however, organisation is fundamentally based on weapons whether individual or demanding a weapon team for their maintenance in action, unless British and American organisations and tactical employment can be brought into line, it is difficult to assess the battle-worthiness of American weapons vis-à-vis our own.[32]

Appealing to the prejudices of Britain's regimental system, these arguments amounted to a powerful battery of technical and organisational reasons for avoiding a changeover to US equipment. Barlow and the British small arms community were employing a number of arguments that would stop existing initiatives to adopt US equipment and in the process give them the time to develop an alternative British solution. In effect, then, this assessment formed the basis upon which to build the case for a completely new standard of ammunition and a rifle to fire it.

In their efforts to develop new small arms technology, the Armament Design Establishment set up an Ideal Calibre Panel in February 1945. Chaired by the physicist Dr Richard Beeching, who went on to author the Beeching Report that closed much of Britain's rail network, this panel was charged with assessing the science of ballistics in order to identify an optimum British calibre of ammunition.[33] Barlow and the engineers intended to use the evidence the panel produced to fill the gap they had created with their arguments against adopting .30′06 ammunition. In March 1947, after much analysis, Beeching reported that future ammunition ought to have a calibre ranging from .250 to .270 depending on the bullet's core material.[34] This report would form the basis of the argument Barlow and the SAG would use to drive home change at the War Office. Despite all this effort, however, the recommendations made by the Panel were not the ones that Barlow took to the War Office for approval.[35] Instead, he proposed a calibre with a larger bore ranging from .270 to .280.[36] Having gone to all the effort of developing the evidence, why did British engineers discount the scientific analysis and suggest something other than that proposed by the Ideal Calibre Panel?

Resisting the engineer

The previous chapter alluded to the ways in which different officers within the Army asserted their power. This was shaped by military convention and wartime realities. Even after the war, however, the director of infantry's position within the War Office did not necessarily mean he could dictate future small arms policy, despite being given the technical responsibility for investigating weapons provision for the Army. In these circumstances, the director of infantry with the help of Barlow and the ADE had to develop a range of arguments that could reframe the problem in the hope of winning over the General Staff. Although the ADE had successfully discredited the .30'06 round, it did not follow that the General Staff would give up on the underlying characteristics embodied by the American ammunition. Far from delivering what might be considered the ideal solution to the battlefield problem, then, the findings of the Ideal Panel Calibre would have to take into account the prevailing preferences at the War Office. At the same time, a decision not to adopt the US round would alienate American military and ordnance officials who otherwise might have been in the prime position to develop British as well as American small arms.

The manner in which Britain's General Staff would think about future ammunition depended on how their expectations were managed. In this respect, the initial talks between Barlow and the director of infantry were concerned with framing the work of the Ideal Calibre Panel by emphatically stating that the British infantry wanted to adopt a weapon whose 'main object was to achieve the ideal calibre for our own use ...' and that the 'primary object was not standardisation with the USA ...'[37] The explicit objective of the Panel was to 'facilitate the design of the most efficient weapons and ammunition compatible with the lightest weight ...', and their starting point was derived from the work of the Standing Committee on Infantry Weapon Development, which had defined a list of requirements for ammunition in 1944 at the behest of the director of infantry.[38]

These requirements stated that the ammunition should be capable of firing out to a maximum of 800 yards with an accuracy grouping for five rounds of 3 inches at 200 yards and have a trajectory that was as flat as possible, especially at 600 yards.[39] The ammunition had to be suitable for use in a self-loading rifle, a sniper's rifle and a light automatic gun. The 1944 requirements also set the ambition of using the same ammunition in a medium machine gun (MMG). This would be a difficult challenge for engineers, as MMG ammunition needed to hit targets at greater distances. The priority, however, was to produce the most appropriate ammunition for the rifles and automatic gun.[40]

Given these initial terms of reference, the Ideal Calibre Panel had reported without considering whether its proposals would satisfy the wider General

Staff's ambition of standardisation with the United States. Unhindered by the need to satisfy American requirements, the Panel focused its investigations on ammunition compatible with achieving the ballistic qualities as defined in 1944. As it became clear just how important US–UK ammunition standardisation was to the General Staff, Barlow and the ADE decided to re-interpret the Ideal Calibre Panel's recommendations. The engineers sought to reframe the ideal solution in such a way as to take into account the reality of the debate within the War Office.

Thus, the new goal was to match the .30′06 round in a few key areas in the hope that the General Staff would agree that standardisation might be achieved on British rather than American terms. Accordingly, in the summer of 1947, Barlow and the ADE stated that they would build a round that would have the striking energy of at least 87ftlbs at 2,000 yards or the equivalent to that produced by a .30′06, 150 grain bullet fired at 2750fps.[41] As only larger bore ammunition could achieve these conditions, Barlow took the decision to modify the findings of the Ideal Calibre Panel. The decision to develop ammunition with calibres ranging from .270 to .280 rather than between .250 and .270 was, therefore, a tactical move designed to help massage arguments and was made in recognition of the types of debates going on at the War Office in 1946–7.[42] Barlow's decision to match the striking energy of US .30′06 ammunition at 2,000 yards was important, for the decision would frame the technical arguments that were eventually employed for defining whether US or UK ammunition would become the NATO standard.

The first technological casualty of the decision to match US ammunition characteristics at 2,000 yards was the idea of developing a .270 round. The .270 round had allowed Barlow to claim that they were following Dr Beeching's scientific advice. Barlow was fully aware, however, that getting a .270 round to achieve the same ballistic qualities as .30′06 ammunition was extremely unlikely. Consequently, after fourteen months of development, the ADE finally acknowledged that the .270 could not achieve the same striking energy as the US .30′06, given the mass of the bullet and the speed at which it could be made to travel. Accordingly, by November 1948, Barlow conceded that in the time allowed it was not possible to bring the .270 to an acceptable level of maturity.[43] Work on this ammunition was not dropped altogether as there was considerable political capital to be gained with both the General Staff and the Americans if it could be demonstrated that the calibre was at least technically viable. Nevertheless, it was put further back down the priority list in favour of ensuring that the .280 ammunition worked properly.

However, even as the British were refining their own technical solutions, there was a great deal of danger that American ordnance experts might also develop a system that would trump them. At a 1946 meeting of the US War Department Equipment Board, known as the Stillwell Board after its chairman General Stillwell, the decision had already been taken to replace the Garand but maintain the .30 calibre. The new American rifle would be lighter than the M-1, capable of selective semiautomatic and automatic fire and have the 'ballistic performance equivalent to that of the present rifle'.[44] The board wanted 'greater firepower—lighter weight', but was not prepared to upset the consensus on .30′06 ammunition to achieve it.[45]

In the spring of 1946, the British Joint Staff Mission to Washington reported that the General Staff could adopt American ammunition without fear that the United States would change to a new calibre 'for some years to come'.[46] However, when it emerged in late July 1946 that the US Ordnance Department was also working on a new round—the properties of which were shrouded in mystery—there was a possibility that the .30′06 might be replaced.[47] The round (eventually known as the T65) was a .30 calibre bullet with a shorter cartridge case. Using the latest propellants, the round cut weight but delivered similar ballistic performance to the existing .30′06 round. More worrying from a General Staff perspective, if the Americans adopted the T65 in advance of a US–UK standardisation agreement, then Britain would be adopting a .30′06 round that had already been made redundant. This new piece of intelligence accordingly presented the director of infantry, Barlow and the ADE with the perfect opportunity to push home their case that a new British calibre would offer Britain's General Staff some certainty over their future small arms.

Consequently, in the summer of 1947, the General Staff found it easier to agree to the compromise range of rounds proposed by the director of infantry, Barlow and the Ideal Calibre Panel. The price the engineers would have to pay in order to get War Office consent was to hold comparative US–UK ammunition trials. In these tests, which were initially scheduled for the spring of 1949, Britain's engineers would have to demonstrate that their round could match US Army requirements.[48] Barlow and the ADE had been willing to put aside the Ideal Calibre Panel's suggestion that the optimal round was between .250 and .270 if it made it easier for them to realise their goal of producing a weapon that would appeal to the War Office. However, just because the War Office might be brought around by this sleight of hand, it did not follow that the US Ordnance Corps could be so easily persuaded.

In effect, the War Office's decision forced Britain's innovators into asking American engineers to decide how far to go in the defence of the US Army's marksmanship tradition. Given the balance of interests and the strength of support that had emerged in favour of the .30′06 round and the M-1 Garand, it seemed doubtful that any voices would bubble up within the US Army to argue for the sorts of automatic weapons envisaged by Barlow and the ADE. After all, the balance of relationships in favour of the M-1 Garand had been extremely difficult to create before the Second World War and no-one in the US War Department was keen to fragment the existing firearms consensus. Consequently, the British were unlikely to find obvious allies within the American military establishment who would help to advance a case for a smaller calibre weapon.

This problem was compounded by the fact that the .280 round the British were working on had negative connotations connected with the American military establishment's pre-war ammunition debates. In fact, the British .280 round was actually .276″ calibre. However, the officer in charge of the post-War US Small Arms Section, Colonel René Studler, had also been proof officer on the Pig Board trials during the inter-war period. It was therefore important to avoid any negative connotations associated with the Pedersen .276″ if the British were to make a successful case for change with their American counterparts. It didn't matter that the .280 ammunition didn't have the same characteristics as the Pedersen round, but it was imperative to give the British round a distinct identity. Thus, in October 1947, Brigadier Barlow decided to remove any references to the fact and wrote, 'I consider it desirable that the .276″ should be referred to henceforth as the .280.'[49] There was no technical reason for making this decision. It was simply about presentation.

However, by the spring of 1949, Britain's innovators had decided that they would have to do more than make cosmetic changes if they were to convince the US Small Arms Section that their solution would meet the US Army's needs. In the first instance, Barlow decided to redesign the ADE's cartridge casing so that the extractor groove complied with US standards.[50] While this might sound trivial, it was in fact an attempt by the British to show that US weapons would not have to have their own extractor mechanism replaced if they were to be re-chambered to fire British ammunition. Consequently, a simple alteration in cartridge design would mean fewer changes to US manufacturing tools, creating considerable savings in both time and money.

More than this, however, Britain's engineers had to further refine their ambitious rifle designs in order to match US requirements and remove any additional counter-arguments the Americans might use to defeat their project. The British consequently decided to push their battlefield solution beyond the proposals they had made at the War Office. This meant that Barlow and the ADE had to reverse-engineer British user requirements in order to create the space that would allow their own weapon design to straddle transatlantic standardisation debates.

Re-engineering the battlefield

To get to the point where Britain's engineers could develop and test a new fully automatic rifle, they had to redefine the battlefield problem such that they could deliver their preferred technical solution. If they were successful in redefining the battlefield problem, then they stood a chance of producing agreement with the user community. This inevitably meant developing sophisticated arguments that could win over those sections of the General Staff who were otherwise happier to select American technologies than buy British. The attitudes of the General Staff largely reflected the prevailing thoughts of Field Marshal Montgomery, who had become Chief of the Imperial General Staff (CIGS) after the war. With Montgomery's departure and replacement by Field Marshal Slim in January 1949, however, the atmosphere at the War Office became more conducive to the proposals that were being made by the engineers. In effect, these proposals would provide the infantry with the means to reverse the decision Montgomery had made when he demoted Lieutenant Colonel Wigram in 1943. This did not mean that British engineers could guarantee sufficient control over the development agenda to prevent their American counterparts from upsetting their own case for change. Nonetheless, it did imply there would be fewer senior British commanders who might stand in the way of any proposals the engineers might make.

Even though the development cycle had been ongoing since 1944, it was only in December 1946 that Barlow proposed building an assault rifle for the infantry. This new weapon would replace both the bolt action rifle and the sub-machine gun.[51] Barlow's suggestions were based on an awareness of the small arms projects then underway at the ADE and his understanding of the infantry's requirements as identified by the Committee on Infantry Weapon development and defined by the director of infantry in 1944.[52] The ADE, under the leadership of Noel Kent-Lemon, a lead engineer and project manager in the Small Arms Group, had been working to refine three existing rifle designs for potential application to whatever small calibre ammunition could be agreed to with the War Office since at least May 1946. On the assumption that the next weapon needed to increase the firepower and reduce the number of different small arms in the inventory, three design teams were set to consider the issues associated with developing a light firearm intended to replace the rifle, the sub-machine gun, the self-loading rifle and the LMG.[53] Until the Ideal Calibre Panel had reported, these weapons were chambered to fire 7.92mm ammunition.[54]

The War Office's Organisation and Weapons Policy Committee officially considered the matter in April 1947. In a paper put together by the director of military training (DMT), General Keightley, the committee stated that 'The last war emphasised the need to reduce the weight [of the rifle] ... and to increase its rate of fire. Accuracy beyond 300 yards was not required.'[55] Accordingly, there was a preference for an automatic weapon that would combine 'the functions of the Rifle and the Machine Carbine [or sub-machine gun] ...'[56] Reflecting the input from the Committee on Infantry Weapon Development, this document stated explicitly that the requirement for scientifically accurate shooting out to 600 yards was no longer necessary and that the new automatic rifle need only be sighted to 500 yards. Other firearms in the inventory would take care of targets at longer distances.

By May 1947, Kent-Lemon and the SAG had to make some choices about which of their three prototype weapons might fulfil the draft specifications outlined by the DMT. Bearing in mind that no definite agreement on ammunition had yet been reached between the British and the Americans, it was decided to proceed with the development of two of the three weapons.[57] Of these, one was already in a bullpup design and the other, which had a conventional layout, was to be re-configured in a similar way.[58] The original bullpup rifle was eventually known as the EM-2 and had been created by Captain Kazimierz Januszewski, a design engineer who had escaped from occupied Europe. The conventional weapon that was re-configured into a bullpup design was renamed the EM-1.[59] Thus, five months before a new General Staff Policy Statement was issued revising ammunition policy, the ADE had already made key decisions about what the future infantry weapon would look like, selecting two rifles as the basis for further research.[60] This could not be described as designing the rifle around the ammunition, a slogan that Brigadier Barlow sometimes used with the General Staff and in talks with the Americans to justify their design choices. Making a decision to develop a new class of infantry weapon based on such an unconventional bullpup configuration, without knowing what ammunition it would use, was bold. How could the choice be justified?

As the central ambition of those developing the EM-1 and 2 was to increase the infantry section's firepower while reducing the weight a man had to carry, there were several advantages that could be derived from a bullpup over more traditional rifle designs.[61] In a conventionally configured rifle, the wooden stock was its heaviest part. The stock had two purposes. First, it was located directly behind the main axis of the firing chamber where it was perfectly placed to help absorb excess recoil energy. Secondly, it allowed the soldier to rest his cheek across it so that he could aim the weapon more accurately. By adopting a bullpup design and removing the stock, the ADE successfully reduced the weight of the weapon. At the same time, however, they created a number of complications related to controlling excessive recoil and aiming the rifle. Developing a new unit sight that sat on a carry handle half way down the barrel meant the infantryman did not have to bend his head into a contorted position to aim the rifle. The question was whether the design teams could restrict the amount of recoil energy generated in the firing chamber to levels that would not result in an uncontrollable or unusable weapon.

Kent-Lemon and the ADE's answer to this problem was twofold. First, while the removal of the stock created challenges related to aiming the weapon, it also beneficially resulted in a straight line action where the barrel of the rifle was perpendicular to the shoulder of the firer. This contrasted with the vast majority of conventional rifles, which had a dropped butt to allow the soldier to place his head in line with the aiming reticule down the barrel of the weapon. In a bullpup weapon, recoil energies are more efficiently absorbed by the shooter's body, potentially making the weapon easier to control. Secondly, firing the weapon in fully automatic mode would put the parts of the weapon under considerable strain that normally would have been alleviated by making the various components more robust. Achieving this invariably meant increasing the weight of the weapon. The ADE, however, recognised that if the calibre of the ammunition could be reduced and the recoil energies of the propellant charge moderated, then this would obviate the need to increase the strength and subsequent weight of the weapon.

When Britain's engineers were making their case for a smaller round of ammunition at the War Office, they were therefore setting up the conditions in which they might more easily design a firearm that could be used both as a sub-machine gun and a self-loading rifle. The flick of a lever would change the weapon from one mode of firing to the other. Crucially, the removal of the stock did not compromise the length of the barrel, so it was still possible to achieve reasonable range and accuracy. If, however, the ammunition became larger, the rifle might still function perfectly well in the self-loading role but would probably become uncontrollable when firing automatically in the sub-machine gun or LMG role. If the aim was to give the infantry a weapon that could fulfil at least two roles, then the question of ammunition would be of extreme importance.[62] If the Americans rejected the smaller calibre ammunition, then the entire project to combine a sub-machine gun and rifle into one weapon might become untenable. The comparative US–UK ammunition trials in 1949 would become the focal point for deciding this issue.

Having won over the General Staff, British engineers still needed to ensure that their rifle and ammunition would go down well with the Americans. In this respect, Barlow, Kent-Lemon and the ADE engineers tried to stretch the EM-2 design to meet US Army requirements. Thus, even though the director of infantry had already decided that the British Army would not need a rifle grenade, the Americans felt this was essential.[63] This prompted Brigadier Barlow to conclude that 'if we cannot prove that we can fire grenades by means of a launcher with our weapons and ammunition we shall not stand a chance of convincing the USA that our .280 calibre solution is the right one'.[64] In relation to both the cartridge case and the rifle grenade, the EM-2 advocates were clearly looking to develop equipment characteristics that would appeal to American decision-makers.

At the same time, it was becoming clear during the course of late 1948 and early 1949 that American engineers were trying to railroad a production order for their own prototype rifle through the US Army. Colonel René Studler, the head of the US Small Arm Section at the Ordnance Corps, was determined to resist the ambitions of the British engineers. Socially ambitious and determined to reach the very top of the Ordnance Corps, Studler intended to make his weapon the best in the world.[65] American soldiers had to be armed with American designed and built weapons. To that end, Studler directly lobbied General Omar Bradley, Army chief of staff, to order 5,000 prototype American weapons called the T25 in the hope of presenting the EM-2 advocates with a *fait accompli*.[66] If successful, Studler would have shown the British that the US Army was committed to an American design of firearm. That he failed can partly be explained by the intervention of the British Joint Service Mission at the UK's Washington Embassy which wrote directly to Bradley asking him not to place an order. Frustrated by the British intervention and unable to deliver his *fait accompli*, Studler was forced into asking for a delay to US–UK trials, previously scheduled for 1949. This would allow American engineers more time to prepare and perfect the T25.[67] Crucially for Barlow and British engineers, however, this interaction revealed that Bradley was not well disposed towards a fully automatic firearm and thought the .280 ammunition rather small.[68]

Studler's efforts to disrupt British ambitions did not end with his direct lobbying of the US Army chief of staff. Having been granted a delay by the British to allow the T25 to be brought up to an appropriate developmental level, the Americans subsequently took as much time as they could in agreeing the details of the 1949 comparative trials. Knowing that Britain's General Staff were in a rush to replace the No. 4 Rifle, Studler hoped that any delays would undermine the British before the Americans had even completed their work on the T25.[69] The Americans, by contrast, were happy to stretch out the length of time it took to reach agreement both in relation to defining the test plan and in conducting the tests themselves.

In the first iteration of the test plan, it was envisaged that the technical would precede the user trials. The technical trials were designed to verify the physical characteristics of the rifle, such as the muzzle velocity or the number of rounds that could be fired before the weapon failed. User trials, in contrast, gave soldiers the chance to fire the weapon on a range, following a test plan that investigated matters such as ease of use, handiness, accuracy or controllability. Usually, the technical preceded the user tests so that weapons that did not meet the specifications could be ruled out. However, with the Aberdeen Proving Ground stating that it needed 385 working days just to complete the technical trials, the British soon protested that it would take too long before a recommendation could be made.[70] Not only would this hamper efforts by the War Office to replace the No. 4 Rifle, it would also prevented the ADE from deploying its resources on other projects. The two sides eventually agreed that it would save time if the technical and user trials were run in parallel. The trade-off was that the British had to agree to submit fewer weapons for trial so that the tests could be completed more quickly. Accordingly, the EM-2 advocates decided to drop the EM-1 from the test plan so that enough time would be available to test the EM-2 and the American T25.[71]

In addition to the debates about when and how long the trials would take, the Americans also went to some lengths to amend the procedures and terms of reference for both the Working Committee overseeing the technical trials and the US Army Equipment Board managing the user trials. With regard to the technical trials, Studler refused to accept that he had no choice other than to take the findings and recommendations of the Working Committee directly to the Pentagon's standardisation officers.[72] Instead, he wanted the results of the technical trials to be sent to the Army Equipment Board, where additional comments would be allowed.[73] The British complained that this amounted to asking the layman to discuss matters of technical detail.

This might have been something that could have been negotiated away. What could not, however, was the fact that Colonel Studler was also trying to define the .280 out of the user trial's remit. The US Army Equipment Board had initially been instructed:

> To review, and, where necessary, revise the War Department Equipment Board Report (1946) [i.e. the report of the Stillwell Board] for the purpose of establishing the principal equipment requirements of the army to serve as a guide to research and development.[74]

By March 1950, however, this had been changed to read:

> A lightweight calibre .30 rifle is required which, with minor modifications, is capable of replacing all present shoulder fired small arms including the BAR.[75]

If this clause had been allowed to remain, then the .280 would have immediately failed the criteria. As it was, the British Joint Service Mission's liaison officers were quick to spot the changes and the original wording was put back. Increasingly, it seemed the Americans were prepared to adopt underhand tactics in order to get their own way, a situation that led Brigadier Barlow to comment in a draft letter that 'this is a back door approach to queer the pitch, and get something on the records on a high enough level in the Pentagon to ensure that our proposals are stillborn, even though the test results may be distinctly favourable'.[76]

But it was not as if the trials were implemented with impartiality in mind. For the fact of the matter was that both sides were guilty of trying to distort the tests in order to show how their respective weapon was superior. The best example of this is related to the rifle grenade investigations. As already stated, Britain had no need for a rifle grenade, but the ADE weapons were modified to account for an American requirement. In April 1950, the EM-2 was subsequently tested at Fort Benning using an M.11.A.2 grenade. The ADE, however, had optimised the EM-2 to fire the wartime US M.9.A.1, as agreed in the test plan. When the British weapon suffered significant damage, it emerged in the ensuing investigations conducted by the ADE that the Americans had deliberately changed grenades.[77] Given the US preconceptions of .280 ammunition, this kind of trick severely undermined the impression the EM-2 advocates were trying to create.

Conclusion

In the face of a user community that appeared to have contradictory perspectives on the weapons they had been issued with and senior officers who had fixed views on small arms, it fell to the engineers themselves to define a range of technical possibilities that they believed would address the problems of the battlefield. This did not represent top-down or bottom-up innovation but innovation from the middle-out.

These designs put forward by the engineers could not be developed simply on the basis of identifying a set of technical characteristics that the weapons needed to satisfy. Engineers had to create a need for those characteristics by reframing existing discussion on marksmanship, firepower, willpower and stopping-power. This resulted in developing weapons and ammunition independently of any guidance being offered by the user community. Given the criticsms that Hastings and D'Este have made of British infantryman during the Second World War, it is perhaps surprising to find out that Britain's engineering community had decided to develop innovative technologies before their American counterparts.

The possibility that British engineers might successfully reframe existing discussion and still develop a sufficiently robust weapon did, however, revolve around the question of ammunition calibre. If a small calibre round was adopted, then it would be possible to build a weapon that met the needs of the infantry as understood by British engineers. However, it would be difficult to make a case stating that the selection of the .280 calibre round proceeded on the basis of an inherent technological logic. Instead, despite the available scientific and battlefield evidence, the efforts of the EM-2 advocates were founded on drawing attention to, and capitalising on, the unclear intentions of the American Army and whether they would replace their ammunition or not. In these circumstances, the General Staff opted for a British solution of ammunition because of their uncertainty about what was happening on the other side of the Atlantic.

However, the argument that the EM-2 advocates made for introducing an untried cartridge reflected the practical difficulties of building a case for change that would work within the organisational context of the post-1945 War Office. This might not have been such a problem but for the fact that the General Staff wanted to achieve standardisation with the United States wherever possible. American .30′06 calibre ammunition was capable of hitting targets out to 2,000 yards. The .250 to .270 calibre range suggested by the Ideal Calibre Panel was too small to match American requirements.

Knowing this, the EM-2 advocates decided to stretch the suggestions made by their scientific advisors in order to give themselves a chance of convincing various members of the General Staff that their ammunition suggestions would meet US demands for engaging targets at distance. The proposed .280 calibre round was not therefore the 'ideal' round, but came about as a result of discussions within the War Office. The .280 ammunition was consequently open to two interpretations. On the one hand, it was optimised for British requirements, which stated that an automatic firearm was necessary for ranges under 500 yards. At the same time, those General Staff who preferred long-range marksmanship believed that the new round would be capable of hitting targets out to 2,000 yards and would therefore satisfy US demands. Both the advocates of the .280 round and those members of the General Staff who remained sceptical could see what they wanted in the ammunition.

In terms of the rifle, the EM-2 advocates believed the ideal solution was to adopt a selective fire automatic weapon. Brigadier Barlow, the archetypal heterogeneous engineer, could use his experience as a shooter, a member of the Army and the head of the Small Arms Section at the Ministry of Supply to try to knit different types of argument together in order to convince the War Office. Certain members of the General Staff, however, remained unconvinced, arguing that this would compromise marksmanship and potentially increase the strain on the supply chain through increased ammunition usage. With this in mind, and in order to keep the Staff on side, the EM-2 advocates worked on a bullpup rifle design which would facilitate long-range shooting. At the same time, a smaller calibre would make it easier to use the rifle in fully automatic mode, thereby giving the infantry the kinds of tactical flexibility that Lionel Wigram had been advocating during the Second World War.

This stance may ultimately have satisfied the various perspectives encapsulated in British ambitions, but American Ordnance officials were equally conscious of the need to protect their own initiatives. Developing arguments that reframed user needs in the UK did not automatically translate into US requirements. Instead, a new set of arguments would need to be developed—specifically aimed at the US small arms and user communities. The result of this was a hotly contested debate in which Anglo-American engineers found themselves at loggerheads trying to protect their respective positions using whatever arguments and tricks they could. How this delicate balance of agreements in Britain might be sustained when confronted with the institutional interests of the American Ordnance Corps and the scientific evidence that they would use to undermine British suggestions is the subject of the next chapter.

4

THE SCIENCE OF KILLING

... from the public point of view, this is a case where ignorance is bliss.

Professor Major Greenwood, UK Medical Research Council, 1939[1]

In October 1939, Solly Zuckerman and his colleague Desmond Bernal sat in a trench in Salisbury Plain testing the effect of explosive shock on monkeys inside bomb shelters. Three years later, and after a great deal of experimentation, Zuckerman would revolutionise the science of killing and in his own words create 'the new subject of wound ballistics'.[2] Developed out of the suffering caused by Luftwaffe raids on London, this new subject was not founded purely out of scientific curiosity. On the contrary, if the process of wounding could be understood, then the public could be more effectively protected from enemy action and the armed forces given weapons that were more likely to defeat the Axis powers. The object of this new science was the more efficient use of national resources in an effort to avoid 'overkill'.

While the science might have aimed at an objective analysis of the processes of killing, the notion of overkill had distinctly social connotations, for the fact of the matter was that different nations viewed overkill differently. The British had been fighting alone and for some considerable time. The resources that the country needed to support its war effort had to be imported from overseas. British engineers had to use what little they had available, frugally and with an eye for wastage. By comparison, as the United States was neither reliant on imported raw materials nor subject to air raids, these same resource constraints did not apply to American industrial capacity. The mathematics of wounding consequently resonated differently with American ordnance officials and engineers who may have understood the potential benefits of this new science but did not necessarily feel compelled to adopt the principles that emerged out of Zuckerman's research agenda.

From the start, then, the science of wound ballistics was framed by political imperatives and national perspectives that shaped the underlying attitudes of those who were called on to engage with this new subject. Consequently, the science was seen through the lens of those engaged in ordnance design. Indeed, the very possibility of developing a pure science—divorced from wider considerations of policy and the practice of killing—was deemed unnecessary by the scientific and medical communities. More accurately, the very reason for a science of wound ballistics was its practical application: to facilitate engineers in their efforts either to protect people from the effects of technology or prosecute war in a manner that they believed would produce more effective results. It was war and the calculations of strategists that gave oxygen to this nascent discipline, but it was the challenges posed by engineers that would ultimately create the conditions from which the field would emerge and entrench itself.

The ability of scientists to establish the facts of wounding was therefore dependent on the willingness of engineers to accede to, and subsequently verify, any theoretical findings that might be offered. In this respect, the science was as much a matter of social relationships between different expert communities as it was an ethical, organisational or societal concern framed by differing outlooks on what might constitute overkill. Into these contexts, scientists were asked to arbitrate between weapons and ordnance design. However, their ability to do this was in turn conditioned by the way a problem was presented to them. Any pure research into wounding that they had undertaken could be turned for or against a technology depending on whether it reinforced or challenged particular engineering or military prejudices. In this respect, the science could confirm strongly held views as much as it could challenge them.

When framed this way, lethality can only be understood within its wider social context. The challenge lies in the fact that lethality constitutes the intersection between a whole range of disciplines from ballistics to surgery, from engineering to the law. Inevitably, then, and putting the grisly nature of the subject to one side, the concept is loaded with interdisciplinary controversy.[3] From the perspective of establishing the genealogy of the field, however, it is important not to let any single interpretation limit the parameters of study. In particular, although a legalistic interpretation of lethality backed by scientific research offers an 'objective' way to protect combatants and engineers from criminal prosecution, such modes of thinking also limit an exploration of the social factors that have shaped how the science of killing as a separate field of study has emerged. Anchoring the science of killing within a specific socio-technical process like developing a gun is therefore important if the interconnected and social processes for defining lethality are to be articulated effectively.

The central theme of this chapter is concerned with showing how scientists emerged as experts in lethality, and the extent to which they could shape the engineering debates that evolved as different technologies for killing were developed. In the process, I will demonstrate that Erik Prokosch and Joanna Bourke have offered insufficient explanations for the science of wounding as it emerged over the twentieth century.[4] While they may suggest there is a one-to-one relationship between the evolution of the science of killing and the emergence of more lethal weaponry, this chapter shows that their ethical stance on militarism has clouded their judgement in explaining how scientific change works as a sociological phenomenon in relation to the weapons of war. In particular, this chapter will show that the science of wounding did not follow a linear trajectory or indeed necessarily define which weapons countries would eventually adopt.

Nevertheless, it is fair to observe that the practices that framed the relationship between science and technology, and the discipline that was born as a result, established an underlying philosophy that moulded the mentality of the military–industrial complex that was fostered by the Cold War.[5] More specifically, from our perspective, the questions posed by the science of wounding played a considerable part in shaping the way small arms and ammunition would be discussed right up to the present day. However, as I will show, this was not a case of the science deterministically leading to the development of new technology, for the science of wounding was developed out of an organisational context that involved transatlantic debate between engineers.

In an attempt to resolve this debate in their favour, American and British engineers recruited scientists and scientific arguments in an effort to strengthen their position in favour of particular technical solutions. In the case of the infantry rifle, engineers appealed to scientists to help arbitrate between the respective technical solutions they had devised. The question that Barlow and Studler wanted to resolve was whose ammunition would achieve the most efficient wounding. The answer would determine which ammunition NATO would adopt. However, the circumstances in which the question was posed produced heavily partisan interpretations of the wounding phenomena under observation and closely reflected the needs of those engineering communities who would use these studies. As I will argue, at its most fundamental level, it also showed that the science was situated and contested, and by itself could not dictate whether the United States or the UK would adopt a particular type of ammunition. Indeed, ultimately, a decision about what constituted an objective science of wounding would eventually be taken on social rather than scientific grounds. For just as the practice of killing was open to argument, so too was the theory.

Lethality: an absolute or probabilistic calculation

That bullets shatter bone seems obvious. In 1939, however, despite the wealth of observations that had already been completed by a number of surgeons and ballisticians, a theoretical explanation for how this happened remained unsatisfactory. Rather than applying what Karl Popper would describe as a deductive scientific method derived from trying to falsify a hypothesis, the pre-1945 explanations of lethality inductively confirmed pre-existing perspectives.[6] The war provided Zuckerman with something of an opportunity to challenge these views. Given the weight of authority already granted to the pre-war accounts of lethality, however, it was not clear that Zuckerman's analysis would gain traction with the wider community of scientists and ordnance designers.

For those of us who are interested in explaining how a particular interpretation of lethality became the authoritative account, the debates Zuckerman started with his American counterparts and among ordnance officials are instructive. This is especially the case because of the way the investigations into lethality evolved, which mirrored the theoretical findings of a number of sociologists who established a new field of study called the Sociology of Scientific Knowledge (SSK) in the 1970s and 1980s.

SSK demonstrated that scientific theories were not considered part of the body of knowledge until some level of agreement had developed among scientists who recognised that a particular theory was scientifically sound.[7] Buttressing the process was the existence of a scientific community whose members understood the need for experiments that generated reproducible results and the use of peer review to assess the accuracy of a particular claim. The evidence produced by SSK scholars suggested that a scientific theory had to traverse a number of steps if it was to count as knowledge. In the first stage, scientific findings were open to more than one interpretation, that is, they were interpretively flexible. In the second stage, various social processes—activities that might include discussion papers, conferences or publications—established the grounds upon which agreement could be reached about how to interpret the findings of an experiment. In the third stage, this process of reaching agreement was related to the wider contexts where scientific knowledge might have societal impact.[8]

SSK was methodologically different from those approaches that simply stressed the importance of the scientific method. Like the Social Shaping of Technology, SSK tracked the narratives, beliefs and the arguments employed by various scientists as an idea moved between and was assimilated or rejected by different scientific constituencies. The starting place was the recognition that different groups developed different scientific explanations for the phenomena they were seeking to explain. By assuming the symmetry of these various explanations, SSK could then trace the path dependency of these different narratives and show how they competed to become scientific fact.

Controversially, SSK showed that there were more social processes going on in establishing scientific truth than the scientists themselves had previously acknowledged. Indeed, for SSK, a scientific explanation could gain traction among scientists for reasons that had nothing to do with the scientific method itself. Social relations between scientific communities framed the way in which experiments were conducted, hypotheses interpreted and conclusions endorsed. The job of the sociologist was to show how and why this happened.

Given the binary concept of life and death, the notion that SSK might have application to the emerging wartime science of killing might seem rather surprising. From the point of view of tracing the arguments about lethality, however, SSK offers some useful coordinates for framing our investigations. Geoffrey Bowker and Susan Leigh Star demonstrate, for instance, that there are a lot of social processes involved in framing the way different communities define the point of death in human beings. This became much more obvious with the creation of the International Classification of Diseases published by predecessors to the World Health Organisation in the 1890s. What emerged out of the practice of collating death certificates was the extent to which various medical establishments from around the world viewed mortality differently.[9] Death certificates themselves were culturally loaded documents that sought to identify single or secondary causes of death but which in effect were medical shorthand that reflected the social mores of a particular country.

Abortion or suicide, for instance, might require their own technical codes to cover up the statistical inferences and social stigma that might be drawn. Of and by themselves, then, death certificates—even when written by a doctor in a field hospital—might not offer an accurate guide for those investigating the theoretical processes underpinning wounding.

A more effective approach to investigating the cause of death clearly involved the direct examination of cadavers. However, no systematic casualty surveys had been undertaken during the First World War.[10] Consequently, the data available before the Second World War was sporadic and fragmentary and pre-1939 explanations of wounding tended to focus on experimental data produced from shooting animals. The alternative was to shoot human cadavers, which were not always readily available. At the same time, it was unclear what inferences could be drawn from making use of dead tissues. While these approaches offered the wound ballistician the opportunity to collect measurements, any conclusions reached could nonetheless be dismissed on the basis that they did not take into account battlefield conditions. More fundamentally, the difficulty of reproducing the exact results, given that bullets and fragments performed differently and performed differently in different types of tissue, made the process of dubious scientific value.

Not that this was necessarily a problem. Most studies of wounding only served to confirm an existing military or engineering prejudice. This in turn helped arms manufacturers make sales of equipment to the Army. Thus, it was much easier for the wound ballistician to pander to particular user communities who typically preferred simple explanations of lethality than it was to offer more scientifically rigorous theories that might undermine a potential weapon sale. As a result, wound ballisticians rarely found themselves coming into direct disagreement with established voices. Instead, by devising clever, apparently scientific methods that demonstrated the effectiveness of a particular weapon system, the engineer could lure the user into purchasing equipment they might otherwise be unwilling to acquire or did not realise they needed.[11] Given the size of an army, it was fairly easy to identify different user groups, one of whom might have access to a budget and be sufficiently influential to guarantee a purchase. According to C.J. Chivers, the former military surgeon Major Louis LaGarde developed a lethality index that could be used by his business partner Captain John Thompson to persuade the US Army to adopt weapons suitable for firing a .45 calibre (Automatic Colt Pistol) round. The Army subsequently adopted the Colt M1911 Pistol, which eventually helped Thompson to sell his sub-machine gun in 1921. That the evidence produced by LaGarde was based on an insufficiently robust scientific method derived from shooting animals was beside the point. The Thompson SMG appealed to various constituencies and so it was eventually acquired.[12]

In these circumstances, the only way to square the technical hurdles and avoid the criticism of a user or engineering community who might be determined to sustain their existing perspective on what constituted lethal ordnance was to go back to the wounding phenomenon itself and survey battlefield casualties. But this was easier said than done. For the fact of the matter was that to generate statistically meaningful results a large number of suitably trained pathologists would need to be present at the right time and place appropriate medical infrastructure close to the battlefield. In the fast-flowing conditions of war, this was nearly impossible to achieve. More than this, soldiers and engineers did not always want to have their views on warfare tested against the evidence.

The genius of Solly Zuckerman and his colleagues Ben Delisle Burns, A.N. Black and later Peter Krohn, was that they had understood the nature of the problem and recognised that it could be addressed by going directly back to the battlefield. Unless engineers could harness the results of this work in particular ways, however, the results could be controversial for those who remained wedded to existing scientific, medical or technical prejudices. Nonetheless, that Zuckerman et al. could inveigle their way into this challenge speaks volumes about the cultural shifts that the Second World War forced on the British military–technical establishment.

That is not to say that the same sentiment was necessarily embraced in the United States. Zuckerman could trade on his relationships with the academic community at Yale, where his friend, Dr John Fulton, had asked him to join the Institute of Human Relations.[13] However, the military and medical establishments already had a common perspective on wound ballistics that would need to be addressed before any fundamental changes might be undertaken. In particular, a number of American authorities including Colonel George Callender (later brigadier general from March 1945), the commandant of the US Army Medical Center during the Second World War, had made extensive investigations into wound ballistics while a member of the Goat Board in the 1930s alongside Colonel René Studler from the Ordnance Corps. The result of these investigations left Callender with a firm belief in the importance of the shape of the bullet, its kinetic energy and the way that energy was transformed into power.[14]

One reason why this interpretation was so widely cited in American military circles was partly because it neatly dovetailed with existing assumptions on lethality. Since the late nineteenth century, investigations into ammunition effectiveness had defined lethality in terms of whether a bullet could penetrate pine wooden boards.[15] Calculations since had demonstrated that a good rule of thumb that offered ordnance officials a quantifiable value involved depositing 58ftlbs (equivalent to around 80 joules) of energy into a body in order to cause death.[16] The kinetic energy criterion was simple, made equipment design moderately straightforward and was easy to evaluate. American engineers would use this criterion to judge all ordnance design. However, as Zuckerman et al. would go on to demonstrate, the problem with the kinetic energy criterion was that it could not explain the phenomena that it was purportedly being used to evaluate. Proving this, however, would require the collection of a considerable amount of data.

Zuckerman's starting point in this regard was in France during the spring of 1940. His analysis, which was based on autopsies carried out on 220 service fatalities, revealed that small shell splinters caused 'dangerous, and even fatal, wounds out of all proportion to their size'.[17] What made this interesting was that, of the 985 splinters found in the bodies of the personnel concerned, for every splinter between 2cm and 4cm there were approximately four splinters of between 1cm and 2cm, seven between 0.5 and 1cm and forty-three below 0.5cm.[18] As some of these sub-0.5cm splinters had produced highly incapacitating results, the 58ftlbs criterion seemed to be open to some doubt.

Specifically, the 58ftlbs criterion implied that for munitions with an average burst velocity of 2000fps, all fragments weighing less than 0.014 ounces (400mg) were harmless.[19] However, it had been observed that a man could be severely wounded while standing 3 metres away from the blast of a 50kg bomb by a fragment weighing less than 10mg.[20] It appeared that the 58ftlbs criterion only served to make a whole swathe of battlefield casualties theoretically impossible. Thus, given that battlefield observations did not support this 'all or nothing' criterion, more had to be done to explain wounding.

This was an extremely important finding because it had direct implications as to what might be considered the area of effect of anti-personnel weapons like mortar rounds or artillery shells. Artillery rounds might actually produce relative effects that could be more or less lethal depending on the distance from the detonation of the shell, the velocity at which the fragment was moving and the area of the body a person might have exposed to the blast. If this claim could be substantiated, then protection from anti-personnel weapons might need to be significantly amended and bombing and artillery plans changed to reflect the theoretical findings about the pattern of ordnance lethality.

In contrast to the assumptions that underpinned the 58ftlbs criterion, the starting point for Zuckerman's research was the insight he had generated out of his work in France. However, the limited availability of biological data from actual wounds meant that the research had to take a more theoretical direction until further data points could be gathered. The Zuckerman team consequently proceeded by establishing the relative vulnerability of various parts of the body based on the limited datasets they already possessed. Perhaps unsurprisingly, this revealed that wounds to the head, neck and trunk of the body were most likely to produce fatality.

Table 1: Bomb Splinter Wounds in Civilian Casualties: Regional Distribution of Multiple and Single Splinter Wounds[21]

	Fatal Splinter Wounds (97 hits)	Non-Fatal Splinter Wounds (303 hits)	Total Hits (400 hits)	Mortality
Head and Neck	10.0%	7.0%	17%	59%
Thorax	3.5%	7.5%	11%	32%
Abdomen	6.0%	5.0%	11%	52%
Upper Limb	1.0%	15.0%	16%	6%
Lower Limb	4.0%	41.0%	45%	9%

However, in many cases the casualties had been hit by several shell fragments, thereby making it impossible to establish a single cause of death. Consequently, the Zuckerman team proceeded to ask a number of surgeons for an opinion on when a wound would require hospitalisation. In particular, they wanted to generate some consensus on how far the projectile would need to penetrate into the various parts of the body such that it would force the victim to need medical treatment. As a result, it became clear that even a small splinter striking and penetrating the skull cap could be fatal, whereas it might take the perforation of the sternum before incapacitation might occur. Incapacitation in this context was not a hard and fast rule whereby any injury would require a certain amount of time for recovery. Instead, it meant that 'sooner or later the casualty would be out of action for a period in which medical treatment would be necessary'.[22]

Having generated a series of physiological definitions that related incapacitation to different parts of the body, the next step was to determine the velocity that would cause a standard missile to produce the depth of wound the surgeons had defined. This meant completing some theoretical work that involved shooting steel balls into human tissues and, having established this as a baseline, doing the same into gelatine blocks made up of 20 per cent gelatine to water, a medium that was deemed to be representative of the human body. As a result of this analysis, it became clear that, for example, when protected by a helmet, a man's head would need to be struck by a fragment with a velocity of at least 2850fps. In contrast, a projectile striking an unprotected abdomen only needed an impact velocity of 1000fps.[23]

This led to calculations as to the relative vulnerable surface area of the body so that calculations of probability of achieving a hit could be reached. For if a person was standing up when they were struck by a bomb blast, more parts of the most vulnerable areas of the body would be exposed for wounding. This vulnerability could, however, be reduced if the person was prone or kneeling down. After photographing various subjects in various positions, it then became possible for Zuckerman to work out the mean average projected surface area of the body and its vulnerability to blast wounds. Further consideration was then given to oblique impacts, strikes to military equipment, and clothing.

As a result of these investigations, two observations could be reached and summarised in research paper RC350. One was that the required velocities would change depending on what someone might be wearing or whether an impact had occurred obliquely. The second and more controversial for those wedded to the 58ftlbs criterion was that the momentum lost by a missile travelling through the body was directly proportional to the degree of tissue destruction.[24] That is to say, the greater the momentum the greater the destruction of tissue. With the use of some statistical analysis, what Zuckerman et al. could show was that for a certain weight of splinter—the example used was 52mg (tiny when compared to observations from the battlefield) and the 400mg all or nothing threshold implied by the 58ftlbs criterion—the probability of hospitalisation went up as the velocity of the projectile increased.

The work by the British scientists thus showed that the 58ftlbs criterion was not sophisticated enough to explain wounding. More fundamentally, their analysis demanded the replacement of the all or nothing criterion with a probabilistic calculation that implied lethality was not a binary affair. In this respect, the anecdotal evidence seemed to back up the analysis by Zuckerman et al. For some considerable time, soldiers had observed that shooting someone did not guarantee immediate death. Yet claims such as these were typically framed by an underlying prejudice about fighting the 'savages' in colonial campaigns, according to which non-Europeans did not know how to behave after being shot.

However, by drawing inferences based on the context of an engagement as much as it did mortality rates, Zuckerman's research was sophisticated enough to explain this anecdotal evidence. This was made clear in Zuckerman's analysis of the 1942 Allied landing at Dieppe in France. Predominantly made up of Canadian troops, many of those on the main landing beach found themselves stuck, unable to clear obstacles or scale the seawall, with their backs to the sea and in the teeth of heavy German fire from deep entrenchments and pillboxes. What Zuckerman's analysis revealed was that soldiers fighting in such desperate conditions would carry on using their weapons irrespective of the wounds they had received. Zuckerman later surmised that they did this because they knew they were helping their comrades who were trying to escape. The failure at Dieppe thus revealed that 'savages' and 'white men' had something in common: they could both continue to use their weapon even after being shot.[25] The implication was that, in circumstances other than a battle like Dieppe, wounded soldiers might well have allowed themselves to be taken off the front line earlier. The interval between an individual receiving a splinter injury and deciding that it needed medical treatment consequently depended not only on the availability of medical aid 'but also on the general morale of the fighting troops'.[26]

For American engineers, physicists and medical practitioners, Zuckerman's probabilistic criterion was controversial and equally as unacceptable as it was for an infantryman who wanted the certainty that an enemy was dead as soon as they had been shot. Consequently, having heard about Zuckerman's research, possibly via John Fulton at Yale, Robert Kent, a Harvard-trained physicist at the Aberdeen Proving Ground in Maryland, contacted Dr Lewis Weed, chairman of the Division of Medical Sciences, regarding the establishment of a project aimed at testing the casualty-producing effectiveness of US weapons. This led to a Conference on Wound Ballistics chaired by Colonel George Callender, the commandant of the Army Medical Center and advocate of the kinetic energy criterion, on 25 September 1943. At this conference, it was decided that an extensive programme of research designed to test the theoretical and empirical assumptions underlying Zuckerman's analysis was to be put in place.

The substantive American fightback got underway following the appointment of Princeton zoologist Professor Edmund Newton Harvey, who was asked to examine the mechanism of wounding. Pulling together a team that included experts in hydraulics and biology, Harvey et al. sought to test in the hope they would undermine the experimental basis of Zuckerman's findings. The starting place for this was the dispatch of a special survey unit that included physicists, ordnance officials and ballisticians to Princes Risborough in the UK to observe Zuckerman's methods. At the same time, Callender decided to undertake large-scale casualty surveys in order to put Zuckerman's more limited research into statistical context. It soon became clear, however, why this sort of activity had been so difficult to undertake during previous wars. For Callender's main sticking point was the availability of enough suitably trained pathologists who understood what data they were expected to collect. Initial ambitions subsequently had to be scaled back despite putting out a call for data via the *Bulletin of the US Army Medical Department*. Instead, during 1944 a smaller number of teams were fielded in Burma, Bougainville, Italy and Eighth US Air Force, undertaking strategic bombing in Europe.[27]

The first round of the dispute over wounding criteria came following the distribution of a report by Ronald Gurney, who argued that a more effective criterion for wounding could be founded on the diameter of the temporary cavity as it related to the mass and velocity of the shell fragments or bullets.[28] Developing the line of enquiry offered by Gurney and using similar equipment to their British counterparts, what Newton Harvey et al. observed was that a bullet travelling at high velocity created a permanent and a temporary cavity within the victim. Photographs showed that the temporary cavity expanded and contracted several times along the path traversed by the missile before collapsing completely. The permanent cavity remained even after the missile had passed through the body. Even though at first sight tissue destruction seemed limited to the permanent track, in fact the trauma to the body was considerably more widespread. Unconvinced by Zuckerman's claim that there was a relationship between a projectile's loss of momentum inside the body, the depth of the projectile inside tissue and the need for hospitalisation, the Princeton Group reported that 'Study and measurement of temporary [wound] cavities show that the total volume of the cavity is proportional to the energy delivered by the missile.'[29] Subsequent research came to the conclusion that 58 ftlbs was indeed a fair approximation for the required energy needed to cause the kinds of cavitation Gurney and Newton Harvey et al. had identified. Consequently, the Princeton Group left many American scientists believing that the energy criterion provided a rough estimate of the wounding power of small missiles.[30]

However, Zuckerman, Krohn and Delisle Burns were not convinced by the argument. Amending their initial research findings to account for American criticisms that the total vulnerable area of the body was much greater than they had initially proposed, the British team issued a revised research report known as RC434. The British then compared the various criteria against actual observations of wound cavities and established that RC434 more effectively accounted for wounding than the 58ftlbs criterion. In fact, the 58ftlbs criterion could not explain mortality at all for fragments below 100 milligrams.

Table 2: The Expected and Observed Proportion of Fragment Masses Found in Wounds[31]

Criterion of incapacitation	58ftlbs	mv^3 R.W. Gurney	RC350 Zuckerman & Black	RC434 Krohn & Black	Observed
Fragment Mass (mgms)	%	%	%	%	%
0–50	0	18	24	49	54
50–100	0	23	16	15	15
100–250	5	24	23	15	19
250–500	23	12	12	7	7
500–1000	26	9	9	5	2
1–5 gms	36	11	12	7	2
5–10 gms	10	3	3	2	1
				Total wounds	119

Consequently, in October 1946, Zuckerman concluded that he was 'not yet entirely certain that the wounding power of a fragment is best measured by its energy', before going on to observe that it may not be a 'purely mathematical problem'.[32] Nonetheless, by the end of the war, with little research having been completed to establish the precise value of energy required, the 58ftlbs criterion retained its place in the United States as an accepted estimation for wounding power.[33]

Conflicting battlefield interpretations

The debates over wounding criteria were to have significant consequences for the engineers who were working on small arms and ammunition after the Second World War. This was not because engineers simply integrated the science into the technologies that they were developing. Rather, it had everything to do with the way that engineers employed arguments in favour of their preferred technology. The science said one thing to an American audience and an entirely different thing to the British. No consensus in the science had been reached. The data were patchy, difficult to reproduce and different scientific disciplines approached the problem differently. Biologists had one perspective, specialists in hydraulics another and physicists yet another. Because the disciplines defined the problem differently, they could not agree an appropriate methodology. More than this, though, the science itself was situated in social contexts that framed the acceptability of different scientific interpretations. Technologies and prejudices already existed among those who would have to implement changes in equipment. American and British engineering, medical, scientific and military institutions were squaring up to each other over which battlefield interpretation was most appropriate and whose vision would survive after the war. Decisions over what would be adopted would have immediate ramifications for the livelihoods of those engineers involved in the process.

All that said, it did not follow that decisions about technology could no longer be made simply because the scientists were unable to agree. What it meant was that American and British ammunition would be evaluated against different yardsticks not only in terms of military preference and technical capability but now also in relation to the science. As I will show, agreement on what constituted a wounding criterion was not brought about by scientists but through organisational and social processes involving engineers and users. In effect, the science decided nothing, but added weight to the powerful voices already in existence on both sides of the Atlantic. If both the engineers and users chose not to agree on what to adopt, then in the final analysis the selection of weapon would come down to which country had the capacity to implement their decision. For the British, Winston Churchill would decide that the UK did not have the capacity to stand on its own and would acquiesce to the American preferences, despite the technical efficacy of the EM-2 and its ammunition.

Given their definition of lethality and their cultural predisposition towards the .30'06, it is no wonder that US ballisticians remained unsympathetic to the British ammunition. Thus, the Americans were quick to point out the different behaviours of bullets and shrapnel in human tissue versus simulants. Bullets performed differently and thus might not be subject to the same variables as the investigations into shrapnel conducted by Zuckerman. More than this, however, the Americans believed that infantrymen still required a round that enabled them to engage with targets out to 2,000 yards. According to the US Ordnance Corps, this meant striking a target with at least 58ftlbs, but maybe as much as 87.57ftlbs of kinetic energy if the .30'06 round constituted the benchmark for lethality. The effect of this argument was to rule out smaller calibres of ammunition.

For Barlow, the American perspective on wounding might not have been such a problem bar the fact that, in their negotiations with the War Office, he had committed himself to matching the striking energy of the US .30'06 round at 2,000 yards.[34] He did this in an effort to convince Britain's General Staff that they would not be losing anything by choosing British over American ammunition. For Britain's engineers, it meant that a British-designed bullet would need to hit the target with 87.57ftlbs.[35]

Nonetheless, whether this amount of energy was needed was open to serious doubt. According to Zuckerman's wartime research, 87.57ftlbs was massively overpowered. However, by accepting the need to match the kinetic energy of the .30'06 at 2,000 yards, Britain's engineers acknowledged the possibility that their ammunition would be subject to American interpretations of lethality. By March 1949, in line with Zuckerman's findings, the British believed that the .280 could deliver an appropriate level of striking energy sufficient to produce incapacitation.[36] What was less clear was whether the round could precisely match the 87.57ftlbs generated by the .30'06 at 2,000 yards. If the Americans were flexible and viewed lethality in the terms defined by Zuckerman, then the British stood a chance of surviving the 1950 technical trials. If they insisted on the kinetic energy criterion and the .280 failed the 87.57ftlbs test, then the British would have to rely on evidence provided by the user trials—being conducted at the same time—in order to demonstrate the wider benefits of their solution.

Unfortunately for the British engineers, the trials at the Aberdeen Proving Ground in 1950 revealed that American ballisticians would insist on defining lethality in terms of kinetic energy, power and wound cavitation. The relationship between bullet velocity and the probability of hospitalisation did not even receive a mention. As a result, the Working Committee overseeing the technical trials was of the opinion that the US Ordnance Corps T65 round was considerably more lethal than the British .280.[37] In response, the Ministry of Supply sent Professor Zuckerman out to the United States to argue the case.[38] In the subsequent discussions, the Americans agreed that velocity was an important characteristic in ammunition design but pointed out that the .280 round had a low muzzle velocity when compared to the .30 T65, and as a result ruled against the British solution.[39] However, the assessment board also noted that 'the higher velocity T65 .30 calibre round does more damage than the lower velocity .280 round but the significance is slight because the .280 round is well above the marginal power required'.[40]

Despite the suggestion that it was capable of achieving sufficient damage, the British round was rejected. The underlying reason for this was that the

.280 round had been designed for shorter-range engagements. According to the requirements laid down by Britain's director of infantry in 1944, the 2,000-yard requirement was considered a stretch target.[41] The British focus had been on producing a rimless round suitable for combat below 800 yards.[42]

In the context of the Anglo-American comparative trials, however, it is what Brigadier Barlow did not say to his US counterparts that really reveals the problems facing British engineers. If Barlow had stated to his American counterparts that the Ideal Calibre Panel had been set up to investigate ammunition appropriate for engagements at closer range, then it would have been impossible to claim that the .280 ammunition satisfied US lethality requirements. At the same time, his admission would have demonstrated to Britain's General Staff that they would not have an equivalent ammunition to the one they had given up in their decision against standardising on the American .30'06 round. The assessment board might have shown that the technical differences were marginal, but the political and organisational ramifications of this margin would shape NATO's choice of weapons for the next sixty years.

The underlying problem for the British, however, was not that their round was sufficiently lethal, but rather that they were unable to state their different conception of the battlefield as part of the design philosophy for the rifle and the ammunition. As far as the director of infantry, the director of military training, and Britain's engineers were concerned, infantry engagements typically occurred at ranges below 300 yards.[43] What American objections had exposed, however, was that certain sections of Britain's General Staff were still of the opinion that marksmanship had a place in the British Army and were still sceptical of the Wigram perspective. Consequently, Barlow was unable to discuss the tactical issues the EM-2 was designed to address and was instead left to try to produce an Anglo-American agreement on the basis of technical data. Unfortunately for the British, the technical detail alone could not force a change in American opinion on the advantages of their existing calibre of ammunition.

Nevertheless, it did not follow that the Americans could simply insist that the British accept the view of the Working Committee overseeing the technical trials. For neither the technical detail nor the lethality criterion would solely determine what would be selected. Bearing in mind that sovereign governments had the ultimate say over what weapons their national armies would adopt, the British could choose not to accept the results of the technical trials and ignore the US science.[44] However, if the Americans could broaden the debate to include countries that had not previously been involved in the selection of ammunition or small arms, then there would be a chance to sink the British ambition or at least slow it down until an American equivalent had been adopted. The active involvement of the Canadians and the French held out such a possibility, and in the next chapter I will show how bureaucratic power was employed to shape the process of delivering wider agreement on the science of lethality. This was not the result of accepting the scientific points per se, points which in many respects remain contested and controversial, but rather by ruling out or delaying British technology and in the process making the Zuckerman criterion irrelevant. Before developing this argument in the next chapter, however, it is important to consider how the science of wound ballistics evolved after the Americans rejected the .280 round and decided to go it alone and standardise on the T65 .30 calibre and cartridge in 1951.

Range, weapon choice and hit probability

Zuckerman's research caused considerable debate within the US ordnance and medical communities, forcing them to justify the technical choices they had made. It also raised fundamental questions about the relationship between lethality, weapon choice, target range and hit probability. These issues had not been subject to serious investigation in the United States previously and were left in the margins of discussion, framed by anecdote rather than evidence. As long as certain favoured weapons, like the M-1 Garand, had the support of influential constituencies in the US Army, then the position on lethality would remain as it was. However, just as the Ordnance Corps believed they had successfully fought off a British challenge, a new threat to the traditional consensus emerged. This time it came from within the US infantry community itself.

In a post-war context framed by strategic aerial bombardment and the emergence of nuclear weapons, the infantry's place in future war seemed uncertain. Consequently, facing the prospect of marginalisation, the Infantry Board at Fort Benning embraced the work of S.L.A. Marshall, who argued that the infantryman would still have a place on the battlefield.[45] At the same time, the Infantry Board were quick to avail themselves of the services of Marshall's colleague Ellis Johnson, the director of the Operations Research Office (ORO).[46] The ORO was a civilian-run organisation made up of statistical analysts and operational researchers based at Johns Hopkins University. Created in the face of opposition from the Army's technical services, the organisation was instrumental in developing the evidence base that would challenge the consensus that had formed around the .30 calibre. Indeed, the ORO would inspire the Infantry Board to push for the M16 in the face of resistance from the Ordnance Corps and senior Army officers.[47]

Based on fieldwork and after action reviews conducted by Marshall and a 150-strong team of analysts, the ORO assessed US infantry performance during the campaign in Korea in 1950–1.[48] What they established was that the changes the Army had made to its post-1945 training regime, combined with intense hand-to-hand engagements in Korea, had led to the infantryman's rate of fire to double.[49] At the same time, they also gathered user opinions on weapons systems and undertook more systematic data collection to evaluate weapon effectiveness in combat. For the first time, this started to produce substantial evidence that reinforced the British argument that most infantry combat typically occurred below 300 yards. Indeed, a 1952 ORO study from Korea showed that 'of the 602 men questioned about their use of the M-1 Garand, 87% said that at least 95% of all their firing was done at targets within 300 yard-range'.[50] Subsequent map study analysis revealed that when comparing different landscapes in Canada, France, Germany, Korea, North Africa and the United States, 'to a total of 18,000 readings, 70% of the ranges at which an erect human target can be seen by a defending prone rifleman are less than 300 yards (and 90% are less than 700 yards)'.[51]

If this was not bad enough for those in the Ordnance Corps who were still trying to defend the marksmanship ethos, the ORO concluded that the general marksmanship skills of the infantryman precluded the possibility of actually hitting a target with an M-1 at ranges beyond 100 yards. The lethality index of the rifle bullet (i.e. the ratio of kills to hits on the battlefield) may have exceeded 30 per cent, but the ability of the infantryman to actually hit the target appeared to be limited.[52] After conducting a test that involved thirty-two men, of which sixteen were expert marksmen and the rest the lowest-qualified marksmen, Norman Hitchman at the ORO established that 'a sharp decline in hit probability occurs and this decline in effectiveness is most marked at the common battle ranges, between 100 and 300 yards'. At 500 yards, all thirty-two men, both expert and ordinary marksman, performed unsatisfactorily and in ways that were 'inconsistent with the design and capability of the weapon and with military specifications'.[53] The Hitchman analysis clearly indicated that the M-1 Garand was over-designed. It was not necessary to take advantage of the full 3,500-yard range of the rifle or the 1,200-yard range for incapacitating a fully clothed and equipped soldier. Indeed, instead of focusing on engaging targets at distance, they argued that in the future the one function that would remain central to the infantry, given the increased availability of ranged weapon systems, was close combat.

In these circumstances, and bearing in mind the potential lethality of the bullet, the most important consideration was to increase weapon hit probability in a way that reflected the range characteristics identified by the ORO and the poor shooting skills of soldiers. Creating effective marksmen while rapidly expanding an army that was mobilising for war had never been successful. Controversially, however, the ORO found that optimising the weapon design of and by itself could not correct for the inability of the soldier to hit his target even after they had perfected their marksmanship skills. The probability of a hit was as likely to come from a random shell fragment as it was from a professional skilled soldier and his rifle.

More contentiously, given the way that contemporary infantryman think about the firefight, the ORO poured cold water on the notion that full automatic fire would resolve the chance to hit. Instead, the study found that only the first shot was likely to hit the target when the rifleman, regardless of their skill at arms, was using aimed automatic fire. All other shots in the burst of automatic fire would wildly miss a man-sized target irrespective of range. According to the ORO: 'At all common battle ranges, with present hand-held automatics, the strike dispersion is so great that moving the center of impact for the burst to the center of the target would not increase the number of hits.'[54]

As far as the ORO were concerned, the engineer's goal ought to be the development of a solution that would compensate for user inadequacies in marksmanship. In this respect, two solutions presented themselves. The first involved what the ORO described as the Pattern SALVO Weapon, a weapon that would fire multiple bullets at the same time and increase the chance of achieving a hit. The second was a small calibre, high velocity automatic weapon that might 'produce dispersion patterns commensurate with the requirements of the idealized salvo weapon.'[55] In both cases, the ambition was to increase the potential effectiveness of the infantryman by increasing the number of dispersed rounds they fired, as aiming errors were 'too great to be compensated by an improvement in the accuracy of the rifle alone.'[56]

These results did not, however, necessarily reflect user opinion on lethality or weapon effectiveness. The ORO had noted that they were mainly writing from the perspective of establishing the effectiveness of aimed direct fire. They were not focusing their efforts on the balance of fire between that which was designed to kill the enemy and that which was intended to suppress them so that others might manoeuvre to close-quarter battle. The ORO acknowledged that 'covering fire' could be tactically useful but that 'it is desirable to increase in both number and rate of the hits which may be inflicted on the enemy by aimed small arms in the hands of the infantry [and that] it is also desirable to increase the mortality from wounds caused by these hits'.[57]

Put simply, the ORO assumed that both the user and their commanding authorities would want a weapon for direct engagements rather than suppressive fire. Consequently, in the twenty years after the initial analysis, comparatively little effort was put into analysing the utility of direct fire suppressive weapons as opposed to fire from indirect weapons such as artillery. As a result, it was only in the 1970s, before another round of NATO talks on ammunition standardisation, that a number of military commands started to take more direct interest in examining suppressive fire effects.[58]

Before this time, suppressive effects were not necessarily the main consideration when investigating the relationship between user psychology and weapon choice. Instead, the question was concerned with user perception of weapon dangerousness as it pertained to their weapon preferences. Thus a US study conducted in 1963 demonstrated that:

> A weapon may have a psychological effect which is not consistent with its known physical effects. The potential danger in a weapon or weapon combination may easily be overestimated or underestimated by naïve troops ... [and] a weapon may have a very different value in a different culture. Psychological reactions, uncorrelated with physical effects, may make a weapon surprisingly effective, because of these cultural differences.[59]

On the one hand, this study provided further analytical evidence to the anecdotal observations by Allied troops that the German MG42—a belt-fed, sustained fire machine gun that could fire 1,200 rounds per minute and caused much panic during the initial phases of the liberation of France in 1944—was a highly effective weapon psychologically. At the same time, it also meant that appropriate training regimes needed to be put in place to help soldiers relate a weapon's technical characteristics more accurately to the psychological fears and preferences that they might have.

From an engineer's point of view, this study also offered some succour to the reality of trying to develop and introduce new technologies. For this kind of analysis clearly backed up the survey evidence that soldiers did not always understand what weapons could do and offered the evidential basis for encouraging engineers to take a more active part in trying to construct user preferences. If the soldier did not know what was best for them, then the engineer would have to step in and offer an education in the technical characteristics and design possibilities of various systems.

Thus, Cold War analysis of range, weapon preference and hit probability as it related to lethality, started to demonstrate the difference between what might be described as the actual physiological effects of a weapon system and its potential to affect soldier behaviour. The Swiss ballistician Dr Beat Kneubuehl has summarised this distinction between effects and effectiveness. In a form of analysis that Zuckerman himself would have recognised, Kneubuehl observes that an effect of a shot in the human body is always a unique event:

> For instance, an airgun pellet with a muzzle velocity of 7 joules that penetrates the spine and damages the spinal cord has a much greater effect than a 44 Rem. Mag. hollow-top with an energy of 1500joules that grazes the upper arm. This means that statements like 'A hollow-point bullet has a greater effect than a full metal-jacket bullet' are meaningless.[60]

The effect of a bullet depends on a wide variety of factors that extend well beyond its physical or design characteristics. In the first place, to be highly effective a bullet needs to strike a certain part of the body. However, the ability to realise this potential lethality depends on the particular climatic and other circumstances on the day as well as the skill at arms of the shooter.

The corollary of these observations is that the ambitions of the engineer and the strategist cannot be predetermined simply by looking at the design characteristics of the weapon system. The effect of a bullet can only be established—and as we have seen this has been regularly misunderstood and contested—after each round has been fired. As each shot constituted a unique event, the results could not be predicted with absolute certainty. A probabilistic calculation might have offered a route for resolving the problem of defining a lethality criterion, but scientists have instead mainly focused their efforts on assessing the potential effectiveness of the weapon system.

In this respect, following the American rejection of Zuckerman's probabilistic analysis of wounding, the only function of the bullet where American engineers and scientists remained in agreement was over the importance of kinetic energy (KE). The 1952 ORO study on the effectiveness of small calibre, high velocity rounds did not challenge the orthodoxy that emerged out of the investigations that had been instigated by Colonel Callender. The ORO still defined wounding power in the same terms that R.W. Gurney and E. Newton Harvey had established in the period after the war and which Zuckerman, Krohn and Black had found unsatisfactory. KE could be measured at the point of impact and so could the volume of the wound cavity. Thus

US scientists continued to work on the hypothesis that the measure of wounding severity was related to the total volume of the temporary cavity produced in the tissue by a penetrating round.

Where Zuckerman did have some impact, however, was in getting engineers to recognise that bullet mass might not be as important as its velocity. For by increasing the bullet velocity, more kinetic energy might be imparted to a bullet than simply by increasing its mass. From an engineering perspective, if the challenge remained depositing 58ftlbs of energy into a human body, then, as the ORO observed, it would be possible to reduce the mass of the bullet and by increasing its velocity still produce the required effectiveness.[61] This analysis concurred with the views of the 1951 assessment board, which concluded that 'Of the three factors that determine the transient cavity, velocity, cross sectional area, and shape, velocity is the most important.'[62] Zuckerman may have lost the argument over the energy criterion, but he succeeded in persuading US officials that velocity might have more to do with wounding than had previously been acknowledged. George Callender subsequently anointed this view in 1962.[63] In effect, then, Zuckerman drew American attention away from the size and calibre of the bullet and refocused it on increasing the bullet's velocity. This in turn encouraged US engineers to pay more attention to small calibre, high velocity (SCHV) ammunition and would ultimately lead to the adoption of the SCHV 5.56mm ammunition and the M16.

Conclusion

Some of the greatest advances in the science of killing occurred in the years between 1941 and the adoption of the M16 by the US Army in 1964. In this period, an evidence base emerged that undermined many of the myths that had sustained an older preference for marksmanship. However, the programme for developing a new technology that might enable greater tactical flexibility in close combat situations did not advance in a linear fashion from proof of concept to implementation. On the contrary, while the science appeared to sustain the battlefield interpretations of Lionel Wigram, it also reflected a growing dissatisfaction within sections of the British and American infantry communities who recognised that their position, relative to that of other service arms, was potentially on the decline. The scepticism of senior officers within the British and American Armies did, therefore, need to be managed through the selective employment of scientific evidence designed to push debate in a direction more conducive to advancing the professional interests of engineers and sustaining the unique status of the infantry.

Those who had a vested interest in sustaining the existing technological status quo might have decided to employ scientific evidence, but this did not mean that scientists would work together to develop an objective criterion of lethality. In practice, the science was hotly contested and reflected the national perspectives and organisational preferences of the British and American armed forces. In the 1950s, the scientists could not come to a consensus agreement about wounding power. As will become clear in the next chapter, this did not prevent decisions being taken about weapons technology. Instead, national governments were left to choose whether to side with the evidence as told by their respective research establishments or opt to cooperate for the sake of realising greater benefits through standardisation.

In 1953, this resulted in the British abandoning what they considered to be the best technical solution available in favour of an American T65, 7.62mm round that they recognised to be over-engineered. While a number of British infantrymen, including several directors of infantry, were unhappy at this decision, the wider General Staff recognised the importance of cooperation with the United States and the value of ranged weapons, combined arms and the nuclear bomb. This wider group of General Staff had not necessarily swallowed the argument in favour of .280 ammunition in its entirety but had always been willing to go along with the engineers' proposals so long as it kept the Americans happy. Given the institutional prejudices sustaining the American belief in .30 calibre ammunition, in 1950 it was impossible to reach a transatlantic agreement on a lethality criterion. Consequently, the science by itself could not drive standardisation. Indeed, the science had proved ineffective at forcing a change in the terms of debate either in the United States or ultimately in the UK. Instead, and as I will show in the next chapter, the Americans wielded their bureaucratic and institutional power in order to bring about technical and scientific closure on ammunition and deliver standardisation on their own terms.

5

THE BUREAUCRACY AS BATTLEFIELD

Churchill: When I was at Omdurman I rode with a sabre in one hand and a revolver in the other.

Field Marshal Slim: Not much standardisation there, Prime Minister.

Downing Street, 20 November 1951[1]

The Battle of Wanat in the Nuristan Province of Afghanistan has generated considerable commentary both inside and outside the US government.[2] Involving forty-eight US soldiers, twenty-four members of the Afghan National Army and three US Marine Corps advisors, the culminating action took place on 13 July 2008 when a large Taliban force attacked Combat Outpost Kahler, leaving nine US soldiers dead and thirty-one others wounded. The scale of the battle resulted in a great deal of press coverage and left many questioning the US counterinsurgency strategy in Afghanistan.[3] As the *Washington Times* alleged, however, it also revealed that the M-4 Carbine, a shortened version of the M16 rifle, was unreliable, having failed to operate during the engagement, and that these failings had been deliberately written out of the subsequent US Army Combat Studies Institute Report.[4] The suggestion was that there had been a bureaucratic cover-up.

This was not the first time the M16 had received negative press. In the late 1960s, during the Vietnam War, a number of GIs reported that the weapon jammed and caused several needless deaths. This subsequently produced at least five different investigations into the problem, after which it was finally recognised that, for a number of interlocking reasons, a change in ammunition propellant by the US Ordnance Department had caused the weapon to jam in the jungle.[5] As in Vietnam, the suggestion in Wanat was that incompetent government bureaucrats had left soldiers exposed to unnecessary danger, danger that more effective processes, less bureaucracy and greater engagement with the user community would prevent.

Similar criticisms can be made about the equipment being introduced by other nations. Over the last ten years, the Australian and American governments have been criticised for the purchase of inappropriate uniforms, the British for inadequate supplies of equipment and body armour. Equivalent problems are also reported at every level of the equipment procurement system beyond the infantry (i.e. from aircraft to communication systems, self-propelled artillery to armoured vehicles).[6] Moreover, such problems are not confined to particular periods of history. On the contrary, every British service rifle since 1880 has been surrounded by controversy. In 1885, the Martini–Henry failed in the deserts of the Sudan at the Battle of Abu Klea during the attempted rescue of General Gordon.[7] The ammunition in the Lee–Metford was considered insufficiently powerful and the Mark IV dumdum bullet for the SMLE ruled illegal. The SA80/A1 suffered serious problems during the 1990–1 Gulf War, and the SAS has never used the weapon.[8] More recently, there have been reports that the SAS believes 5.56mm ammunition is inappropriate, apparently because it allowed 'fanatical insurgents to keep on fighting despite their wounds'.[9]

It would seem, then, that one of the least expensive weapon systems in the military inventory is capable of stirring up some of the greatest controversies, controversies that politicians, soldiers and journalists will typically blame on bureaucrats and bureaucracy. In this chapter, I develop this argument by drawing on the debates and controversies swirling around the British government as it looked to adopt an automatic weapon in the 1950s. These debates were particularly controversial because the Labour government had adopted the EM-2, naming it the Rifle No. 9 Mk I, in April 1951. Less than eight months later, however, the newly elected Conservative government put this decision on hold, and in late 1953 the Cabinet decided to abandon the EM-2 and .280 ammunition altogether. Churchill had decided to adopt US T65 .30 ammunition and the Belgian FN Fusil Automatique Légere (FAL) self-loading rifle instead.[10]

The introduction of the semiautomatic FAL and the 9mm Sterling SMG would eventually ensure the Infantry Section could engage targets at range and then close for the assault. The FAL and the Sterling would replace the

venerable bolt action SMLE/No. 4 Rifle and the Sten SMG. Despite considerable protestations by Field Marshall Slim, Winston Churchill and the
Conservative Government had decided to sacrifice tactical flexibility, the battlefield evidence and the aspirations of the Wigram apostles in favour of
American equipment and the prospect of standardisation. Bearing in mind
the conflicting scientific evidence and the subsequent American decision to
abandon standardisation on the .30 calibre round in favour of 5.56mm ammunition in 1964, how ought we to interpret Churchill's logic? This chapter aims
to provide an answer via the lens of bureaucratic politics.

Bureaucratic politics: an exercise in advancing 'Interests', 1950–7

In the context of governmental decision-making, finding ways to explain the
process by which agreement between actors might be achieved have tended to
focus on the relationships between bureaucratic actors. Framed this way,
organisational or sectional interests shape the manner in which decisions are
made. This in turn is dependent on the relative position of the actors in the
bureaucracy and their willingness to bargain and trade off alternative possibilities before arriving at some form of agreement. The classic exponents of this
approach argued that actors 'choose in terms of no consistent set of strategic
objectives but rather according to various conceptions of national security,
organizational, domestic, and sectional interests'.[11] According to this
Bureaucratic Politics Model, government decisions are not necessarily the
result of rational calculation but rather of a complex interplay of bargaining
which has different players pulling and hauling to promote their organisational interests.

In many ways, this mode of explanation offers a useful theoretical lens for
developing an appreciation for how NATO standardisation agreements
emerged. Thus, it is possible to argue that the policies and perspectives
adopted by various NATO ordnance communities reflected their sectional
interests. In the immediate years after the Second World War, American and
British actors took different stands on technical questions which were in turn
dependent on where they sat in relation both to each other and their own
bureaucratic politics. Research and design in the British small arms community had traditionally been underfunded. The post-war fear was that funding
and support would be withdrawn and once again Britain's ability to develop
a firearm would fall into decline.[12] When put in this context, the development
of the EM-2 and .280 ammunition offered British engineers the vehicle

through which they could sustain their existence. This demanded that the users' perspectives be reconfigured so as to create the space that would allow British engineers the opportunity to develop a sufficiently radical and compelling alternative to that being contemplated by Britain's General Staff. The US Ordnance Corps, by contrast, were adept at ensuring their weapon solutions closely aligned to the strongly held views of the powerful marksmanship lobby within the US Army. They could not afford to have Britain's engineers foist an alternative solution on them for fear that they too would find themselves an unnecessary expense for US taxpayers.

In 1950–1, then, these two distinct sets of interests clashed during comparative user and technical trials, trials that would potentially result in the demise of one engineering constituency in favour of the other. Although these different actors did not technically form part of the same bureaucracy, they still sought to defend and advance their position relative to each other for fear of being left worse off. When it came to making a decision about what might be the best technical solution, the optimum choice was not necessarily the one that best addressed the battlefield evidence. On the contrary, the solution that emerged might only tangentially relate to the battlefield.

Either way, however, without any clear scientific guidance on lethality, a decision about the future of Anglo-American small arms would have to be taken on non-scientific grounds. From our point of view, what was particularly interesting was the way these non-scientific factors would eventually fold back on questions of lethality and shape the way the science of killing was subsequently understood. At the time, without a definitive scientific perspective, what forced the decision in favour of the Americans was the broadening of the immediate post-war debate to include actors with conflicting opinions to those of the British. These actors would water down or complicate British calculations and make it easier for the Americans to achieve their technical goals.

The opening challenge to British ambitions started with the Canadians. The Canadian interest in the transatlantic small arms debate stretched back to 1946, when the British General Staff had asked Canadian officials what they thought about the British Army adopting the US .30'06 round.[13] When the General Staff changed their minds, the Canadian military were subsequently asked for help with experimental facilities so that the British could speed up the development of the .280 round.[14] In addition, the Canadians were directly involved in the post-war 'America, Britain, Canada' (ABC) agreements related to small arms standardisation and acted as the weapon handlers and observers to the 1950 comparative ammunition and rifle trials in the United States.[15]

For the Canadians, the EM-2 represented a difficult proposition. Canada had fought the Second World War as a Dominion power, but with the fall of the Axis, Canadian politicians were seeking to reposition the country so as to take part in a new world order. Key to this was Canada's pursuit of a dual strategy to build security arrangements and maintain export markets with both America and the UK.[16] Ideally, transatlantic harmony would give Canada the greatest opportunity to maximise its export potential and create the ideal conditions for a full change of the country's economy from war to peace footing. While the EM-2 represented only a minor piece of that story, for the Canadians it was true to say that any disharmony between the UK and the United States on something as simple as a rifle would not bode well for standardisation of all transatlantic military equipment.[17] A failure to agree on this would mean that the Canadian government would be required to establish more industrial capacity to cater for differing US and UK equipment needs with a consequent decrease in financial return. This was something the Canadian government would have preferred not to do. Achieving agreement on the rifle issue was, therefore, the first step in resolving the perennial Canadian problem of having to apply both American and British manufacturing standards to their manufacturing processes.[18] As far as the Canadian government was concerned, the question of military utility was of secondary importance to reducing manufacturing complexity and the costs of production. If the Americans refused to accept the EM-2, then Canada would also prefer an alternative solution.

While the comparative user and technical trials were underway, there was some hope that an agreement could be reached amicably between the ABC nations. When the trials ended in September 1950, however, the Canadian position started to become more difficult. As alluded to in the previous chapter, the immediate cause of this was that both the American T65 and the British .280 round could be deemed appropriate for use depending on the battlefield requirement. In this respect, while the technical tests had indicated that the .280 round was as lethal at the T65, the user trials came out much more favourably to the British rifle. Indeed, as far as Brigadier Barlow was concerned, the US Army Equipment Board had concluded that neither the T65 nor the .280 was satisfactory in their current incarnations, but that of the two submitted, the British SAA was preferred.[19]

US ordnance officials and the American General Staff, in contrast, were considerably less happy with the direction in which the US Army Equipment Board was headed. Accordingly, in December, while ostensibly still examining the details of the joint comparative trials, the Americans asked a NATO Standing Group to consider standardising the M2 .30'06 SAA for all NATO countries.[20] This was followed up with communications to British diplomats stating that 'The future US round will be the .30 calibre T65.'[21] By all accounts, the Americans had decided to disregard the trial agreements and go it alone.

On hearing this, the UK's military and technical establishments felt the need to consider the question of adopting the EM-2. The United States had apparently ignored the results of their own Army Equipment Board. The British therefore believed they had every right to decide what they wanted to do without concern for standardisation. The matter was consequently accelerated through the War Office and ultimately presented for consideration to the Chiefs of Staff and the Cabinet Defence Committee.[22] With all in agreement, the secretary of state for war, Emanuel Shinwell, announced to the House of Commons on 25 April 1951 that the UK had decided to adopt the EM-2 as the Rifle No. 9 Mk.I.[23] At this point, what were previously the private and somewhat abstract discussions of a discrete technical community became the stuff of debate on the floor of the House of Commons. Shinwell's announcement finally polarised the divide within the transatlantic community, bringing Winston Churchill out in favour of the American position.[24]

Given their difficult geopolitical situation, it was the Canadians who first sought a reconciliation of the respective positions with their call for a ministerial level conference to discuss the issue.[25] The intention was to bring together the respective defence ministers and secretaries of state from the United States, the UK and Canada. Reluctant to discuss technical details and no doubt conscious of the potential for a bureaucratic ambush, however, Emanuel Shinwell was cautious about accepting the Canadian suggestion.[26]

The reason for this lack of British enthusiasm appears to have been the suspicion that the Americans were going to use a summit as an opportunity for gathering support for their T65 ammunition. In this respect, Shinwell's fears were well-founded. The Canadian minister of defence had suggested a meeting between the ABC powers, which was originally scheduled to take place in August 1951. Upon agreeing and offering to host the meeting in Washington, DC, the American Secretary of State for Defence, General Marshall, also took the opportunity to invite the French government.[27] Having an additional party at the discussions, one that had not been involved in any of the agreements on small arms, would complicate the process of achieving agreement, effectively making standardisation a NATO issue, not just a transatlantic matter.[28]

The French had previously shown no interest in the rifle debate, primarily because they had not been party to the early agreements on equipment standardisation, but they were clearly more than happy to attend the August meeting following Marshall's overtures. French involvement had not been automatic. It was only with the establishment of NATO in 1949 that they had a legitimate pretext for being present. Their attendance, however, presented the British with a difficult political problem. The French were clearly reliant on US small arms in their efforts to regain control of their former colonies and were unlikely to bite the hand that fed them and argue in favour of the UK proposals.[29] The British delegation was, therefore, at a distinct disadvantage as the decision to adopt the EM-2 was likely to be opposed by the other three powers attending the Washington meeting.

For the British, the August 1951 meeting did not go well. As Shinwell no doubt guessed, the French and Americans opposed the British decision, while the Canadians stated that they were stuck in a difficult position which they increasingly found hard to maintain.[30] Brooke Claxton, the Canadian minister of defence, made the point that they were caught between the UK and the United States and that they were being forced to choose between the two nations. They could choose one standard of ammunition and firearm, but that would leave the NATO powers at a disadvantage, as Canada could not manufacture both types of ordnance. At a deeper level, Claxton questioned the whole standardisation programme by arguing that the UK and the United States were failing to make transparent and compatible decisions. As a result, it was extremely difficult for Canada to organise its own equipment procurement and programme of manufacture.[31]

The French and the Americans, in contrast, were considerably more forthcoming in stating their views of the British decision. Although the French had not seen any technical information on the .280 round, they were of the opinion that the stopping power of the British ammunition was likely to be inadequate. They therefore believed that NATO ought to adopt the .30 calibre and made it clear that France would support the United States in questions relating to small arms.[32] It was consequently left to the Americans to outline the technical reasons for rejecting the joint comparative trials, stating 'That none of the test rifles, or ammunition, was suitable or acceptable, and none could be considered as a replacement for the popular battle tested M-1.'[33] Accordingly, they argued that the only possible solution was that they adopt the T65 round and standardise it across NATO.[34] Backed into a corner, Shinwell was eventually forced into accepting that the matter would be referred to a Working Party of the NATO Standing Group on Standardisation.[35]

This was bad news for the British delegation, but even worse was to come. Upon his return home, Brigadier Barlow went back through the minutes of the conference and found that the US Ordnance Corps, and Colonel René Studler in particular, had used data that described an older prototype version of the UK's .280 ammunition.[36] In the course of a US presentation that made use of many charts and graphs, it was difficult to spot the error. In fact, British engineers had been working on increasing the velocity of the .280 ammunition, something the Americans chose to ignore. Instead, they preferred to use the older data in their efforts to make a case against the British design solution. Clearly, both sides were a long way from coming to any sort of agreement.

Unfortunately for the EM-2 advocates, the decision to adopt the EM-2 had also brought Winston Churchill, the leader of the opposition, into the fray. Churchill could now openly voice his own views in the House of Commons. Aware that Churchill would taunt him, Shinwell agreed to refer the British decision to adopt the No. 9 Rifle to the NATO Standing Group in order to show that he had achieved something by his visit to the United States.[37]

It was not, however, the view of this newly appointed Standing Group that forced a change in War Office policy; rather, it was the Conservative Party's re-election in October 1951 that was the final turning point for the EM-2. For what the NATO Standing Group eventually decided effectively left it open to the British to stick by their decision should they so wish. This was because the Group only agreed a list of military characteristics that the NATO powers, with the notable exception of Britain, wanted to see from their ammunition. In the future, a standard round ought to more closely resemble the .30 T65 than the .280 British round.[38] However, the Canadian delegation also indicated, on the basis of the Standing Group's own ammunition trials, that the UK 'be urged to continue work on the .280 ...' as 'it shows such promise.'[39] British engineers, it seemed, had been given enough permission to stick to their decision. Whether policymakers would concur with their perspective would soon become apparent.

Resisting the engineer: policy-based evidence

For those British engineers and officers pursing rifle technology suitable for increasing the tactical flexibility of the infantry, the prevailing attitude towards their proposed solution changed with the election of the Conservative government on 25 October 1951. Churchill was suspicious of the British design of rifle and had been arguing against the Labour government's decision since April of that year. In the first instance, it seems likely that his counter-arguments were not based on anything more than an instinct for creating a political debate and his active interest in firearms. Over time, as he gathered information from a variety of sources, Churchill put himself in a stronger position to object to the Labour decision. His objections were twofold. First, he was not convinced by the arguments concerning the need for increased rates of fire. Logistically speaking, Churchill was of the opinion that automatic firearms were impracticable given the strains on the supply chain during war. Secondly, he viewed standardised equipment as an essential prerequisite to gaining emergency wartime access to the North American manufacturing pool. This section explores these views, exposing the mechanisms by which Churchill finally forced the CIGS to back down.

Churchill's initial objection to the EM-2 stemmed from his belief that there was no advantage to be gained from increasing the number of rounds that an infantryman could fire per minute.[40] This view remained with him throughout his opposition to the EM-2 and quickly surfaced once he was re-elected prime minister. Indeed, one of the first things the new prime minister did was to write a brief note to the chiefs of staff stating his personal view on the EM-2. Churchill wrote:

> There is no doubt that the .280 is a far better rifle than the .303. It may well be technically the best so far designed. The rate of fire is not, however, important or usually an advantage. The existing rifles can fire away more ammunition in ten minutes than the soldiers can carry. Indeed, the practical problem has been, and I believe still is, to husband the use of ammunition by the forward troops.[41]

This contention was the exact opposite to the view held by all directors of infantry since 1944. Moreover, the CIGS and a growing number of staff officers were also coming to the conclusion that, in the face of an increased threat to Europe from the Soviet Union, it was absolutely necessary to replace the bolt action No. 4 with a weapon with increased rates of fire.[42] If this was becoming the received view of the General Staff, then Emanuel Shinwell was doing nothing more than agreeing to the wishes of the professionals advising him.[43]

Thus it seems remarkable that Churchill believed it necessary to intervene and put a brake on the EM-2's development given the weight of military opinion in favour of its adoption. If the new prime minister had taken note of the arguments put forward by the EM-2 advocates, then he would have seen that the .280 ammunition had no logistical implications. This was because it was in fact both lighter and smaller in size than the existing .303 round.[44] Indeed,

British engineers had specifically explored this issue in a number of documents designed to illustrate the logistical advantages of .280 over .303 and T65 ammunition.[45] This had shown, for example, that .280 calibre allowed 828,000 more rounds to be carried by a British infantry division without any increase in transport above that already required to carry the .303 cartridge.[46] If there was a logistical debate to be had, then the real issue related to the fact that the US Army had the luxury of motor transport to carry their troops and supplies to the front lines in quantities that the British did not. They could, therefore, afford to transport a larger and more powerful calibre round without causing significant strain to the supply chain.[47] In contrast, the British infantryman needed a smaller, less weighty round as they would be required to carry it to the front lines in their webbing. As one commentator put it, 'The U.S. infantry lives off or near to and moves in jeeps, peeps and lorries. The British infantry's mobility is the mobility of the man on his feet. This fundamentally different attitude to infantry is at the root of the different approach to this rifle.'[48] In these circumstances, it can come as no surprise that the CIGS, Field Marshal Slim, took a dim view of Churchill's line of reasoning and that their meetings on the subject were acrimonious.[49]

The argument that had more purchase on the General Staff, however, was Churchill's belief that standardisation with the Americans was a manufacturing imperative. The prime minister was well aware of the production potential of the United States and was insistent that Britain should do nothing to jeopardise access to it in times of war.[50] On this basis, what was at stake was whether Britain had the capacity to deliver sufficient weapons and ammunition in preparation for and during the next conflict. After receiving advice from his secretary of state for war, Anthony Head, Churchill quickly concluded that Britain's need for rifles outweighed the capability to produce enough EM-2s in the time allowed. Indeed, Head stated that the UK needed 1.5 million rifles when the newly re-formed Home Guard was included in the totals, whereas Britain could only produce 9,000 EM-2s per calendar month from 1955 to 1956.[51]

The need to provide the Home Guard with the same weapon as the regular force alongside the re-equipment of the standing army was a new line of reasoning not previously considered at the War Office. When the original decision had been taken to adopt the EM-2, it had been on the basis that the total number required was 329,446, which would take six years to manufacture, allowing for ramping up production.[52] Churchill, however, could use the Home Guard as a way of pointing out that Britain did not have the production capacity to go it alone and that standardisation was the only way to ensure that the UK would have enough weapons in the future.

The War Office, in contrast, was unconvinced by the case for reintroducing the Home Guard, while the CIGS was more interested in ensuring his front-line forces had the equipment that they needed.[53] In the circumstances, Slim did not view the production issue the same way as the new prime minister. This belied the fact that, at a deeper level, Slim's concerns were not about manufacturing but rather with the job he was directly responsible for: the defence of Britain and what remained of the empire, and the possibility of future conflicts with the Soviet Union in Western Europe. Slim believed the EM-2 to be the most appropriate weapon in the circumstances, and he wanted to ensure that his troops were issued with it. Indeed, he was known to have stated that the best way to show the other NATO powers the virtues of the EM-2 was for Britain's forces defending West Germany, known as the British Army of the Rhine (BAOR), to be issued with the weapon so that it could speak for itself.[54] For Slim, to have to repeat the arguments that had been reproduced over the previous twelve months to a new and sceptical prime minister was, therefore, not something he relished when they met in November 1951. After all, the arguments concerning the appropriateness of the EM-2 had not changed in the month after Churchill's election.

To be fair to Churchill, the position he took when he met President Truman in January 1952 was the position he agreed with Slim in November the previous year. However, even though he praised the .280 rifle, Churchill implicitly sided with the Americans at this meeting. For he also pointed out that in times of war, it was important to have a large pool of rifles and that, as both the United States and Britain were fighting in Korea, there was little benefit from making any changes in small arms until there was a substantial period of peace.[55] The Americans could be happy with this conclusion as they had no urgent need to make the change from the M-1 Garand. In contrast, the CIGS could not find much that satisfied him in this arrangement, for it meant that the British Army would be compelled to use the .303 until a new round was agreed. Increasingly, it seemed that without political support at the very top of government, the efforts of the EM-2 advocates would be blocked and the War Office compelled to use American equipment. The final *coup de grâce*, however, did not come from the Americans, but rather the Belgian company Fabrique Nationale.

Contingent events: Fabrique Nationale d'Armes de Guerre

With political support for the British weapon waning, the question was no longer about when the EM-2 would be adopted, but how long the Ministry of Supply could put up a rear-guard action to keep the idea alive. In this context, it was demoralising for the engineers and Barlow that the final blow to their efforts came from a company that had been working with them both during and after the Second World War.[56] This was especially the case as FN had only been invited to work on the .280 project because of the limited amount of time available and the need to guarantee the production of a working rifle to fire the British engineer's ammunition.[57] The EM-2 advocates never intended to adopt FN equipment. However, the fact of the matter was that the Belgian company was very effective at taking what chances it had in order to promote their system over all others. This section is therefore concerned with showing how FN exploited their opportunities and created an opening that ultimately led the British to adopt the 7.62mm FAL in 1957.

FN policy was shaped by the determination to have its weapons selected by one of the major powers. Accordingly, in 1946 they hawked their products around, asking for advice and direction from British engineers as well as the design departments of other nation states while changing features of their own weapons, principally the FN49, in the hope of picking up work. Initially, this involved approaching the Ministry of Supply regarding their newly redesigned self-loading rifle chambered to 7.92mm calibre.[58] Although the controller of supplies (munitions) was sceptical at first, Barlow eventually convinced his superior that the company should be used in a limited capacity so as to make up for any shortfall in capability within the Ministry of Supply.[59] However, this attempt to make use of external resources was not well received by the then director of weapons development at the War Office, Major-general Francis Festing. He wrote, 'As regards the standardisation aspect, I do not at all like the idea of having to go to the US with a rifle produced in a foreign country ...'[60] Festing was reassured, however, to know that FN would be employed only to ensure that the British had a working rifle to fire the .280 ammunition.[61]

Consequently, between 1948 and 1950, FN worked alongside Noel Kent-Lemon and Britain's engineers in the refinement of its own self-loading rifle, rechambering their 7.92mm model to take the .280 round and converting an additional weapon into bullpup configuration.[62] They also made a point of working on the .280 round ostensibly in an effort to improve its performance.[63] To certain members of the British small arms community, it seemed that the company was building 'hand-made' ammunition to impress decision-makers.[64] By August 1949, it was the view of the Ministry of Supply that the conventional design of FN weapon should be retained because it had reached a more advanced stage of development, having completed its 5,000-round endurance test before any of the other weapons including the EM-2.[65] The Ministry of Supply consequently went to the 1950 comparative trials with two types of weapon: the FN .280 in conventional configuration and the EM-2 in bullpup.

The problem that FN had, however, was that the British never really had any intention of purchasing their weapon. Major-general Festing, for example, asked the Ministry of Supply whether there was 'some way we could pick FN's brains and still truthfully be able to say that the rifle was a British product' as such a course 'would avoid purchasing manufacturing rights and payment of royalties … if the [rifle adopted by the UK] had to be recognised as an FN design'.[66] The British view of FN was therefore conditional on how the company could be used to advance the campaign for the EM-2. The problem was that when the decision was taken to adopt the EM-2 in April 1951, the veneer of friendly relations quickly disintegrated as FN scrambled to emphasise the qualities of its own weapons to all those that might listen.

In these new circumstances, one of the first requests made by the company was that the British government invite FN representatives to all trials of weapons where FN-designed equipment and ammunition were being displayed. In addition, the company insisted that all its designs be properly accredited before any display. Finally, FN pursued the Ministry of Supply for damages, claiming that it had been involved in the development of the .280 ammunition.[67] On the basis that the British were going to adopt the EM-2, FN also rechambered its own weapon to fire .30 ammunition and made it available to the Belgian armed forces fighting in Korea, thereby recruiting the Belgian government to its cause.[68] The company then asserted its independence from the EM-2 advocates who were by that time concerned with whether the British Army would adopt the .280 calibre and continued to make its weapon available for additional, US-sponsored trials held during 1952. All of this activity underscored FN's determination to protect its intellectual capital.

An opportunity to emphasise FN's independence presented itself following Churchill's re-election in October 1951. With the CIGS battling and eventually failing to maintain support for the decisions made by the previous government, the director of infantry was forced into siding with the General Staff and breaking ranks with Barlow and the engineers at the Ministry of Supply. The pretext for this was a re-evaluation of some trials that had been held in the spring of 1951. Ironically, these check tests, as they were known, had been ordered on the basis that the advocates needed to placate FN after the Labour government's announcement that the British Army would adopt the EM-2.[69]

Ever since that decision was made public, FN had been complaining that the 1950 comparative trials had shown that their weapon was more appropriate for taking into service than any other. Therefore, they argued that the choice of the EM-2 was unfair and politically motivated; a claim to which there appeared to be some substance. That this was the case was entirely down to the fact that, in the spring of 1951, Brigadier Barlow had continuously interfered in the workings of the check tests. Indeed, the examining board stated that they believed their examinations showed that FN's assertions about the 1950 trials were broadly correct and complained that 'the amount of interference with their powers, and direction of their opinion, was not warranted. It is difficult to take an impartial decision when one side of a question only is being continuously and forcibly emphasised ...'[70]

Subsequently, in December 1951, the director of infantry wrote to Brigadier Barlow stating that he believed the Ministry of Supply had 'doctored the patient' with regard to the EM-2 during these trials.[71] In the process, the director of infantry revealed the presence of a fault line between the views of Brigadier Barlow and the engineers at the Ministry of Supply on the one hand and the War Office on the other. The condition that brought this to the surface was Churchill's election in October, as well as Barlow's forceful intervention in the workings of the 1951 check tests, which made it easy for the War Office to break with the views of the Ministry of Supply. FN was now presented with the chance to appeal directly to the War Office with regard to future firearms without having to go through the Ministry of Supply.

Experts versus policymakers

For those who developed and supported the idea of the EM-2, what was crucial was the careful marriage of ammunition with rifle. A smaller calibre round would make it possible for the military to have a lighter weapon with increased firepower. In addition, adopting the EM-2 would reduce the number of weapons in the inventory, simplify training and decrease the logistical support required for small arms. In the face of the prime minister's decision to achieve standardisation with the Americans, changing the calibre of ammunition to .30 severely undermined the chances of attaining all of the organisational and tactical possibilities. Yet in 1952, with the .280 round effectively stymied by

Churchill's intervention, this was being contemplated. In this respect, the period up to the government decision to adopt the FN FAL was characterised by a bureaucratic fight between the expert engineers at the Ministry of Supply and policymakers who had determined that standardisation was more important than delivering flexible infantry tactics.

Entering into this bureaucratic maelstrom, the Canadians were the first to suggest a compromise round following the report of the NATO Standing Group.[72] However, with the Americans flatly rejecting the .280 calibre early in 1952, stating that they would not adopt any ammunition other than the .30, any new compromise ammunition intended for the NATO alliance would not have the support of its largest power.[73] Consequently, this new developmental cycle could not come to anything more than slowly coaxing the Ministry of Supply into accepting that their technical ambitions were not to be. This final section is therefore concerned with showing how the War Office finally managed to realise its aim of procuring an automatic rifle without having to wait until the Americans adopted something to replace the M-1 Garand.

The difference between the efforts of the Ministry of Supply before the US–UK comparative trials of 1950 and those after Churchill's election was the fact that Barlow, Kent-Lemon and the Armament Design Establishment were now forced into working collaboratively with the Belgian and Canadian governments.[74] A Belgian, British and Canadian (BBC) committee was established to look into the technical problems and partition out experimental work between the three powers.[75] For the Belgians, this involved employing FN to act on their behalf, thereby forcing the British to accept a degree of equality and openness with the company that previously did not exist. It also meant that both the Canadians and Belgians now had access to staff at the War Office in a way that had not previously been available.

The underlying problem, however, remained the fact that the Americans would not back away from their commitment to the .30 calibre. And yet the chairman of the BBC committee, Brigadier Barlow, insisted on continuing with tests and trials of both ammunition and weapons despite the growing evidence to indicate that there was no future benefit from doing so.[76] In this respect, even Kent-Lemon was becoming increasingly frustrated with having to work on new ammunition that he and his engineers believed provided no tangible benefits when compared to the T65 round.[77] In the end, the ADE believed that the War Office ought to adopt the T65 round and tap into American production capacity rather than continue work on a round that policymakers had ruled against and a new round that satisfied no-one.

However, Brigadier Barlow was not quite ready to concede defeat. His ambition was still that the British Army ought to adopt a British design of rifle even if the Churchill government was not prepared to take the .280 ammunition. During the course of 1952, a number of EM-2s were rechambered to fire both the compromise round and the T65 with a view to undertaking trials in 1953.[78] Barlow was confident that the EM-2 would perform strongly in any future test, but in his eagerness he also demonstrated that claims about a British design philosophy which emphasised the importance of building the rifle around the ammunition were as much about marketing as they were about optimum design. In reality, the ADE had opted for a bullpup design in 1946 before the ammunition issue had been resolved. Now with Barlow busily rechambering the EM-2 to take larger ammunition, what was clear was that the most important thing for him was for the British Army to be equipped with a British rifle.

Thus it was with a deep sense of irony that at a meeting with the director of infantry at the War Office, FN insisted that the real issue at stake was deciding on the future calibre of ammunition before selecting a rifle.[79] They argued that, if the Americans insisted on the T65, then what would be the purpose of the other powers going it alone? As it was, when faced with representatives of the Canadian government and FN, the director of infantry was not quite ready to let go of the idea that the British Army should be equipped with a British design of infantry weapon, and so in October 1952 he sided with Brigadier Barlow for the last time and allowed the trials to continue.[80] It was at this point that higher authority at the War Office finally intervened to bring to a close the question of whether or not to adopt the EM-2.

In April 1953, the War Office decided that they had had enough of waiting for the technical establishments to catch up with the government's views on the need to work with the Americans. Accordingly, the General Staff wrote to the Ministry of Supply asking him to consider an Army Council paper that set out the reasons why Britain should adopt the FN FAL.[81] This document said that the selection of a new automatic rifle was an imperative and that a choice about which weapon the British Army should have could be made without having to examine the ammunition question any further. Moreover, the paper continued by stating that while both the EM-2 and FN were excellent weapons, there were two advantages the FN possessed which the British weapon did not: that it cost less and that it would take less time to get the weapon into the hands of the British Army.[82]

Following a meeting between the Ministry of Supply and the director of infantry, it was stated that they were 'solidly of the opinion that there is a real urgency to equip the Army with a new rifle as early as possible ...' and that the 'development of the EM-2 should continue as an insurance ... [as] ... it would have to show a greater superiority in performance and an improved cost ratio for it to supplant the FN at some future date'.[83] Moreover, as Canada was prepared to adopt the FN but not the EM-2, this weighed heavily in favour of Britain doing the same. Needless to say, Barlow protested, but the War Office had made up its mind.[84] By late 1953, after some further discussions between the French, American and British governments, the Army finally accepted that the US .30 ammunition was satisfactory.[85] By 1957, following further negotiations with the other treaty organisation countries, it was clear that it would also prove acceptable to the wider alliance powers and was subsequently renamed the 7.62mm x 51mm NATO Standard.[86] The next weapon to be adopted by the British Army was to be a semiautomatic, self-loading rifle of Belgian design using an American standard of cartridge, all of which bore no relation to the battlefield conditions that inspired its selection.[87]

Conclusion

The British government's decision would have dramatic effects that would shape NATO's choice of small arms from the 1950s to the present day. Not only would it lead to considerable debate within select NATO circles about the rights and wrongs of small arms technology and tactics but it would also set the tone for future discussion on alliance interoperability and burden sharing. For if NATO partners could only barely agree on the types of ammunition that they would use in the 1950s, then what hope was there for the alliance to realise the wider benefits of standardisation? The question of small arms and ammunition was, then, a test case for establishing the benefits of the entire NATO standardisation project. At the same time, engineers and soldiers would use the 1950s debates as a point of departure when considering future ammunition during the 1960s, '70s and even into the present day.

Bearing in mind the fact that the 1950s discussions would have dramatic effects on the way soldiers would fight over the next sixty years, how might we explain the British decision to abandon the EM-2 in favour of 7.62mm ammunition and the FAL? The traditional answer is that the decision was based on a careful weighing up of the factors and that, on balance, the War Office made a determination about what was most important. There are a number of reasons why such an account has some virtue, most notably that the explanation typically concurs with the personal accounts of those making the decision. However, when considering the process of decision-making in more detail, it becomes readily apparent that there is much more going on than simply an individual actor or group choosing one possibility over another. Indeed, what becomes clear from this chapter is just how many different actors were making contingent choices based on partial information or information designed to advance a particular position. Decision-making was not unitary but rather dispersed across a number of intellectual domains and over multiple organisational levels and actors.

In the first instance, then, the Bureaucratic Politics Model successfully reflects the empirical ebb and flow of decision-making within a distributed bureaucracy. Different actors asserted their interests, arguing their case for different types of solutions to the bureaucratic and battlefield problem that faced them, taking into account their specific and situated needs. To this extent, actor preferences were rational and emerged from within the situated contexts that they were operating within. However, what is also clear from this chapter is how decision-making was bounded by the availability and careful control of different types of information. Contingent, practical and pragmatic considerations shaped the logic of the various actors, framing particular preferences in light of the constraints they were operating under at the time.

Nonetheless, the bureaucratic strategies employed by various actors also point to the possibility that a great deal more can be said about the way technical choices were framed and resolved and about how these interests themselves were constructed. In particular, it asks us not just to think about how different descriptions of the battlefield come to dominate particular bureaucratic decisions but also how power is used to arbitrate between those different perspectives: how power is used to exclude particular types of debate so as to avoid conflict or lead discussion down a particular path. When considered in this way, bureaucratic politics is not just about the free market of ideas and the pushing and hauling between actors who are making choices after weighing up the factors involved. On the contrary, and as I will show in the next chapter, it also has to take into account the characteristic modes of reasoning that shape the practices and language that are used to describe battlefield problems in the first place.

6

ALLIANCE POLITICS
AND NATO STANDARDISATION

INTERESTS, POWER, RATIONALITY

We Americans still see ourselves as the great Arsenal of Democracy. We prefer to go it alone, to meet any challenge, and so forth. We conduct our national defense debate in terms of 'Who is Number One—the Soviet Union, or the United States?'[1]

In 1957, and much to the annoyance of Duncan Sandys, the then Britain's minister of defence, the US Army reneged on its agreement with the UK to adopt the FAL and instead chose the M-14 automatic rifle designed by the US Ordnance Corps.[2] The following year, the British government decided to significantly reduce the UK's capacity to research and design small arms such that, in the future, the Royal Small Arms Factory (RSAF) would only 'retain an evaluation and modification capability'.[3]

Having adopted the M-14, the US Army once again changed its mind in 1964 and adopted the small calibre, high velocity 5.56mm M16 for out of NATO area operations, including Vietnam. By 1968, after the first round of NATO standardisation agreements had expired, the US Army subsequently retired the M-14 and adopted the M16 for general issue.[4] In that period, having delivered the vast majority of Anglicised FALs (i.e. weapons produced to imperial rather than metric design drawings and subsequently renamed the L1A1 Self Loading Rifle (SLR)), Britain's small arms capacity was further reduced from its wartime high of three manufactories to just the RSAF at Enfield. By 1967, it was clear that even Enfield was no longer economically viable and was merely being kept on for strategic reasons. Decisions taken by American officials on the other side of the Atlantic were not only having direct effects on the way that Britain's infantry would fight; their policies were also costing British workers their jobs.

Against this backdrop, a small 'skunkworks' design team working at Enfield proceeded to develop the concept for a replacement to the L1A1 SLR, later known as the SA80 and adopted in 1986.[5] This bullpup weapon had a similar form factor to the EM-2 and was initially chambered to an even smaller 4.85mm calibre in preparation for a further round of NATO standardisation trials that were scheduled for between 1979 and 1980.[6] Facing stiff competition that included an innovative German 4.73mm caseless round—a round that saved considerable weight by obviating the need for a brass cartridge case—this time British ordnance designers were forced into accepting 5.56mm ammunition as an agreed NATO standard (STANAG 4172).

Curiously, for those interested in explaining technology change, the new specification of 5.56mm ammunition was not the same as the American 1962 variant. Instead, the Belgian company Fabrique Nationale had once again managed to find a way to optimise ammunition design and persuade the whole of NATO to adopt it. In effect, STANAG 4172 established yet another type of 5.56mm ammunition. As far as the British teams working at Enfield were concerned, the new 5.56mm ammunition, designated SS109, would contribute to the poor performance of the SA80 during the First Gulf War and eventually result in the weapon's suspension from the NATO-nominated list of approved equipment in the mid-1990s.[7]

Thus the 1979–80 decision trials had multiple consequences. In the first instance, the United States reconfirmed its commitment to the 5.56mm standard despite the annoyance caused from having to re-barrel existing M16s to accommodate the technical qualities of the new ammunition. At the same time, the advantages of the German caseless round were so great that a number of NATO countries indicated an unwillingness to adopt 5.56mm for all mission types. Conscious that NATO powers might choose to assert their sovereignty over equipment purchases and buy German, the Americans started their own research and development programme into caseless ammunition.[8]

Even as this was going on, however, NATO powers continued to accept that there were potential advantages in standardising equipment. In the face of the material and manpower advantages of the Soviet Union, interoperability would free up design and manufacturing capability and allow different nations within NATO to specialise their production and research in set areas. Duplication of effort would consequently be reduced and the overall financial burden of trying to defend Western Europe more equitably shared across the alliance.[9] However, the benefits of interoperability were dependent on a bureaucratic process that mapped the different battlefield interpretations of various NATO powers together into a coherent standard. Yet as this chapter will show, by 1980 it was becoming clear that the economist's ideal pattern of planned armament design was not necessarily working out and that national military considerations trumped burden sharing.[10] The American decision in 1957 and the subsequent ammunition flip-flops had left many in NATO's armed forces unwilling to simply adopt the same weapons for specific roles or even standardise their tactics, techniques and procedures.

Such a state of affairs could partially be explained in terms of the sectional interests and power relations between NATO partners. However, as the previous chapters have explained, there was more going on than simply the entrenched national interests of different ordnance communities. Indeed, in many respects, the process of standardisation was itself dependent on the way in which knowledge about the battlefield, lethality and the infantryman was produced. The science could not decide the outcome of these early discussions on small arms and ammunition, because in the early 1950s the Americans and the British disputed the evidence and no agreement had been reached by the time the initial decisions were being taken.

Bearing that in mind, and in an effort to explore and develop a deeper appreciation for how social factors framed the standardisation debates, this chapter is divided into three parts. The first considers the challenge of reaching agreement during the period between 1957 and 1980. This part of the chapter will develop the main historical trajectory of the standardisation debates and describe how the doctrinal perspectives and battlefield interpretations of a number of key actors in NATO started to coincide. The second part of the chapter, by contrast, will show that there are a number of social processes buried within this narrative that help to frame the standardisation debate in a particular way. Reflecting the prevailing state of power between the actors involved, these social processes show how knowledge about a technical problem was produced and used to make one technical solution more attractive than the others. This will make it possible to draw the themes together in the third part of the chapter and assess the underlying rationality of the stances being taken by various parties. In the process, I uncover the modes of reasoning that were being used to decide on NATO's future technologies. This will afford us with an opportunity to consider the way that power operates in a bureaucratic context.

Part 1: Small arms standardisation between 1957 and 1980

The ability of the Americans to dictate the terms of standardisation was not dependent on their ability to compel the other NATO powers to accept 7.62mm ammunition. This was not a case of America having power over Britain to the extent that the United States could get the UK to do something that otherwise it did not want to do.[11] British engineers resisted American ambitions. However, an effective American bureaucratic strategy delayed the point of decision over the .280 ammunition until a new set of actors could be recruited to their cause. The technical artefact that emerged out of this process met the minimum requirements necessary to satisfy all the NATO partners.[12] That is to say, it produced an agreement on what constituted an acceptable minimum threshold ammunition for all the actors, but it did not necessarily result in a consensus on either the nature of the battlefield problem being faced, or the benefits of the solution that had been identified. Indeed, even as early as 1961 it is clear that the Federal Republic of Germany (FRG) felt that 7.62mm ammunition was far from optimal. As a consequence, the FRG had made moves to adopt the Spanish CETME rifle, a rifle initially designed for the German Kurz round.[13] This had initially caused some consternation at the UK's Ministry of Defence because Britain was half way through the introduction of the SLR. However, having dissuaded the FRG from pursuing its policy further, it was not long before the UK and the West Germans would find common cause in their dissatisfaction with the 7.62mm, eventually forming an axis that would work to undermine US thinking on small arms and ammunition.

The 1950s debates had made it abundantly clear that if standardisation on rifle designs were to occur, then there would have to be greater agreement about the nature of the battlefield problem even before consideration was given to the kinds of technical solutions that might resolve them.[14] Consequently, a number of 'Non-Material Standardisation Conferences' were held between the ABC countries to try to work out common terminology on tactics, organisation and training. The goal was to synchronise doctrine such that individual country tactics, techniques and procedures conformed to a NATO-wide standard. In effect, this meant that different armies would have to try to find agreement about their requirements.[15]

The problem was that if it had proven hard to deliver agreements between just the UK and America, then with even more NATO partners it would become even harder to align the non-material processes and knowhow associated with weapon design and use. Different armies thought about the battlefield differently. Earlier chapters in this book have shown how different conceptions of the battlefield were related to sectional interests within British and American Armies. More actors meant even more complex negotiations before agreement might be reached, negotiations that would reflect completely different conceptions of the infantry battle. These different perspectives reflected the situated nature of gathering combat data as much as it said something about each nation's unique experiences of war.

Thus, the American strategy of broadening the debate with other powers during the 1950s may have succeeded in undermining the British argument for .280 ammunition, but it also had the potential to make standardisation on anything other than the most consumable of equipment types harder to achieve. This certainly appeared to be the case as the key NATO protagonists (the FRG, UK and the United States) continued to develop their own weapon systems according to their own battlefield interpretations in preparation for the 1979–80 comparative trials. That this did not happen, however, has much to do with the fact that a number of contingent variables coincided in the 1970s to bring the FRG, the UK and the United States to accept a unifying doctrinal principle built around the use of armoured infantry. This potentially allowed these NATO partners to agree on the tactical arrangements for the employment of small arms. At the same time, the French had ruled themselves outside NATO's military command structure in 1966, consequently making it easier to harmonise doctrine among those powers making the largest military contribution.

However, several features of the standardisation debate leading up to the comparative trials demonstrated how the Americans could powerfully affect the terms in which the trials were conducted and the way in which the FRG, US and UK submissions would be evaluated. In particular, the Americans could successfully make use of their long-standing research into wound ballistics to define the underlying parameters in which standardisation would occur. In the process, they forced other nations to make ammunition choices within narrow technical constraints. Effectively, then, the United States could use its scientific analysis to rule out technical solutions it viewed as unfavourable.

This was particularly important to the Americans, as the British and West German armies were not only dissatisfied with 7.62mm ammunition, but also felt that the 5.56mm round and the M16 rifle did not resolve the battlefield problems as they understood them. As far as the West Germans were concerned, 7.62mm ammunition might be suitable for a medium machine gun, but they considered it to be far too powerful for an infantryman's rifle.[16] The Bundeswehr was responsible for defending the plains of West Germany from Soviet threat. In order to do this effectively, German preferences were for soldiers to fight close to, if not directly from, the armoured vehicles that had transported them to the battlefield.[17] MMGs mounted on the armoured vehicle would provide the supporting fire while firing ports on the armoured vehicle allowed infantry to fire while on the move. Once the armoured vehicle was close to the objective, the infantryman would dismount and engage the enemy at close quarters using lighter automatic weapons.[18] The Bundeswehr's design philosophy was for this lighter weapon to be built around ammunition that had been optimised for close-range engagements below 300m. This type of weapon would replace the 7.62mm G1 (the Bundeswehr designation for the FN FAL) rifle that they had been forced into selecting instead of the CETME, and their 9mm SMGs.

Just as important as the doctrinal considerations, the Bundeswehr's weapon preferences also reflected an awareness that soldiers struggled with marksmanship. For example, in 1969, German officers established that 10 per cent of the infantry failed to hit a man-size target during their marksmanship training. If this was not worrying enough, they also established that as many as 40 per cent of the total number of shots fired were within 10cm of the outside edge of the target.[19] Thus, the main concern was the need to increase hit probability, especially at close ranges. Indeed, according to British commentators, the Germans were more interested in hit probability than they were in lethality, snootily and inaccurately observing that this was a problem of conscript armies. In these circumstances, the German preference was to develop a weapon with an even smaller calibre of between 4.6mm and 4.9mm.[20] By American standards, this might compromise the lethality of the round, but for the Germans, the lack of recoil from a weapon using sub-5mm ammunition would mean less discomfort for a soldier who would ordinarily be dissuaded from using his weapon when armed with a high-powered rifle. Moreover, when combined as part of a handy automatic weapon, the round would increase the firepower of the German infantry and make up for any shortcomings in marksmanship. When utilised as part of an armoured infantry doctrine that deposited troops directly on to the objective, the technical choices being made by the Bundeswehr formed part of a coherent logic.

Initially, the West German idea for a small sub-5.56mm calibre round bore no relation to post-1957 British Army requirements. Instead, during the 1960s, Britain's General Staff were extremely reluctant to make any early changes from 7.62mm, despite the fact that by 1969 the Americans had entirely shifted to 5.56mm. The chief constraint, in this respect, was the recognition that the American Ordnance Corps were working on the Special Purpose Individual Weapon (SPIW), a weapon they believed might soon replace the M16.[21] What Britain's General Staff could not know, given that they were not party to American military–technical politics, was that the SPIW had been an attempt by the US Ordnance Corps to recover their position after the M-14 had been retired by the US Army in favour of the M16.[22] However, the defense secretary, Robert McNamara, and the US Chiefs of Staff had quickly closed down this effort and instead decided as early as November 1966 that the Army would adopt the M16 and the SPIW would be relegated to an exploratory development programme.[23]

Unaware of this, the British were keen to replace the unsatisfactory 7.62mm round, but were unsure about America's long-term intentions in relation to 5.56mm ammunition. With many still annoyed that the Americans had forced the British to abandon .280, British requirements emphasised the need to combine a round suitable for both a rifle and a Light Machine Gun (LMG). This reflected the infantry's ongoing commitment to operate in a dismounted role without the support of vehicles. However, the General Staff were not convinced that 5.56mm ammunition would be especially effective for use in both a personal weapon and an LMG where engaging targets at range remained a concern. Consequently, they were reluctant to make any wholesale acquisitions of the M16 in case it compromised their ability to acquire a hybrid personal weapon and LMG.

That is not to say, however, that the M16 might not have had some utility in certain conditions. Indeed, at just over 6lbs 4oz (2.9kg), not only was the fully automatic M16 considerably lighter and shorter than the SLR but it was easier to fire from the hip or quickly bring to the shoulder, thus making it easier to engage a fleeting target.[24] Consequently, the General Staff's scepticism did not stop the British Army from acquiring 5,000 M16s in 1965 for operations in Sarawak and Sabah against Indonesia insurgents.[25] Following this decision, Colt Industries were extremely keen to visit the British small arms community in March 1965 in the hope of cementing further sales to the UK.[26] Nevertheless, the move to bring about the wide-scale adoption of the M16 was resisted by a number of groups within the military–technical establishment, including the Royal Small Arms Factory and the master general of ordnance, as well as the General Staff more widely.[27] In battlefield terms, British officers believed that the M16 could not provide the infantry with the means to defeat both a conventional Soviet Army in Europe and insurgent forces in various worldwide locations. To realise both these missions, calibres above 5.56mm but below 7.62mm were considered the most viable. This would combine lethality at range with logistical flexibility and potentially facilitate the replacement of the 9mm Sterling SMG and the 7.62mm SLR, the L4 Bren LMG and the General Purpose Machine Gun (GPMG).[28] Indeed, one study by the Royal Armament Research and Design Establishment (a successor department to the Armament Design Establishment) had already been undertaken that questioned whether a weapon might be designed that entirely obviated the need for an LMG.[29]

Consequently, the General Staff could use their lack of information on the progress of SPIW and their underlying prejudices against 5.56mm to conclude that a new ammunition type was necessary, one that could hit targets out to 600 metres and would facilitate the replacement of entire classes of small arms. For the RSAF, this meant evaluating ammunition with calibres of between 6mm and 6.5mm.[30] Subsequent investigations conducted at Enfield concluded that a 6.25mm round could provide a good balance between lethality and soldier burden as new materials could potentially produce a 63 per cent weight saving over the existing 7.62mm NATO round. More than this, they believed that 6.25mm ammunition would cover the requirement for effective LMG fire out to 600 metres when compared with the 450m of the 5.56mm M16 ammunition.[31] A 6.25mm round thus reflected the British Army's continuing strategic problem: balancing the requirements of high-intensity fighting in mainland Europe against the logistical demands that arose from the ongoing post-colonial effort to leave stable governments favourable to UK interests. On balance, then, whereas the Germans could afford to produce specialist weapons designed specifically for armoured infantry, British soldiers might be expected to deploy anywhere in the world as part of a counterrevolutionary or counterinsurgency campaign.

However, by the early 1970s, the initial impulse to defend vulnerable post-colonial governments had shifted considerably in line with the 1968 and 1974 UK Defence Reviews.[32] In the future, Britain's strategic priority would be the defence of Western Europe, working as part of the NATO alliance. This renewed emphasis revitalised British military thinking in relation to the Army's role in the defence of Western Europe. In the period immediately after the Second World War, the General Staff's thinking on how to deploy the BAOR was conditioned by financial stringency and the availability of nuclear forces.[33] In this context, it was readily accepted by politicians that NATO's armies mainly acted as a tripwire for the early use of atomic weapons.[34] This in turn created little incentive for the British government to go to the trouble of creating proficient and well-armed military formations.[35] In the context of a nuclear engagement, however, the General Staff were well aware that mobility would enable quick dispersion, which might mean the difference between annihilation and survival.[36] As a result, the British Army placed a greater emphasis on tactical mobility centred on the use of armoured formations and tracked armoured 'battle buses' like the FV432 that could transport soldiers to and from the battlefield. However, the ongoing use of light infantry for operations outside of Europe meant that the General Staff would not go as far as to create armoured infantry along the same lines as the Bundeswehr.[37]

The Defence Reviews emphatically refocused the British Army away from policing Britain's former empire towards offering a credible military defence of the plains of West Germany as part of a strategy of flexible nuclear response. In the process, the switch encouraged the General Staff to look again at the Bundeswehr's military doctrine and reconsider technological imperatives that had previously been framed by the challenge of balancing global against European commitments. Specialist weapon systems could now be designed for the specific circumstances in which strategic planners had determined the Army would operate. This logic in turn emphasised the utility of an armoured vehicle along the same lines as the Marder Infantry Fighting Vehicle (IFV) being developed for the Bundeswehr. Known in the UK as the Mechanised Combat Vehicle (MCV), this new system would eventually be called the Warrior, have a turret-mounted 30mm RARDEN cannon, 7.62mm Hughes chain gun and be able to transport seven soldiers and three crew members.

The logic of the MCV, which was designed to deposit the infantry directly on to their objective, was compatible with the German approach to small arms and encouraged the British to switch attention towards small calibre sub-5mm rounds suitable for battle at close quarters. In 1974, after considerable debate with what was left of the RSAF small arms design community, Britain's General Staff reversed their focus from 6mm to 6.5mm ammunition and agreed to conduct trials into a conventional 4.85mm round. However, a lack of suitably qualified engineers at Enfield ensured that investigations were directed towards adapting existing cartridges and bullets rather than going back to basic design principles.[38] The directors of the RSAF accepted this trade-off knowing that, potentially at least, an Enfield-designed weapon might revive the fortunes of the workforce and stave off what appeared to be the inevitable closure of the factory.

At the time the British were reconsidering their own military doctrine, the US Army was itself in the process of an ignominious withdrawal from South East Asia. Against this background, senior American officers sought to rebuild the shattered morale of the Army by refocusing attention back towards what some re-described as the main challenge: the conventional defence of Europe. Doctrinally, this heralded the development of FM 100–5 and the concept of Air–Land Battle. Technologically, this demanded the Army look again at how they were making use of the M113 Armoured Personnel Carrier and whether it offered the most appropriate basis for a new IFV.[39] By the 1980s, this would result in the introduction of the US M2 Bradley, a platform that had a number of similarities with the British and German vehicles. While the specificities of the technology and the tactics employed remained unique to each nation, the underlying concept was to have soldiers rely on an IFV's protection and mobility to get them safely to the objective, at which point the vehicle's auto-cannon and sustained fire machine gun would provide covering fire for debus-sing troops. The key contributors to NATO were shifting away from engagements that emphasised light-infantry operations and towards the Bundeswehr's approach to armoured infantry. For the United States as for the UK and the FRG, a number of disparate and contingent events were starting to produce a convergence of opinion about the relative importance of the armoured infantry and the nature of the future battlefield.

Part 2: Standardisation as an exercise of power

By the mid-1970s, the preconditions that had previously been identified as being necessary for delivering standardisation—conditions associated with standardising NATO tactics—were starting to fall in place. British and American armoured infantry doctrine was taking on recognisably similar forms to that already adopted by the Bundeswehr. By the estimation of those trying to bring about standardisation, this was a good indicator that future agreement on a NATO ammunition standard would be possible in the com-parative trials scheduled for the late 1970s. Having similar processes for how a technology would be used did not, however, necessarily equate to agreement over standard weapons. On the contrary, as the NATO powers assembled in Bavaria for the year-long military and technical trials, six countries (Belgium, France, the Netherlands, West Germany, the UK and the United States) submitted eight different types of ammunition and six completely new weapons for evaluation.[40] Selection between these systems, after they had been examined by technical experts, including engineers, statisticians, wound ballisticians, shooters and armourers from various NATO countries, would require detailed agreement on ammunition and weapon performance, agreements that had to be orchestrated well in advance of the eventual test.

Table 3: A History of NATO Non-Standardisation.
Rounds Used in Various NATO Rifles, 1960 to 1974, Compared with the Rounds and Weapons Submitted for the 1979–80 NATO Standardisation Trials

Country	1960	1974	1979–80 Trials	
	SAA	SAA	New Ammunition	Weapon submitted Rifle/LMG
UK	7.62mm	7.62mm	4.85mm cased ball, tracer, blank	Enfield Weapon System
United States	7.62mm	5.56mm	XM777 ball SM778 tracer	5.56mm M16A1(2)
France	7.5mm	7.5mm/ 5.56mm	French 5.56mm cased: ball (brass & steel), tracer (brass & steel)	5.56 MAS
Federal Republic of Germany	7.62mm	7.62mm	4.75mm caseless: ball, tracer, blank	4.75mm MK-101 7.62mm MG-3
Belgium	7.62mm	7.62mm	5.56mm improved: ball, tracer, blank, API	5.56mm FN Minimi
Italy	7.62mm	7.62mm		
Netherlands	7.62mm	7.62mm		5.56mm MN1
Denmark	.30	.30/5.56mm		
Norway	7.62mm	7.62mm		
Greece	.30	.30		
Turkey	.30	.30/7.62mm		
Portugal	7.62mm	7.62mm		

On the face of it, then, the process offered a transparent means for establishing which of the various systems was the best for NATO to standardise on. Unlike the Anglo-American tests of the early 1950s, where various bureaucratic devices had been employed to engineer an acceptable result for the Americans, these trials had been designed and agreed upon by all the NATO powers themselves. The experts were from across the NATO alliance, including from powers that had not submitted a weapon system for evaluation. The trials were thorough, involving a number of technical tests to establish which was most reliable and which was easy to manufacture. More than this, the trials tested a range of variables including ammunition performance in extreme weather and weapon effectiveness both when on the offensive and under stress conditions, and (among other things) when firing from a fixed point at moving and static targets. As all parties had agreed to, and were responsible for, administering the process, there was every reason to believe that the result reflected the fair opinion and sound analytical judgement of those involved.

This uncritical reading of the standardisation debates nonetheless belies the fact that the process was itself implicitly framed by the power relations of the various NATO powers. In terms of political theory, Stephen Lukes recognises this in his consideration of the three dimensions of power.[41] According to Lukes, we can think about power relations in pluralist terms—the first dimension of power—whereby power relations are determined by the ability to get someone to do something that they would otherwise not be willing to do. In the next chapter, I will consider how Lukes' third dimension of power, the power to prevent people from even thinking they have a choice, has application in a discussion of technology change.

Before I get to this point, however, I want to show that a pluralist reading of power hardly does justice to the way in which the United States went about realising its standardisation goals in the lead up to the 1979–80 NATO trials. A more persuasive reading of the power of the Americans to realise their goals emerges out of Lukes' second dimension of power. Instead of considering the observable conflicts and actual processes by which decisions are being made (i.e. the focus of the first dimension and much of the previous chapter of this book), Lukes observes that we should also pay attention to the way that non-decision-making occurs. Put simply, this means that the ability of an actor to shape the agenda even before a decision has to be formally reached by the other actors engaged in the process. In terms of the NATO standardisation trials of 1979–80, this second dimension of power appears to have more resonance.

By the mid-1970s, it had become clear that the NATO Conference of National Armaments Directors was an unwieldy bureaucratic means for developing agreement between alliance partners. The level of detail necessary for discussing small arms and then debating the challenges that these decisions would produce were too great given the demands of a plenary meeting. Consequently, and much to the annoyance of countries like Italy, quadrilateral and trilateral talks were held to engineer agreements between the FRG, the UK, the United States and sometimes France. Positions could be explored within the smaller grouping before going back to the full NATO membership for wider discussion.[42]

However, while such manoeuvrings might keep each nation abreast of the positions of the big NATO countries, it could not bring about entirely harmonious perspectives on either doctrine or technology. In this respect, further manipulations in non-decision-making had to be put in place if agreement was to emerge on American terms. For despite the convergence of opinion on the utility of armoured infantry, there remained an underlying difference in tactical philosophy that went to the heart of the small arms debate. For the FINABEL countries (France, Italy, the Netherlands, West Germany, Belgium and Luxembourg), 7.62mm ammunition remained important for sustained fire machine guns mounted on vehicles or firing from fixed points. The utility of a light machine gun, however, was viewed suspiciously, as the soldier's personal weapon was considered sufficient. This contrasted with the US position, which continued to investigate the possibility of acquiring an LMG for light infantry operations outside Europe.

The differences in small arms philosophy did not end there. The defence of West Germany may have been the unifying principle that brought the alliance together, but like their American counterparts, British infantry officers continued to have an eye on operations on the fringes of Europe (especially in Norway) and remained wedded to the notion of some kind of LMG. Even in this respect, the British and American militaries had different perspectives. Whereas the UK felt it important to balance the logistical and tactical advantages of precision fire in the form of a magazine-fed Light Support Weapon (LSW), the United States was unconcerned by the logistical implications of a belt-fed, sustained fire solution. Consequently, the Americans investigated a number of belt-fed LMGs that were potentially compatible with the switch to 5.56mm. Eventually known as the Squad Automatic Weapon, the new LMG would supplement the squad's existing firepower and allow the M-60 or another 7.62mm belt-fed weapon to be retained for use at the level of the infantry company, either in defence or from fixed firing points.[43]

By contrast, Britain's General Staff could see the logistical, training and financial benefits that might be realised by replacing the GPMG, LMG, SLR and SMG with one class of weapon. This led to the Small Arms post-1980 concept as stated in General Staff Requirement 3518 (GSR 3518), promulgated in 1974. GSR 3518 asked engineers at Enfield to design a weapon in which 80 per cent of the parts were interchangeable between an LSW and a soldier's rifle. If the 4.85mm round being designed by Enfield could be sufficiently lethal out to LMG-type ranges, then one family of weapons might reduce soldier burden, increase training efficiency, ease logistical and maintenance concerns and balance the demands of light and armoured infantry operations all in one go. The question was whether a round could be made that was sufficiently lethal such that it covered the range of tactical uses envisaged by GSR 3518.

In this respect, persuading the Americans to switch to a sub-5mm calibre would be difficult, not only because of their existing investments in the M16 and 5.56mm, but also because much of NATO had stopped undertaking significant primary research into the question of wounding power.[44] In the early 1970s, for example, unsure of American intentions on the science of killing, British scientists evaluated the effectiveness of 4.85mm ammunition against at least two different criteria of wounding power, both of which originated from the work by the US Ballistics Research Laboratory. Each one gave a slightly different reading of the effectiveness of the ammunition, suggesting that 4.85mm could have utility in an LSW role as it was more effective than 5.56mm out to 300 metres.[45] The scientists at Porton Down recognised, however, that unless a wounding criterion was agreed upon across the alliance, then there would be little chance of guaranteeing the Enfield ammunition design would prove acceptable for NATO standardisation. Unfortunately for the engineers at Enfield, this was made more complicated by the Americans who would sometimes prevent lethality information being shared by the NATO Agency for Standardisation.[46]

For Britain's political–military establishment, the lethality question was, nonetheless, a particularly pressing issue. For just as the Army was being asked to take the possibility of a Soviet invasion of Western Europe more seriously, they were now also being deployed in support of the civil power in Northern Ireland. In this situation, the need for precise marksmanship was reinforced by the sensitivities of trying to carry out what some in the Army considered a counterinsurgency campaign in front of television cameras on home British soil.[47] From a training perspective, this re-emphasised the need to improve weapon handling and marksmanship skills. In this respect, a crucial indication of an infantryman's skill at arms was his ability to achieve a tight grouping of hits on a target when firing on the range.[48] However, whereas GSR 3514 stipulated that troops, while prone, should achieve a grouping of 4" at 100m, the reality was that they were only capable of producing a 10" group with the SLR.[49] Thus, from a technical perspective, operations in Northern Ireland encouraged engineers to investigate whether it would be possible to develop a cheap, lightweight optical sight that could be fitted to every rifle as, in effect, this might help to design out the poor shooting skills of the solider.

Marksmanship, however, was but one aspect of the problem. The post-war lethality arguments had shown that 7.62mm ammunition was overpowered and likely to pass through the intended victim. In these circumstances, if 7.62mm was used to maintain order on the streets of Northern Ireland, then there was every chance it could unintentionally kill or injure several people who might be passing by. Overpowered ammunition that undermined the precision shooting of a soldier was not appropriate in situations that demanded the use of minimum force. Indeed, according to the Home Office/ Ministry of Defence working party, the ideal solution would be the development of ammunition with 'the same accuracy as afforded by the rifle (SLR) but which does not penetrate nor make a wound of dreadful appearance'.[50]

If avoiding wounds of a dreadful appearance was an important criterion to take into account when designing future small arms, then even 5.56mm ammunition might be considered overpowered in some quarters of the British government. When the M16 was first introduced in Vietnam in 1962, for example, a number of the American and Vietnamese users observed that the weapon was capable of causing extremely destructive wounds.[51] Indeed, some of those who had trialled the weapon on operations claimed that the M16 was capable of causing explosive wounds. By 1965, these statements chimed with the views of British Special Forces operating in Borneo, many of whom would agree that the M16 was more than capable of 'throwing [a victim] backwards about two yards' or 'blowing the top of [their] head off'.[52] According to Eugene Stoner, the designer of the M16, the experience of troops fighting in Vietnam and Borneo underlined the virtue of his small calibre, high velocity ammunition because

> bullets are stabilized to fly through air, and not through water or a body, which is approximately the same density as water ... When they hit something, they immediately go unstable ... If you are talking about a .30 caliber bullet, that might remain stable through a human mass ... while a little bullet, being it [*sic*] has a low mass, it senses an instability situation faster and reacts much faster. This is what makes a little bullet pay off so much in wound ballistics.[53]

The possibility that the M16 might produce dreadful wounds meant the weapon would potentially fall foul of the 1899 Hague Conventions on avoiding superfluous or unnecessary suffering. In 1964, this had prompted British government lawyers to check the legality of the weapon.[54] At the time, 5.56mm was approved for use in the Far East. By 1977, however, the M16 had been approved for use in Northern Ireland as part of SAS covert operations against the Provisional IRA.[55] Following a number of mistaken shootings by the SAS, most notably the accidental killing of John Boyle (a sixteen-year-old Catholic who had strayed across an IRA arms cache), the government had been forced to defend the deployment of the M16. They justified the choice of weapon on the basis that it was lighter, handier to use and more accurate at close range. They downplayed the lethality of the small calibre, high velocity round.

Thus the question of ammunition lethality was an extremely sensitive topic that had implications for those working on tactics and engineering as well as those trying to win the media war or manage government public relations. More than this, getting it wrong could also have significant consequences in the courts. For if British troops were using weapons that might be considered illegal, at least in terms of international law, then the government might find itself being prosecuted by the families of those shot by the Army. Thus, in the context of Northern Ireland, the British desperately needed some resolution on ammunition lethality as it pertained to 5.56mm and sub-5mm rounds. However, whether the British Army would use 4.85mm ammunition was entirely dependent on getting agreement across NATO on what was meant by lethality.[56]

Given the vehemence of the lethality debates in the immediate post-war years, it might come as something of a surprise to note that agreement on the science was achieved at all. However, by 1975 a working panel finally agreed on a NATO criterion for wounding. The starting place for this had been the initial US acceptance of Zuckerman's findings that velocity was an extremely important variable in wounding and the British recognition that the Americans would not give up the kinetic energy criterion. In the subsequent bilateral and then NATO-wide meetings during the 1960s, continued iterations of US research postulated that expected kinetic energy (EKE) was the most appropriate means for defining wounding power.[57] This measured the probability of a bullet still being inside the body at a certain point given the range of decelerating forces acting on it. Thus the EKE formula was an approximation for the energy transfer between the bullet and the victim. While this was still open to contestation, given the reliance on modelling and the inability to verify all the data, an insufficient amount of primary scientific research was being done among European members of NATO to effectively challenge US findings.[58] Consequently, US research played an ever more dominant role in furthering the science of wound ballistics. This is clearly denoted by the number of papers being produced in the United States and the way that these dominated the citation indexes of other non-US reports on the subject.[59]

Table 4: Summary of US Effectiveness Criteria
(Information based on summary by Beat Kneubuehl, 2008)[60]

Author	Criterion	Year
Benton	Bullet passes through fir plank	1867
Rhone	Kinetic energy 58 ftlbs or 80 joules	1896
Zuckerman	$m^{0.4}v$ (bullet passes through)	1942
Sperrazza and Allen	$mv_{3/2}$	1956
Dziemian	$E_{1-15cms}$ energy transfer in 15cm of gelatine	1960
Sturdivan	Expected Kinetic Energy	1975

In this respect, we can start to discern the manner in which Lukes' second dimension of power might be understood to apply. The Americans could shape the NATO standardisation trials in 1979–80 primarily by ensuring that their definition of lethality formed the index against which all ammunition types would be judged. To be sure, there were other evaluation criteria that would be applied. However, the application of US structural power through their investments into the science of killing created the conditions for establishing a body of knowledge that would define which of the eight different types of ammunition and six completely new weapons submitted to the trial would prove to be acceptable. Bearing in mind that these weapon systems would be evaluated against the EKE wounding criterion, the Americans could be sure that whatever emerged out of a subsequent NATO standardisation trial they would be in a prime place to maintain their existing position on 5.56mm ammunition.

At the same time, by carefully controlling the timing of agreements on lethality, the United States could ensure that it could manage the amount of time other NATO powers would have for developing a mature weapons technology. Lacking clarity on the criteria that would be used as part of the evaluation consequently reinforced US dominance in the lead up to the trials. For if other NATO powers had been working on a technology that had markedly different design parameters, it was unlikely that they would have enough time to demonstrate that they were viable alternatives to the M16.

Having enough time to develop a sufficiently mature technology was, therefore, an important consideration for those engineers involved in developing a strategy for dealing with the NATO trials in 1979–80. However, when it came to weapon maturity, the American advantages did not end with definitions of lethality, for one of the other significant criteria by which a design might be evaluated was the cost to manufacture a particular system. In this respect, the M16 had already gone through an entire development cycle and a vast amount of investment in manufacturing plant had already been made. The unit cost of making both the M16 and 5.56mm ammunition had already been given the time to reach a level where development costs no longer needed to be factored in. Indeed, according to Edward Ezell, the United States would have to spend another $360 million to replace all the M16s it had already purchased.[61] As 1.3 million M16 rifles were already in service, it was unlikely that the United States would want to change small arms unless other countries chose to spend the money ironing out the design specification and manufacturing quirks associated with producing a new technology.[62]

What is fascinating to note, however, was that even with these structural advantages in place, the Americans could not dictate the outcome of the trials once they had signed the Memorandum of Understanding, and this had been made public in late 1976.[63] Consequently, by the end of the trials, the Americans were forced to accept a Belgian design of ammunition, optimised for destructiveness at range, developed by engineers at Fabrique Nationale. Designated SS109, this new ammunition would replace the M193 standard that the Americans had used up to that point and in the process force the US Army to spend $110.5 million on re-barrelling existing M16s with a different rifling twist.[64] At the same time, the new round encouraged a mid-life upgrade of the M16 and prompted the Americans to bring forward their development of the M16A2.[65]

Having cannily outwitted British engineers in the early 1950s, FN had decided that there was little value to be gained by designing a completely new ammunition type when the Americans had already established that only 5.56mm would pass the lethality criterion. According to this logic, the route to successfully selling a future rifle would therefore depend more on the ammunition agreement than it would on optimising a complete weapon system built around a new calibre. However, if the Belgians could optimise the existing 5.56mm round, then they would be in a good position to sell on their selection of rifles and Light Machine Guns after a new NATO ammunition standard had been defined. With the Americans considering the purchase of the FN 5.56mm Minimi for the Squad Automatic Weapon in the mid-1970s, the FN strategy was a calculated move designed to put this weapon in the best possible light.[66]

The Belgian and FN approach contrasted with the Bundeswehr strategy which was to pin their ambitions on a completely revolutionary technology: caseless ammunition.[67] Without a brass cartridge case for the propellant, a caseless round weighed significantly less than conventional ammunition. This would reduce soldier burden, ease the strain on the ammunition supply chain and, as the round made it possible to fundamentally redesign the rifle, potentially ease maintenance. Backed by a consortium of German companies, including the privately owned Heckler & Koch (H&K), this sort of technology led to the development of the G11 rifle, a weapon that might reduce the total soldier burden by 20 per cent.

A 20 per cent reduction in weight was sufficiently advantageous to leave the Bundeswehr unwilling to sacrifice the potential of caseless in favour of a 5.56mm weapon, even though the G11 was eventually withdrawn from the NATO trials because of poor reliability.[68] In these circumstances, the Germans indicated that they would hold off from adopting 5.56mm ammunition until the G11 had been given more development time. At the same time, the possibility of this new technology forced the Americans to reconsider their entire approach to small arms, leading some to conclude that US small arms research was in the doldrums. This criticism in turn pushed the Americans to start their own research programme into caseless ammunition, leading them to establish the Advanced Combat Rifle programme (ACR).[69] Despite this increased interest in caseless ammunition and the fact that Heckler & Koch were one of several companies engaged in American research, by 1991 the investment in caseless was too great for the German manufacturer. Consequently, when the newly unified German state, now overwhelmed with an abundance of AK-47 rifles, decided not to purchase the G11 rifle, H&K found itself bankrupt. At this point, British Aerospace was quick to step in and purchase the company.[70]

Overall, US officials found themselves in a position to exercise power to shape the agenda of the NATO trials. What they could not do, however, was to precisely determine the outcome of those trials especially given the strategies adopted by the Germans, Belgians and British. That the British continued down the route of developing a traditional cased sub-5mm solution demonstrated a certain naiveté about the distribution of power across NATO and the likelihood that the Americans would give up their standard. Lacking the research capacity of the German manufacturing consortium and the canniness of the Belgian company Fabrique Nationale, the British attempted to do too much with too little.

As far as FN were concerned, the outcome could not be better. The new SS109 cartridge—defined in the new NATO Standard STANAG 4172—had been optimised for destructiveness at range. This put FN in a strong position to secure the contract with the Americans for their Minimi LMG, subsequently acquired in 1984 and redesignated the M249.[71] By contrast, the risky strategy adopted by the Germans failed to pay out, and consequently H&K found itself vulnerable to the unexpected circumstances brought about by the fall of the Berlin Wall. Most surprisingly of all, despite achieving success on the calibre of ammunition, the trials demonstrated to the Americans that they would have to accept that Europeans would play an increasingly assertive role in the evolution of NATO's technology choices. Overall, however, that the Belgians should find themselves the winner of the trials offers us a curious insight into the way that NATO's big powers could all agree to disagree if none of them won out on their particular technical offering. For in many respects, the Belgians offered NATO a way to show that standardisation could work, but only if none of the big powers ended up dominating the procurement decisions of the alliance.

Part 3: Assessing the rationality of standardisation

In the period between 1957 and 1980, the battlefield interpretations of the British and Americans evolved from First and Second World War iterations of fire and movement. In the face of the Soviet threat, the challenge became one of integrating the demands of light and armoured infantry operations in the context of NATO standardisation and the uncertainty of being deployed globally. The debate about balancing marksmanship against firepower, willpower against stopping power, reflected a different set of concerns associated with alliance politics and bureaucratic and battlefield imperatives. Within this framework, different NATO powers developed unique views about how to arm themselves given the specific and contingent set of variables that they faced. These different perspectives spilled out into the open during the NATO trials in 1979–80, pitching the big powers of the FRG, the UK and the United States against each other in a nuanced technical debate over ammunition calibre. Conventional explanations of the choices that emerged out of these circumstances tend to emphasise the bounded rationality of decision-making and the manner in which innovation occurred as either a bottom-up or top-down phenomenon. What has emerged out of this chapter is how such arguments downplay the way in which knowledge and power work hand in glove to frame debates.

Thus, the Americans hoped that by constraining the choices available, they could secure the compliance of their alliance partners. However, to suggest that a science of killing emerged out of an uncontested process does not reflect the manner in which the debates on wounding power emerged in the 1940s, '50s and '60s. In the 1950s, accession to the American view on lethality had been produced as a result of the British decision to reconsider its .280 ammunition. The result was a truce in the discussions, after which the British withdrew, ceding the field to the United States. Subsequently, the US analyses of wounding emerging out of the 1960s and 1970s dominated discussion of lethality, a dominance that was directly linked to the number of scientists undertaking primary research on the subject when compared to other countries. In terms of the Sociology of Scientific Knowledge, a process of non-decision-making by actors who might previously have taken a different point of view ceded the domain to American scientists who could effectively determine scientific closure on their own terms, codifying it through the 1975 NATO agreements on lethality.

However, given humanity's propensity to violence, it seems unlikely that the EKE criterion constitutes the end point of the scientific debate. Indeed, even at the time, the effectiveness of the new FN SS109 ammunition was contested by a number of critics, including, for example, Dr Martin Fackler, an influential (now retired) colonel and surgeon in the US Army's Medical Corps. Fackler criticised much of the process for selecting the SS109 ammunition, arguing that the changes to US rifles produced a unique 'error waiting to happen'.[72] Contrary to what been established over thirty years of research, he claimed this was the result of weapon designers being overly influenced by the 'mystique of high velocity' and the interdisciplinary conflicts produced from investigations by ballisticians, physicians and biologists. Contending that an intelligent surgeon has more appreciation for the projectile-tissue interaction than the other disciplines, Fackler appeared to side with Zuckerman in recognising that the problem of wounding was not simply a mathematical problem. What Fackler could not know, however, was that Zuckerman had tried to persuade the United States small arms community of this point, but because of their fixation on Kinetic Energy, had been forced into redirecting American officials towards velocity as the crucial variable in wounding.

Irrespective of the scientific validity of Fackler's argument, the observations do raise an interesting and important underlying question concerned with the relative power of the different disciplines involved in shaping the process of selecting weapons. There has clearly been a tussle between engineer and scientist, surgeon and soldier. For much of the post-war period, this had left soldiers having to find ways to shape an agenda that has typically been set by engineers and scientists. Engineers and scientists have been able to reinforce their arguments by working closely together. Indeed, the science of killing and the technology required to evaluate, test and make the science work have been dependent on each other. However, engineers and scientists have needed different things out of this process. Engineers needed to design solutions within absolute parameters if they were to stand a chance of making something they could actually manufacture. This worked in tension with those scientists who offered up a more probabilistic account of the wounding mechanism.

What is clear from the way that the 58ftlb criterion was forced on NATO during the 1950s is that engineers were mainly driving the changes in small arms technology given their preference for design certainties. By 1979–80, scientists working on lethality had provided the NATO panels working on standardisation with an agreed index for engineers to arbitrate between systems. In this respect, the science now framed the process in ways that it had previously been unable to do. This reflected a subtle rebalancing of the underlying relationships between engineer and scientist, one that recognised the partnership between the disciplines when it came to advancing a case for a new weapon system.

At the same time, it is interesting to note that even having established the relative terms of the debate, the Americans still failed to realise their immediate goals: standardising on their existing M193 round. Instead, the Americans were compelled by their own agreement to the Memorandum of Understanding to comply with the outcome of the NATO trials and adopt SS109 ammunition and re-barrel their existing weapons so that they could fire the new round efficiently. Ammunition standardisation in the late 1970s thus offers a window into the balance of alliance politics and the imperatives shaping the decision-making cycles of the respective NATO powers. When alliance politics is viewed through the lens of weapons acquisition, scholarship tends to focus on one of two approaches. At one end of the argument, scholars have noted that nationalism tends to trump cooperation in the NATO defence market.[73] At the other, there is a tendency to play up the benefits that emerge from a pluralistic free market in procurement such that the market will define areas of specialism and optimise production.[74]

What we find with the post-war debates in small arms ammunition, however, is the way in which NATO power relations have fluctuated over time. The

Americans may have been in a position to compel the Bundeswehr to under-take actions it otherwise would have chosen not to do during the 1950s—in rebuilding the Luftwaffe as a large independent organisation fully integrated into NATO, for instance.[75] However, by the early 1970s, the balance of rela-tionships had shifted away from the Americans. The Americans themselves realised this and a countervailing narrative within US government circles began preparing a hostile Congress, still intent on buying American.[76] This new reality in part reflected the rebalancing of NATO bureaucratic power as various FINABEL countries reestablished the capacity to manage their defence infrastructure after the war. Nevertheless, even as alliance partners started to develop the capacity for undertaking a more systematic analysis of their specific strategic predicaments, the conditions for bringing about stand-ardisation on US terms remained propitious. Not only had US scientists shaped the way NATO would understand lethality, but American, West German and British strategic thinking started to coalesce on the techniques needed for the defence of Europe as well. Armoured infantry would become important for countering Soviet armour as it poured through the central front.

Superficially, this chapter suggests that written agreements between part-ners could allow a certain degree of pluralism in the selection of equipment. However, it is also clear that there were limitations to US power despite the otherwise favourable conditions they had worked hard to create. The successes of the Belgian company Fabrique Nationale accordingly afford us another chance to think about how resistance to dominant perspectives and narratives can be out into practice and made effective. For FN, it was a corporate impera-tive to work within the dominant US narrative and assert an alternative tech-nical solution that had previously lain unconsidered. In the process, the Belgians showed that the US narrative could not construct alliance partners in precisely its own image. In effect, FN subverted the process the Americans had put in place and gave them something they did not realise that they had needed or thought possible: a new, standard ammunition that apparently offered even greater benefits to US forces without having to adopt an entirely new weapon system. At the same time, by accepting the Belgian round, the European partners could claim some equality with the United States in NATO by not having to buy American yet again.

When it comes to evaluating the FN strategy, it is not important to know whether the SS109 ammunition could actually do what was claimed for it. Rather, it is important to reflect on what different parties believed and wanted the ammunition to do. In this respect, in the next chapter I will lead discussion away from a consideration of the NATO trial data from 1979–80, and towards developing an appreciation for the way that the preferences, ambitions, needs and wants of the various NATO powers, might be produced. Specifically, I want to refocus discussion back on the frontline itself and reflect on the relative power relations between those in the back office and those on the battlefield. For what has emerged since the end of the Cold War is a subtle shift in emphasis in which the status of the infantry has risen vis-à-vis those experts working far away from the battlefield. Part of the means that they have employed for achieving this rebalancing of the science/engineer/soldier relationship emerges out of the increased power of manufacturers like Fabrique Nationale. In our consideration of this in the next chapter, I will start to move towards an analysis of weapons selection based on Lukes' third dimension of power.

7

IS IT GUCCI? INDUSTRY, STATUS ANXIETY
AND THE FN MINIMI

Gucci Kit = non-issue kit. Most of what a soldier carries with him in the field falls under the definition of Gucci. Issue kit is mostly bollocks, Gucci (sic) kit is normally the dog's bollocks.[1]

As I shot I became calmer. I realised how much I needed to shoot. Shoot something, anything.

Robert Mason, Dak To, Vietnam 1966[2]

At 07.00 on 10 September 2000, elements of Britain's 1st Battalion, the Parachute Regiment (1 PARA), started their assault on positions held by a gang known as the West Side Boys in Magbeni, Sierra Leone. Armed with SA80s, a number of belt-fed 7.62mm GPMGs and various other pieces of combat paraphernalia, the soldiers jumped from the back of hovering Chinooks and landed chest-deep into a swamp.[3] Though they knew they would land somewhere marshy, the troops of 1 PARA did not expect to have to carry their weapons above their heads as they struggled to get to dry ground.[4] Once out of the wet, the objective was to support the SAS as they rescued members of the Royal Irish Regiment held hostage by the gang. Now carrying link ammunition covered in mud and grime, the GPMGs would be prone to stoppages at inopportune moments. Professional and well-trained, however, the soldiers of 1 PARA would be up to the task of suppressing opposition from the West Side Boys.

Even though the Paras recovered from their initial surprise at landing in a swamp, a number of questions might be asked as to why they would take heavy and unwieldy equipment like the GPMG into the close and difficult terrain around Magbeni. For a civilian analyst to question this kind of decision does of course expose them to the charge that they lack the professional skills and experience to know what might be most appropriate in any one engagement. Soldiers have been 'flesh witnesses' and only they can really understand the situation that was faced.[5] The decision to take GPMP, nevertheless, poses an interesting set of tactical–technical questions about 1 PARA's preferences. Of course, in relation to Sierra Leone there were a number of contingent and practical considerations that framed weapon selection. Lighter 5.56mm support weapons like the belt-fed FN Minimi or SA80 LSW may not have been available or deemed insufficiently reliable. The choice of the GPMG, however, not only says something about how soldiers understood the tactical situation they faced but also, and as I alluded to in the previous chapter, to the way that choices had been constructed in the first place.

From the soldier's point of view, a first order challenge lies in the professional desire to do the job and do it properly. The soldier's ability at fieldcraft and weapons' handling speaks to this sentiment directly. The objective is to do the technical aspects of the job correctly, but more than this, the goal is to do it with some 'style'.[6] To do this in battle, a place of well-documented chaos and sensory overload, demands a great deal of psychological and physical strength. In the circumstances, however, and as Robert Mason attests in the quote at the beginning of the chapter, there is a sense in which the act of doing something actually offers a feeling of being in control. Technologies that support this desire to 'crack on' and take action offer soldiers the opportunity to master events rather than be subject to them.[7]

Set in this context, the central challenge of this chapter is to show how technological choices do not simply reflect a tactical situation but also say something about the different forces that are responsible for 'framing, shaping and distorting' the way users think about weapons.[8] In this respect, the one set of actors who we have yet to consider but who still retain the power to affect choice include those working in industry. Industry's ability to shape the rifle choices made by soldiers is not, however, just about Lukes' first or second dimension of power. Rather, it is also based on how the needs of the infantryman are managed and their technological imaginations configured. In effect, industry's strategy for framing the rifle choices of the infantry draws on Lukes' third dimension of power.[9]

Lukes' discussion of power considers the way that powerful actors direct the choices of free agents through the production of a false consciousness. Unlike critical or Marxist scholars, Lukes attempts to sustain the idea that individuals themselves can express their agency and play their part in co-constructing various outcomes. Although some scholars contest that Luke's third dimension of power is 'illiberal and paternalistic', Ian Shapiro argues that the only way we might establish whether this dimension of power is in operation, is by working through an empirical account to show 'when, where, how and why' interests are being manipulated.[10] It then becomes easier to see when actors are subject to false consciousness such that they might work against their real interests.

In a complex selection environment like that associated with small arms, it would be too crude to suggest that soldiers' perspectives were directly manipulated by industry. Rather, the infantry's attention can be diverted in favour of solutions that benefit certain regiments or sections of the Army but that might not benefit the whole and that do not necessarily reflect the wider interests of the armed forces. This mode of analysis acknowledges that the user community cannot be reified but is made up of a number of constituencies. As we will see in this chapter, a more sophisticated approach to shaping user preferences recognises this and then exploits it by playing on a soldier's professionalism and their desire for status. From a material point of view, we can see this happening in the way that soldiers increasingly look to modify their kit and weapons in order to make it peculiar to themselves.

While the activity of shaping technological choice might simply be interpreted as industry marketing its wares to potential consumers, industry's framing of the Army's weapon choices typically draws upon and feeds into an underlying desire for status among different military communities. In this respect, industry has long recognised that the key to selling equipment is not simply to show that it 'does the job' but that it also 'looks the part'. In many ways, then, arms manufacturers are doing much the same as any other purveyor of technology: trying to make weapons that reinforce the social standing of one group relative to that of another in order to increase the appeal of their brand of design. Professional armies want to look like they have professional-level gear. As I will argue in this chapter, industry's key recruits in this process are the elite regiments of an army. To show how this works in practice, the focus is on one case study: the British Army, the SA80 and the adoption of Fabrique Nationale's Minimi Light Machine Gun.

In an effort to show how a range of factors have brought about the conditions in which private industry can exploit the infantry's desire for control and getting the job done properly, this chapter is broken down into three parts. The first describes how the traditional relationship between the British Army and its historic supplier of armaments, the government-owned ordnance factories, unravelled during the roll out of the SA80. With the Army having lost all trust in engineers and the procurement system, the second section shows how the Army went about asserting itself in the replacement of the Light Support Weapon. This section demonstrates how combat experience and unit status has become a dominant arbiter in the selection of weapons at the expense of scientists and engineers applying analytical and statistical techniques. The final section explores the values of the contemporary British infantry so as to show how arms manufacturers can exploit these preferences. In particular, by putting the way British soldiers define 'Gucci kit' into a wider cultural context, the way arms manufacturers influence the buying preferences of the infantry is revealed. Thus in this final section we will see how Lukes' third dimension of power has pertinence for exploring the way industry has helped to create the needs of the soldier.

The changing soldier–engineer relationship and the privatisation of Royal Ordnance

As we've seen in previous chapters, the process by which users have defined their requirements has been contested and open to interpretation. Throughout the selection process, however, equipment has always gone through a range of tests and evaluations to ensure that it meets the stated requirement. The tests are important because they represent a point at which different technical imperatives are mediated.[11] At the same time, even as engineers and scientists try to skew a test to put their particular technologies in the best possible light, they must work to maintain the idea that the whole exercise is neutral and objective. By doing so, they legitimate the findings from the trials, build confidence in the decision-making process and underline the suitability of a specific technology. Being seen to maintain the neutrality of those conducting the test is therefore of great importance for everyone involved in technology development, from users to engineers to industry.

In the contemporary British Army, the testing and evaluation of infantry equipment is managed and undertaken by the Infantry Trials and Development Unit (ITDU). Formally named the ITDU in 1968, the unit can trace its origins back to before the First World War when it was part of the Experimental Establishment at the School of Musketry, Hythe.[12] Now based at Warminster, the ITDU is a small organisation made up of a select group of officers and men with technical skills—for example, in marksmanship or as armourers—that, until a recent reorganisation of the Army in 2010, traditionally reported to the director of infantry. It is this unit that now offers a technical perspective on the worthiness of any weapon for certain military duties, acting as the guardian of, and the channel for, the infantry's needs.

It would be inaccurate to suggest that the ITDU in particular and the infantry in general are simply a malleable tool of industry. On the contrary, the analysis offered by the ITDU gives decision-makers in the Army the opportunity to make up their own minds about the equipment that ends up in service. Nonetheless, it has become a lot easier for industry to influence the thinking of those decision-makers involved in weapon selection. Indeed, over the last twenty years it is clear that industry has put a lot of work into developing their own techniques and analytical methods for describing and evaluating solutions to battlefield problems. The result is that the Army has to work harder to develop its own views and assert them in the face of industry specialists looking to sell certain types of equipment.

The process by which this particular soldier–industry dynamic emerged is complex, but it started as a result of the privatisation of the British government's Royal Ordnance Factories. The 1982 Falklands War may have been an infantryman's war, but it had little direct impact on the selection of the SA80 (or indeed small arms in general) other than to leave Army chiefs convinced that the old 7.62mm SLR and L4 Bren needed to be replaced as soon as possible. However, it was only after the disastrous introduction of the SA80 that the infantry began to realise they had to take more direct control over small arms selection if they were to ensure that they were equipped with reliable and effective weapons.

Nonetheless, it was not until the mid-1990s that infantry officers at the Ministry of Defence sought to change the balance of small arms in the Infantry Company and started to fight more assertively for resources vis-à-vis the other branches of the Army.[13] In their efforts they could rely on the support of what remained of the British government's civil service engineering and scientific community. However, the ability of these specialists to offer the kind of independent advice that they would have provided to their predecessors was curtailed by the procurement initiatives developed by McKinsey management consultants and introduced into the MOD in 1998.

Smart Procurement, as these initiatives were known, attempted to integrate private industry and public procurement teams into partnerships. Consequently, those government engineers and scientists that might previously have taken a more independent perspective of weapon selection, and whose views might have even carried the day in previous years, had to maintain their position in the context of partnership with industry. Properly independent engineering and scientific experts thus found themselves caught between the demands of the infantry and the ambitions of an industry and consulting market that had access to the sorts of resources and capabilities that no longer existed within government post-privatisation. This fundamentally altered the balance of relationships between the user community and industry, forcing experts in the civil service to fight to get heard. By 2012, it was clear that this fight had been lost when it was revealed that 60 per cent of all engineering support provided to Britain's armed forces came from outsourced agencies.[14] Thus the trend was towards greater industry involvement at the expense of providing independent advice to both users and taxpayers. This is set to continue with the government's ongoing attempt to introduce more privatisation to the MOD's Defence Equipment and Support organisation.

However, it had not always been the case that users and government would rely on the private provision of industry advice. Traditionally, the RSAF would make the weapons that the War Office chose, but as the manufactory did not have a design department, it was not responsible for weapon design.[15] Instead, during the nineteenth century, the War Office established various Small Arms Committees made up of officers and the RSAF's superintendent who would evaluate submissions from weapon designers. Nominally given the rank of colonel in the Army, the RSAF superintendent would establish the design implications of a weapon from the perspective of production. It was only following the outbreak of the Second World War that a formal department dedicated to small arms design properly emerged, not within the RSAF itself, but within the Ministry of Supply. After 1958, this design function was severely reduced for weapon evaluation purposes only and relocated from its wartime location in Cheshunt to Enfield. Lacking the depth of design expertise that had been marshalled during the Second World War, it was eventually this group of RSAF engineers—most notably including Ted Hance, a trainee apprentice working with Noel Kent-Lemon during the development of the EM-2—that were responsible for coming up with the Enfield Weapon System (EWS).[16] This prototype system was eventually renamed the Small Arms post-1980 or the SA80, Individual Weapon (IW i.e. the rifle) and Light Support Weapon (LSW).

In 1984, the RSAF was made a division of the newly renamed Royal Ordnance Factories (ROF), which had been set up as a new state-owned company. This new company was formally given both the intellectual property rights to the SA80 and a contract to produce the first tranche of the weapon before full privatisation. With the government keen to ensure that the spin-off of the ROF was a success, ministers subsequently took the decision to prevent foreign contractors bidding for the second tranche production run of the SA80, a competition that would be held before the formal sale of the ROF.[17] This excluded H&K and FN from bidding for the work and allowed the government to claim that it was protecting British manufacturing. This move was, however, clearly also designed to make it impossible for any other British contractor to make a credible bid for the Tranche 2 contract for SA80.

What was clear, however, was that the government could not be sure that the taxpayer was getting value for money out of the Tranche 2 tender process. Consequently, after the government announced the winner of the competition in February 1987, Treasury civil servants wrote to the MOD complaining that the MOD had not followed the due process for running a public tender. In practice, however, as one senior civil servant observed, 'the Minister (of Defence Procurement) [Lord Trefgarne] was not anxious to see RO [Royal Ordnance] undercut by a bid with a substantial foreign content since this would undoubtedly prejudice a successful float ...'[18]

The government's decision to protect British industry thus ensured that a privately owned ROF would have a Tranche 2 contract to produce the SA80, significantly increasing the potential value of the business. Indeed, James Edmiston, the former director of Britain's Sterling Armament Company, was clear in his criticism when he noted that, by excluding foreign competition, the ROF—a company that had already invested £100 million in the SA80— would be left in the prime spot for winning the Tranche 2 contract.[19] At the same time, ministers were aware that British Aerospace was interested in purchasing ROF. What ministers could not be sure of, however, was whether BAE wanted to get into the small arms business. Fearful that the RSAF at Enfield was not capable of turning a profit, given the Tranche 2 contract that the ROF had signed with the government, BAE subsequently asked for time to review the deal and figure out their business strategy before deciding on whether to honour the tender process. After agreeing to sell the ROF to BAE in April 1987, the government subsequently allowed the company a further two and a half month grace period to decide whether they would take on the SA80 Tranche 2 contract. By mid-July, BAE told the government they would honour the Tranche 2 contract but that they would close Enfield and move the whole manufactory to a new 'state of the art' plant in Nottingham.

During much of the 1980s, Enfield's workforce had been aware that their jobs were unlikely to survive privatisation. As privatisation approached, however, workers felt increasingly demoralised, leading some to conclude that the government had left Enfield 'shattered as a working community'.[20] This sentiment came to a head following the formal sale of ROF and the announced closure of Enfield. The state of the art plant in Nottingham took a new approach to the production of the SA80. This new approach did not, however, demand a particularly large or skilled workforce. Consequently, the RSAF Apprentices Scheme, a scheme that had produced some of Britain's most highly skilled craftsmen, was abandoned and the number of workers dropped from 1,200 at Enfield to just 475 at Nottingham.[21] At the same time, very few RSAF employees opted to move north to Nottingham to help set up the new plant.[22]

Underpinning the changes in manpower levels was BAE's conclusion that the Nottingham plant would only prove to be financially viable if the production philosophy switched from manufacturing components to assembling them as part of an assembly line. This was most readily observed in the SA80 itself. When the weapon was being made at Enfield, 40 per cent of the 120 components were being machined in-house. Following the move to Nottingham, the total number of components produced in-house dropped to just thirteen. Sub-contractors employed by BAE were making the rest.[23] Managing sub-component quality in this context proved to be essential for maintaining the overall integrity and reliability of the weapon. The changes consequently introduced a number of significant variables into the production of the SA80 system, variables caused by having two different production standards associated with a despondent and soon to be unemployed workforce closing down one plant, while another was ironing out new processes as it was worked up for full production.

Unfortunately, these production issues were compounded by a weapon configuration that had gone through a number of revisions after the 1979–80 NATO Standardisation Trials. Before the trials, designers had allowed for the possibility that the EWS would have to fire 5.56mm ammunition as directed by the General Staff Requirement. Little did designers realise, however, that the 5.56mm ammunition that would eventually be adopted would not be the existing American M193 standard, but a completely new Belgian version. At the time the design team were working, it was completely reasonable to assume that the round would conform to existing US standards. After the trials, however, the SA80 system had to be recalibrated if it were to accommodate the Belgian SS109, the new NATO standard. The problem was that

British ammunition had traditionally been loaded with nitrocellulose tubular cut propellant, a propellant that had been optimised for fighting across the empire. This ensured that ammunition was suitable both for long-term storage and was robust in a range of global environments. Unfortunately, however, British propellant also had a different burn rate to the Belgian design. The result of these ammunition changes would leave the SA80 either needing further recalibration, or a decision would have to be taken to ignore NATO STANAG 4172 in favour of British ammunition.

None of this was necessarily a problem, except for the fact that the Army itself was becoming increasingly desperate to replace the SLR, a weapon that had been in service since 1957. This was particularly the case as the costs associated with maintaining the SLR were becoming rather substantial. In 1974, for example, it had been estimated that the base cost for the MOD to repair the SLR was £1 million per year.[24] Thus, with the SA80 tantalisingly close to introduction, the prospect of spending additional funds on refurbishing worn out SLRs was not something that the General Staff were keen to pursue given the pressures that already existed on the defence budget. However, the change to British ammunition standards further slowed the 'In Service Date' for the weapon as engineers worked to adjust the robustness and cyclic times of various parts. As a result, when the SA80 Individual Weapon finally came in front of the Acceptance Board in 1984, the Army's representatives were extremely keen to see the rifle introduced into service. More than this, in the context of a government determined to privatise the ROF, the Army was very keen to see the RSAF given the contract for Tranche 1 production, precisely because it believed that this offered the best chance for maintaining the 170-year relationship with an expert community of engineers.

Nonetheless, it quickly became clear that the SA80 was being introduced into service before the production problems caused by the demoralisation of workers at Enfield and the switch over to the new Nottingham plant had been ironed out.[25] The result was that 1st Tranche weapons produced at Enfield were believed to be considerably less reliable than 2nd Tranche weapons produced at Nottingham. Moreover, because the contractual liabilities associated with the failure to deliver Tranche 1 were considerably less onerous than failure to deliver Tranche 2 on time, BAE decided to start delivery of weapons against Tranche 2 before finishing the Tranche 1 contract. With the MOD deciding to undertake an early, phased roll out of the SA80 system, further design changes were quickly identified once the weapon was in the hands of the user. However, making iterative changes to the design as new weapons were coming off the production line was made more complicated by BAE's decision to start delivering Tranche 2 and the fact that the ROF owned the design rights to the weapon. Consequently, the Army had to put in place special measures to ensure that they had enough of the right iteration of the SA80 ready to fight the First Gulf War in 1990–1.

Although the production challenges associated with SA80 were slowly being overcome, the Army's unexpected deployment to the Gulf meant that any latent problems caused by the use of SS109 5.56 ammunition manufactured to NATO specifications would quickly come to the fore. In this respect, the Ordnance Board had previously identified a large number of reliability issues with the SA80 even before the weapon was introduced to soldiers. In particular, Ordnance Board officials had shown the weapon had not been perfected for out of Europe operations and especially suffered with a problem of sand ingress.[26] Clearly, in Kuwait, this presented a challenge. However, the sand ingress problem would be severely complicated by the Army's purchase of supplementary wartime ammunition produced by Belgian and Swiss manufacturers.

SS109 ammunition manufactured to Belgian and now NATO standards used ball rather than tubular cut powders. These ball powders had a faster burn rate and would change the cyclic rate of the SA80 system, potentially putting the internal components under more stress and causing them to break more quickly than had been allowed for in the initial design specification. This might be alleviated by making slight modifications to the gas port, the feature of the weapon that controlled the movement of propellant gasses that re-cocked the firing mechanism and loaded a new round into the chamber. Before the Gulf War, at least one study had been carried out by the Small Arms Tactical Support Unit at the Royal Military College of Science to establish whether such changes were warranted given a switch to SS109 loaded with ball powders.[27] This detailed study considered whether a solution to the ammunition problem could be engineered without having to undergo a complete re-call and systematic re-evaluation of the weapon. Arguing that it was better to take a systematic approach to ensure that any changes were based on establishing whether there were any underlying design faults, the RMCS warned against the sticking plaster approach. Taking the short route by modifying the gas port risked the creation of further problems once minor modifications had been made. With the MOD unwilling to totally recall the SA80 for further design evaluation, however, the weapon continued its phased roll out.

None of this was particularly satisfactory for the General Staff. Saddled with the ageing SLR, the Army chose the sticking plaster approach. No doubt this decision was also backed by ministers who could not face the political fall-out that would result from having to admit that privatising the RSAF had materially contributed to the failings of the SA80. More than this, however, the government itself was complicating the process of resolving the ammunition problem, as it sought to reinforce the message that privatisation of the ROF was a success. In particular, the head of the Defence Procurement Agency, Peter Levene, was keen to explore ways to save money on ammunition procurement as part of a five-year agreement with the ROF known as the Explosives Propellants and Related Products (EPREP) deal.[28] As it was expected that this agreement could save the government as much as £4 million on small arms ammunition, ROF Radway Green—the UK's main supplier of ammunition—was also keen to press ahead with the deal as the subsidiary company wanted to access wider NATO markets by making more NATO compliant SS109 ammunition.

As it was, the existing contract to make ammunition with tubular cut propellant left the ROF making a significant financial loss. Making the change would, however, force the project management teams already struggling with ensuring that ROF delivered enough weapons into service, with the additional problem of making further design changes to the SA80. But if the financial savings could be realised, then the government could claim that the ROFs were more efficient under private ownership than when they had been managed by the dead hand of the civil service. Although EPREP was eventually signed in July 1988, the government deferred to the SAA project management team at MOD and paid the premium demanded by ROF Radway Green to ensure the continued supply of tubular cut ammunition over the immediate future.[29]

Nonetheless, following the outbreak of the Gulf War, the SA80 would still end up being used with non-British ammunition. Luckily, however, troops rarely used the SA80 in anger. Consequently, many of the ammunition questions that had arisen out of the changeover in NATO standards never resulted in the unnecessary deaths of British servicemen. However, it did not take long before stories about the poor reliability of the SA80 emerged in public. According to various newspaper stories based on the leaked LANDSET Report, the SA80's inadequacies were so bad that bayonets broke, magazines fell out of weapons and soldiers had to use tape to stop sand ingress into the working parts of the IW and LSW.[30] As infantrymen had only had to use their weapon twenty-two times in anger throughout the entire campaign, it was clear that soldiers had come to doubt the reliability of the weapon as they trained and prepared for operations before the beginning of Desert Storm. With the MOD subsequently releasing the LANDSET report for scrutiny by the House of Commons Select Committee on Defence in 1991, the SA80 and the privatisation of the ROF would come under increasingly close public scrutiny.

Unfortunately for the Army, there can be little doubt that spinning off the government manufactories complicated the process of acquiring the SA80 system, making it exceptionally difficult to resolve the problems that subsequently emerged as it was being phased into service. The problems with the weapon, which underwent more than twenty-two Modification Instructions, had serious repercussions for the infantry as they prepared for the Gulf War.[31] Feedback from units equipped with the SA80 universally praised its accuracy and the way it had improved soldier marksmanship. However, poor finishing, breakages and its inability to generate firepower without stoppages—especially in sandy conditions—resulted in soldiers losing confidence in the weapon.[32]

In the five-year period after the Gulf War, the problems facing the SA80 took a number of further turns. In particular, the problem of converting British ammunition standards to the new NATO standard continued to dog those trying to resolve the reliability issues made public by the weapon's failings in the desert. In the first instance, the Defence Select Committee looked into the controversies that had surrounded the introduction of the SA80 and in 1992 recommended that the government seek compensation from BAE for poor workmanship and delivering weapons behind schedule. The government subsequently sought legal advice and threatened the company with a demand for compensation. This in turn prompted BAE to countersue, claiming that the government had set a price for the SA80 Tranche 1 and 2 contracts when the RSAF was still technically publicly owned. Consequently, the Tranche 1 and 2 contracts had established a unit price for each weapon that belied the fact that the government was acting as both seller and buyer. BAE thus accused the government of offering the RSAF for sale, having manipulated the price of the weapon before privatisation.

Although the government and BAE finally agreed to settle their differences out of court in 1994, the problems with the reliability of the SA80 continued. Indeed, the Gulf War highlighted the need to ensure that all ammunition across NATO conformed to the SS109 standard.[33] Convinced that the reliability problem was bound up with the question of managing the weapon's cyclic rate, the Army continued its programme of alterations to the gas operating system. However, the design authority for the SA80 remained with BAE. As a result, the solution to weapon reliability effectively remained beyond the ability of the MOD to resolve given the existing contractual arrangements and the lack of in-house expertise and capability. If the MOD wanted to properly solve the challenge of adopting SS109 ammunition, then the government would have to pay for changes to the SA80 to be made.

With the alterations to the gas operating system proving to offer inconclusive results, matters started to come to a head.[34] In October 1997, a Reliability and Interoperability Programme was established in the Defence Procurement Agency (DPA).[35] H&K was the Design Authority for the SA80 after the German company had been acquired by British Aerospace and reorganised with the Royal Ordnance division in 1992. Consequently, H&K was commissioned by the DPA to systematically investigate the inconsistent reliability of SA80 and suggest a way forward. At the same time, concerns were being expressed within NATO about the impact the SA80 was having on ammunition types being presented to NATO for qualification. The NATO Nominated Weapons List comprised weapons that were used for conducting specific tests of ammunition as outlined in 'Evaluation Procedures for Future NATO Small Arms Weapon Systems', SA80 being one of the weapons.[36] Matters came to a head in October 1996 when the NATO group responsible for this activity was given the task by the North American Regional Test and Evaluation Centre (NARTEC) to define the problems experienced with SA80 during ammunition testing.[37] A deadline was set for March 1997, and in April NARTEC informed the European Regional Test Centre (ERTC), based in Pendine, that they had identified the issues and were going to propose that SA80 should be withdrawn from the NATO Nominated Weapons List at the September 1997 meeting.

In the event, the UK head of delegation, Lieutenant Colonel Tony Thornburn, persuaded the sub-group to temporarily suspend SA80 from the list rather than withdraw it completely—a subtle but important nuance given the political ramifications that could result. Indeed, the sub-group now included Partnership for Peace Nations, many of whom attended the meeting. Thornburn recalls asking all members present 'not to divulge the decision nor, in particular, speak to the media, until the UK had time to staff the matter, informing them that they had already commissioned H&K to study the design and reliability of SA80 and make recommendations for its improvement'. He argued that 'if the information leaked out prematurely, the Ministry of Defence, and/or their political masters, would merely become defensive and it would slow the whole process down with defensive briefs etc.'[38]

He promised to come back to the next meeting with a proposed solution. In the subsequent H&K three-month investigation, two million rounds of mostly non-NATO qualified ammunition (forty-two types in total) were cycled through an appropriately modified weapon to prove its reliability. ITDU subsequently fired another one million rounds through the weapon to guarantee, statistically and beyond reasonable doubt, that the proposed H&K modifications worked.[39] The programme to improve the reliability of the SA80, euphemistically named Mid-Life Upgrade, became more palatable within the MOD following the election of the Labour government in May 1997.

In 2001, the new SA80A2 was finally rolled out to soldiers, nearly thirty years after the initial design specifications had been put in front of the General Staff for approval. Both the SA80 Individual Weapon and Light Support Weapon have since demonstrated that the original design might have been successful if the problems with it had been addressed systematically. As it was, the £95 million upgrade resulted in the Army having a weapon that was 95 per cent reliable in sandy conditions. This proved to be more reliable than all of the other service weapons being used by various major armies around the world, including the M16A2. The whole saga of delivering one of the simplest pieces of equipment into the military inventory had been acrimonious, and unnecessarily complex, and drove home to the infantry that they needed to take more direct control over the way it acquired future weapons. For it seemed that the only way to guarantee the acquisition of the right equipment was to find ways to reframe small arms discussions so as to privilege military judgement over the perspectives of the other expert professions. The painful divorce between Enfield and the government had left the user community distrustful of expert advice.

The LSW and the Light Machine Gun

The SA80 debacle finally revealed the illusion of control the Army had over the selection of weapons for what it was. The previous chapters in this book have shown how many actors were involved in weapon development. In the late 1980s and 1990s, however, the Army had to recognise that it was not the dominant actor in that process. No longer could the Army rely on and trust that engineers would provide them with reliable weapons. Now it was crystal clear that the Army was but one of several groups competing to shape the way in which weapons were chosen.

Given the central place the rifle has in the psyche of the Army, this was a formative experience for many. It not only shaped the way the LSW was replaced but it also framed the way equipment was subsequently purchased.

As the Army was conscious that the usual procurement process was lengthy and subject to considerable analytical oversight, equipment programmes were invariably delayed and costly.[40] In recognition of all these issues, the Army was, therefore, more than eager to make extensive use of the Urgent Operational Requirement process during the wars in Iraq and Afghanistan rather than be waylaid by a system it no longer trusted.

Symbolic of this breakdown in trust in the procurement process, was the infantry's replacement of the SA80 Light Support Weapon in favour of the FN Minimi LMG. If RSAF engineers had traditionally underwritten the paternal bargain between officers and men, soldiers and the state, then the LSW came to represent the failure of that arrangement. A weapon that suffered from poor reliability throughout its development and into its early deployment, it never acquired much status with the infantry and was typically given to a battalion's newest recruits, known as Crows.[41] Since 1999, however, the Army made a point of acquiring the FN Minimi belt-fed, 5.56mm Light Machine Gun. It has been argued that this apparently minor equipment change was simply the result of the Army finally grasping the firepower realities of the contemporary battlefield.[42] Such an analysis does not, however, do justice to the underlying sociological processes that were happening within the Army at the time.

A more accurate statement as to what has been going on would need to reflect on the emergence of more assertive professional soldiers who more actively shaped the technical demands of the infantry and in the process refashioned Army attitudes towards marksmanship and firepower. What emerges out of this kind of analysis, however, is that professional soldiers did not agree on what was necessary from a marksmanship/firepower perspective, and that different units were equally not able to mould the technological agenda. In the first place, the Ministry of Defence only has a certain number of staff posts available for officers to engage in processes associated with weapon selection. This inevitably limits appointments to a sub-section of the Army's officers rather than a representative sample. Consequently, and in terms of Lukes' second dimension of power, the person selected to manage small arms requirements was extremely well placed to direct the research, development and acquisition agenda.

In the second place, soldiers from different units have differing levels of status. This no longer simply reflects the cap badges and regimental identities of the units formed out of the nineteenth-century Cardwell Reforms.[43] Rather, the currency of this new Army pecking order lies in the combat experience of the soldiers themselves.[44] This is made clear by Captain Bury of the Royal Irish Regiment, who writes,

> We had all been tested in battle. We had learned more about ourselves and each other in those intense hours than in all the time that had gone before. Most of us were proud of the way we had acted, relieved that we hadn't let anyone down, and honoured. Honoured that we had fought with the Paras, that we had held our own with them.[45]

Units with a lot of combat experience are deemed to set the benchmark for the performance of the rest of the Army. This in turn reflects what Professor Anthony King argues is the professionalisation of the infantry. Non-elite regiments have striven through training to raise their combat drills and tactics, techniques and procedures (TTPs) to the standards set by those units that have a lot of combat experience.[46]

The notion that there are differences of opinion or disagreements over TTPs and technology within the user community is not, however, something that is regularly accounted for either in the literature, or by those officers responsible for writing the technology user requirements that are given to engineers. Instead, users are either aggregated and referred to as a homogenous group, or the effects of one user community's thinking on the efforts of the whole organisation are improperly mapped. While there is a lack of specificity, the notion of the user offers a shorthand way of representing the different perspectives of the infantry as coherent and agreed. It is, however, a move that ultimately covers up the underlying political discussions that are going on among infantrymen. This is not a new phenomenon. Indeed, Major-general E. Clarke, the 1942 director general of artillery, noted that, 'There is no such thing as "User policy" or "User opinion" in the singular, though they are frequently quoted as a valuable and insufficiently appreciated asset.'[47]

Such nuances are difficult to identify. In the wrinkles of weapon selection, however, the differences of technological opinion among the infantry can be discerned. This is particularly obvious in relation to the adoption of the Light Support Weapon in 1987 and its replacement the FN Minimi in the late 1990s. Although many commentators claim that the switch-over was 'obviously correct', the nature of the arguments associated with this change are poorly contextualised and reflect a poor understanding of modern firepower.[48] Indeed, it must be remembered that a number of NATO countries were not convinced by the need for an LMG-type weapon, including the Bundeswehr who did not adopt a 5.56mm LMG but preferred to retain a 7.62mm sustained fire machine gun.

Where evidence could be found that considered the relative merits of fire-power over marksmanship, it was not entirely clear that automatic fire from an LMG necessarily increased hit probability. The 1950s ORO Hitchman Report, for instance, demonstrated that fully automatic fire weapons did not increase the probability of a hit when compared with SALVO fire ordnance. Similarly, studies undertaken by the ITDU in mid-1969 determined that the Self-Loading Rifle was more likely to realise military objectives than the belt-fed GPMG.[49] They concluded that 'one rifleman firing three rounds or two riflemen firing one round show these to be more successful and more eco-nomical than the five round GPMG burst'. Although the discussion of aimed fire ran counter to the ORO Hitchman report, in 1969 the ITDU in effect argued that the movement of the weapon and the inability of the shooter to control it made it extremely unlikely that an automatic burst would result in enemy incapacitation.

None of this stopped the British Army adopting alternative small arms that might compensate for these inadequacies. On the contrary, after the war, the Army recognised they urgently needed to replace the aging fleet of Vickers Heavy Machine Guns. This held open the possibility that, like the German MG42, a weapon could be acquired for both a light/medium and heavy role.[50] This prompted the General Staff to consider acquiring a new Sustained Fire Machine Gun. However, after the Americans unilaterally chose the M-14 over the FN FAL, the British General Staff adamantly refused to buy the US M-60 belt-fed machine gun.[51] Instead, the General Staff decided to buy the FN Mitrailleuse d'Appui Général (FN MAG), which was subsequently renamed the L7A1 General Purpose Machine Gun in 1962 (GPMG).[52]

Unfortunately for those soldiers working in the dismounted or light infan-try role, the GPMG was both heavy (10.9kg/24lbs) and unwieldy. More than this, the belted ammunition was cumbersome and slowed the entire infantry section as everyone in the unit took responsibility for carrying it.[53] Soldiers may have found the GPMG a reassuring and confidence-building piece of equipment when it was given, or made organic, to the Infantry Section. However, the weapon did not always facilitate the ambitions of those officers responsible for combining firepower and manoeuvre, an issue that solders became acutely aware of when fighting in the jungles of Malaya and Borneo between the late 1940s and early 1960s.

In Borneo, the dominant terrain over which the British Army fought was mountainous and covered in jungle. With forward bases along the remote border regions with Indonesia, resupply by air put a premium on helicopter support.[54] This necessarily restricted the equipment load that could be carried to the frontlines. But logistics were not just a problem for battalion commanders seeking to ensure they had sufficient material to maintain offensive operations. Individual soldiers as well as section, platoon and company formations also had to wrestle with the problem of generating fire and balancing this demand against the need for mobility.

What was peculiar to the South East Asian tropics, however, was that both the environment and tactical doctrine demanded more from infantryman.[55] Experience in Burma and Malaya had shown that troops should not restrict themselves to travel by road but must be prepared to fight in the jungles and make use of active patrols and ambushes while avoiding well-used tracks.[56] In these conditions, excessive equipment weight could make hacking through the forest even more difficult than it might otherwise be, factors that had considerable bearing on the tempo of operations.[57] Thus in Malaya in 1953 one report observed that, 'The effectiveness of the LMG on patrols is very small.'[58] In such conditions, the fully automatic M16 had been acquired in small numbers to offset this problem. At just over 6lbs 4oz (2.9kg), the M16 was considerably lighter than the SLR.[59] The GPMG, by contrast, required too much effort to manhandle through the back woods and was consequently less likely to be taken on patrol. Through trial and error in the jungles of Malaya and Borneo, the Army thus demonstrated the sense of re-chambering the old .303 Bren gun to fire the new 7.62mm NATO standard and re-adopt it as the L4 Infantry Section weapon, a programme that only finished in 1960.[60]

The SA80 and LSW were therefore designed against a backdrop in which the Infantry Section had never been equipped with either an automatic rifle or a belt-fed sustained fire LMG. Moreover, after the 1968 and 1974 Defence Reviews, reviews that saw Britain's military commitments reduce to east of Suez, the General Staff started to view the notion of a belt-fed LMG even more cautiously. The previous chapter set out the context surrounding these decisions. What is important to note here, however, is that following an extensive briefing by Enfield staff in 1973, the General Staff were fully supportive of the IW and LSW concept. The LSW was not a straight replacement for a belt-fed weapon like the GPMG but would complement the rifle by giving the Infantry Section an option to use skirmishing tactics and engage targets out at a longer range.[61]

Thus appreciations of the effectiveness of the LSW ought to be contextualised against the Army's use of both the GPMG and the L4 Bren gun in the Section firepower role. When looked at this way, it is clear that the LSW concept emerged out of an Army that had a great deal of experience working in remote parts of the world in difficult terrain where logistical support was limited. Whereas the SA80 Individual Weapon was optimised for close engagements and precision fire against sub-300 metre targets, the bipod on the LSW and the longer barrel provided more precision for hitting targets out to 600 yards. Retaining a magazine instead of adopting a belted ammunition machine gun was designed to minimise the logistics burden if forced to operate outside of Europe. Inside Europe, the LSW would find itself working in concert with sustained fire weapons in fixed positions or mounted on vehicles. The combination of firepower and range offered by the SA80 family was intended to maintain the momentum of an attack in difficult terrain where carrying a belt-fed machine gun was awkward. By the time that the operational requirements for the SA80 system had emerged in 1973, the intention was that the LSW would cover a number of roles in the section while the GPMG would be retained at company level. This was subsequently picked up by the ITDU in 1984 as they discussed the utility of the LSW over that of the GPMG.[62]

Although the tactics associated with this family of weapons had not been formulated in their entirety in the early 1970s, by the time the SA80 system was adopted in the mid-1980s, the Army had honed its drills and techniques so as to take full advantage of the new weapons. This optimisation process started during operations in Northern Ireland. When the Army first arrived in Northern Ireland, the infantry was still using what a subsequent director of infantry described as 'duck waddling' in its approach to patrolling.[63] This involved patrolling in column such that the leading and end soldiers provided security for the rest of the section. Reliant on the wits and observation skills of just two men, gunmen could wait for the leading member of the patrol to pass before firing on soldiers in the middle or rear of the line. Given that the IRA preferred to engage troops and then escape without being detected, the standard technique for patrolling did not provide sufficient force protection for troops.

With casualties mounting, the Army decided to establish a training team charged with developing tactics to overcome the threat from the IRA.[64] In this respect, Major Colin Shortis, a member of the Devonshire and Dorset Regiment, would play a key role in the iteration of infantry tactics.[65] Eventually becoming a major-general and director of infantry between 1983 and 1986, Shortis would go on to play an instrumental part in the selection of the SA80. While in Northern Ireland, however, Shortis evolved an approach to patrolling that provided greater force protection.

Instead of patrols advancing in column, the eight-man infantry section would split itself into two, four-man teams. These four-man teams were known as 'bricks', any number of which could be combined to form a 'multiple' to meet a range of tactical requirements. Commanded by corporals or lance corporals, each member of the team would observe and cover a quadrant down the patrol's line of advance, thereby providing 360 degree observation of the surroundings. With several of these bricks working interdependently along similar axes and communicating by tactical radio, the approach provided the building block for more secure and effective combat patrolling.[66] In particular, by a process of rotating the 'multiples' like a satellite across the route of the patrol, the IRA could never be quite certain where the next soldier might appear from. This in turn made them less inclined to take a passing shot.[67]

The four-man brick lent itself to a complete change in the balance of equipment provided to the infantry section in the mid-1980s.[68] The strength of the new tactics was that two bricks could use fire to facilitate each one leapfrogging over the other. By implication, then, both fire teams would need to have a balanced range of small arms if they were to flexibly support each other. Conversely, if only one of the two bricks had an LSW, then the ability of the section as a whole to fire and move forwards by mutual support would be greatly curtailed.[69]

Unfortunately for Shortis, maintaining the balance of firepower within the Infantry Section was to become considerably more complicated by the reliability problems with the SA80. While the SA80 only just passed the safety trials being run by the Ordnance Board, the LSW failed to meet its 1984 In Service Date because of its inability to consistently group shots when fired in automatic mode.[70] The result was a delay to the introduction of the LSW while additional modifications were made to ensure that the weapon could achieve a revised accuracy criterion.

At the same time, questions started to circulate as to whether the LSW was the best weapon for service given the various reliability and accuracy problems. In order to put this question to the test, the ITDU was asked by Shortis, while he was director of infantry, to establish the comparable accuracy of the LSW with that of other infantry weapons of similar type.[71] Comparing the LSW with other 5.56mm LMGs, including the H&K 13, the Steyr LMG and the FN Minimi, Major Tony Briard for ITDU concluded that the LSW met revised accuracy criteria for 100 and 600 metres and could be adopted if the weapon was more reliable.

The trials left the director of infantry with a difficult decision to make. Either he could buy a commercial off-the-shelf weapon or accept the RSAF's assurances that they could make the LSW more reliable. If the director of infantry opted to buy off the shelf, however, then the MOD would only commit the financial resources to buy one support weapon per section.[72] Should he opt for the LSW, and if the reliability problems could be resolved, then the infantry would have balanced fire-teams. In this situation and given the amount of time, effort and organisational and political capital invested in developing the LSW, the director of infantry found it exceptionally hard to abandon the weapon in favour of something else.[73] Consequently, in the end, the infantry accepted the guarantees provided by the Enfield engineers and decided to accept the LSW into service.[74]

Twenty years after Shortis's decision, the Army reappraised the LSW and decided that a weapon that used a magazine had inherent limitations compared to the belt-fed FN Minimi LMG. It is interesting to note, however, that a number of British Army reports have repeatedly downplayed the effectiveness of the Minimi for service. During the 1980 NATO Standardisation trials at Hammelburg, for instance, one British armourer was noted as saying, 'It is felt that the accuracy of the weapon is not up to standard due to a short sight base and a short barrel.'[75] Major Briard further substantiated this in the formal 1984 ITDU LSW comparative trials. These trials showed that the FN Minimi was 'robust and reliable' and 'easy to strip, assemble and handle ...' but that its burst group size was 'much larger than that of weapons currently in service and [that] it fails to meet the GSR accuracy amendment'.[76] Major Briard was not alone in his observations. British commentators such as retired Lieutenant Colonel Jim Storr have since remarked that the Minimi was not as effective at suppression as the LSW,[77] while American critics of what would later be designated the M249 Squad Automatic Weapon also felt that the Minimi was not accurate enough for the US Army.[78]

Nonetheless, the Minimi had its advocates in Britain, advocates who by 1998 included a new director of infantry, Brigadier Seymour Monro.[79] Of all the new protagonists pushing for greater quantities of infantry firepower, however, the most vocal within the infantry was Colonel David Benest. Starting his career with the 2nd Battalion of the Parachute Regiment, during the 1990s Benest would be responsible for setting the Army's small arms requirements while he headed up Land Systems Operational Requirements (LSOR) and the Defence Equipment Capability team for the Special Forces community. Having fought in the Falklands at Goose Green with 2 PARA, Benest's experience of war had led him to strongly support the selection of a belt-fed weapon like the FN Minimi.

Based on advice offered by the Normandy veteran Sydney Jary, 2 PARA had gone out to the Falklands with twice as many GPMGs as usual.[80] Jary had a lot of experience of the German MG34 and MG42 and was convinced that the L4 Bren would not guarantee fire superiority over the Argentinians. This was especially the case as Argentinian forces were armed with the automatic version of the FN FAL and the direct equivalent to the British GPMG, the FN MAG.[81] As far as Benest was concerned, in the culminating fight at Goose Green on 29 May, Jary's suggestions were prophetic.[82] By 10.30 in the morning, overwhelmed by fire, the Parachute Battalion had been forced to ground at the foot of Darwin Hill. Pinned down and frustrated, the Battalion's inertia led 2 PARA's commander, Colonel H. Jones, to launch his suicidal charge on the Argentinian trench line. Following Jones's death, the acting commander, Major Dair Farrar-Hockley, concluded that if Goose Green was to be taken then he needed to bring more fire to bear on the Argentinian position. This led to the repositioning of MILAN anti-tank rockets to where they could more effectively support the final phases of the attack. This additional fire helped to unlock the stalemate and convinced Benest of the importance of firepower over human will.[83]

Benest's attitude towards firepower may have been formed out of his combat experience, but his views were most certainly at odds with the prevailing attitude of the Army before 1982.[84] Airborne forces in particular had always been conscious of the need to maintain fire discipline. Dropped behind enemy lines, soldiers would usually have to fight and survive on what they had available until they were relieved by ground forces. As a result, there had always been an emphasis on ammunition conservation. Thus, in 1949 the former commander of the 1st Airborne Corps, General Richard Gale, argued that contemporary problems with marksmanship stemmed from the false belief that automatic weapons would replace the rifle. In his view, 'Compared with the rifle in capable hands, automatic weapons are poor killers and heavy users of ammunition. The rifle is still the main and most economical weapon for killing infantry—one shot, one man.'[85]

In the twenty-year period after the Falklands, however, the Parachute Regiment's traditional emphasis on fire discipline was being actively challenged by Benest who advocated more aggressive use of fire over marksmanship. Arguing that history was on his side, Benest and his staff in Land Systems Operational Requirements wrote several papers undermining the LSW and advocating a belt-fed LMG in its place. This led to a number of studies that investigated the utility of sustained fire weapons, the results of which helped

Benest champion the replacement of the LSW among several infantry constituencies including successive directors of infantry at Warminster.[86]

The turning point in the argument over whether to replace the LSW came with the deployment of 5th Airborne and 4th Armoured Brigades to Kosovo in the summer of 1999. With Serbian forces under air attack by NATO, British units faced the possibility of entering Kosovo with unreliable small arms. Consequently, Major-general Mike Jackson, another officer who had served in the Parachute Regiment, put in a request for a more reliable section support weapon. This led to the purchase of the 'Para' version of the FN Minimi as part of an Urgent Operational Requirement (UOR). Colonel Benest did not have any direct input in the writing of the UOR, but given his extensive agitation against the LSW, it seems reasonable to conclude that his efforts had successfully shaped the perspectives of a number of senior officers within the Army.[87] As they helicoptered into Kosovo as part of the initial Kosovo Protection Force, the Parachute Regiment would finally be equipped with a belt-fed LMG.

However, the whole process by which the infantry had gone about selecting the Minimi was contested by a number of officers connected to the ITDU. These included its commandant, Lieutenant Colonel Tony Thornburn.[88] Thornburn had served in the Devonshire and Dorset Regiment under Colin Shortis and had a long-standing appreciation for the reasons underpinning the adoption of the LSW. Aware of the firepower benefits of the GPMG (given the right round), Thornburn was also conscious of the encumbrance such a weapon caused to the Infantry Section.

Nevertheless, during a series of LMG trials conducted in 2003, it appeared that HQ Infantry had insisted that the requirement for a new weapon specify the need to fire a continuous burst of 100 rounds. Despite the fact that by this time the SA80 had gone through its mid-life upgrade and both the IW and the LSW had no known problems whatsoever, HQ Infantry's decision effectively ruled the LSW out of the trial. What was also clear was that the requirement on accuracy, lethality at range and rate of fire had been relaxed in such a way as to offer the Minimi the best chance of selection. The Defence Procurement Agency had framed the selection criteria in a way that demonstrated they had bought into Benest's arguments, and the result was that the elite regiments, and especially the Parachute Regiment, had got what they wanted. The usual practices of the ITDU could be elided if enough of the right sort of influence could be brought to bear on weapon selection. Subsequently, in 2003, General Mike Jackson, by that time the chief of the

General Staff, would agree to adopt the FN Minimi for general service across the Army.

Unable to persuade the Army of his point of view, Thornburn had to wait until he'd retired before he could generate the evidential basis that might sustain his claims about the LMG. As part of a contracting team to the MOD in the late 2000s, System Design and Evaluation (SDE) Ltd created an acoustic target system that could track every bullet fired within several metres around a target. According to SDE, this demonstrated that 'most rounds fired in a typical, realistic scenario are simply not accurate enough to suppress'. Even more controversially, SDE claimed that the LSW was 'extremely good at suppressing targets out to 500m or more' and that the LMG was 'far worse' in such trials.[89] According to this analysis, the prospect of fixing the enemy with suppressive fire so that troops might close to engage them did not appear to be working given the existing weapon mix and state of training within the Army.

Gucci kit and the manipulation of desire

> Oh yeah, everyone's got their favourite weapon ... I'm a .50 [calibre Heavy Machine Gun] guy. I don't know if it's true, but they say the round only has to come within eighteen inches of you to sear flesh. That's badass. It doesn't have to hit you and it can still tear you open. It's just a sexy weapon.
>
> Private Jones, 2nd Platoon, Battle Company, 173rd Airborne Brigade, Korengal Valley, 2008[90]

As Private Jones from Alpha Company, 173rd US Airborne Brigade, makes clear, everyone in the Army has their favourite weapon. In the case of the modern British Army, soldiers love the FN Minimi.[91] There can be little doubt that the introduction of the weapon has been very well received and that it is highly successful with the troops. Indeed, unlike the LSW, soldiers are very happy to be photographed with the LMG. Yet if the technical features of the LMG can be contested, then what else might explain soldier attitudes towards Fabrique Nationale's weapon? Why does the infantry choose to emphasise the validity of the LMG dataset over that of the LSW?

The short answer is that the LSW was encumbered with a reputation that no amount of analytical data could correct. The longer answer, indeed the answer that has been driving much of this book, has to trace the way that beliefs about these weapons have been constructed and relate these to wider patterns of beliefs about tactics and technology. Clearly, the LMG was perceived, rightly or wrongly, as the weapon that could deliver battlefield results in the same way that it was felt that the GPMG could do the job. Indeed, when it came to the LMG, it might be fair to characterise the situation as soldiers wanting the firepower of the GPMG without its weight and encumbrances.

There is, however, something deeper going on that cannot simply be explained in these terms. The best way to make sense of this is to draw parallel arguments between small arms technology and the way that British and American soldiers have been issued with digital camouflage. Here the question of uniform selection is not just about the effectiveness of the technology but also what it says about the relative martial prowess of those using it.[92] Cap badges, insignia and battle flashes have long been important ways to distinguish different groups and inculcate military culture. What is important is to convey the martial prowess of the wearer of the uniform. Thus as one commentary on a prominent British Army discussion website puts it,

> Army stuff, it's great innit? Looking ally [Parachute Regiment slang for 'cool'] and that. But how does it all fit together? What goes in all those exciting pouches and pockets? How do you complete your ensemble so you look like a hollow-eyed Helmand veteran ...[93]

In this respect, uniform selection is a contextual activity. The most salient issue is not the technical features of the uniform but the social context of the artefact. The uniform says something about the 'otherness' of the person that wears it but also says something about their relative status in a particular social context, too.

There is no reason to assume that weapons are necessarily any different. When it comes to uniforms, as far as Professor Tony King is concerned there is no need to challenge the underlying science.[94] Instead, he takes on face value the effectiveness of the new types of camouflage and the methods that have been developed to assess it. By contrast, throughout this book I have shown that across a number of different dimensions, a seemingly closed and well-understood technology is subject to a number of contestable claims that frame the way it is interpreted. The science has not offered a way through the social processes that have been at play in the development and acquisition of small arms. Rather, what we have seen is how technologies are subject to powerful constituencies asserting their preferences and worldviews. In this respect, the FN Minimi instructively offers the means for tracing the arguments of these constituencies once the pretensions of science and technical evaluation have been stripped away.

The British Army's selection of the LMG following the Kosovo War certainly lends itself to this kind of analysis. In 1999, members of the Parachute

Regiment were given the Para version of FN Minimi as part of an Urgent Operational Requirement pushed through for Major-general Mike Jackson. Unlike the conventional Minimi, the Para version of the weapon had a telescopic stock and shortened barrel that reduced its overall length but facilitated movement and de-bussing from vehicles and aircraft. Putting aside the fact that a weapon with a shorter barrel and telescopic stock is usually less accurate—and is the reason why soldiers typically add an optical sight to the Minimi—the message went out to the rest of the Army that the best equipment was going to the elite regiments.

This mirrored a pattern of small arms acquisitions that occurred over the 1980s and 1990s by specialist teams in Britain's Royal Marines and Parachute Regiment. Instead of adopting the SA80 weapon system, these units selected the M16 or the Canadian equivalent built by Diemaco (now known as Colt Canada). This in turn followed a pattern of small arms acquisition that had been established by British Special Forces when they adopted the M16 in the 1960s for operations in Borneo, upgraded to the M16A2 and FN Mimimi in the 1980s and the C7/C8 Diemaco in the 1990s.[95] In effect, this produced two tiers of infantryman: the battle-hardened experts who were trusted with an M16 and the rest of the Green Army who had to make do with a weapon that did not work properly. Not only did this signify combat status but it also demonstrated that different parts of the Army had the organisational power to go their own way. To be elite meant to live by different rules and to have better kit.

To be elite also meant that soldiers had to be demonstrably aggressive or even warrior-like. This is reflected in a 'can do' culture where anything is possible and troops get on with things despite the difficulties they might face. In this respect, technology can either reinforce or hinder this cultural preference. Small arms that slow the tempo of battle by being too heavy, too unreliable or cannot be made available at the point of contact with the enemy will not fit a preference for 'cracking on'. The LMG's noise and its sustained fire capability when fitted with a hard plastic container for belted ammunition (colloquially known as the 'nutsack' by US soldiers) appeals to soldiers under great psychological stress. This chimed with a British study undertaken in 1995 into the psychological benefits of sustained, direct fire weapons. This showed that the benefits of sustained fire were not necessarily the effects on the enemy (although this may well also have occurred) but the confidence that was generated among the users who were firing the weapon.[96]

In terms of small arms, however, the focus on action also results in high ammunition usage.[97] In Afghanistan, for example, British forces fired 27 million rounds of 5.56mm ammunition at the Taliban over an eight-year period, equivalent to seven rounds every minute.[98] Even before the war in Afghanistan, evidence from the LMG trials conducted in Kenya suggested that ammunition usage would be high. During the trials, Sections initially ran out of ammunition before 'firing in the final assault'. Consequently, ammunition conservation drills had to be perfected and re-learnt so as to ensure troops would not waste rounds before the culminating point.[99] The weapon fits with a culture that values action and combat experience.

That is not to say that weapons necessarily form the most important status marker for the British Army. For example, Paul Higate argues that former British soldiers working as private military contractors (PMCs) do not view weapons as the main axis along which identity construction occurs. Instead, Higate observes that for British PMCs weapons are central to the identity of Americans who might overindulge in 'verbal diarrhoea about some fictional new weapon'.[100] Nonetheless, within the British Army itself, proficiency with firearms clearly does constitute a signifier of status and professionalism. And in this respect, the units that set the credibility markers for a piece of equipment are those units with the most combat experience. The values of these gatekeepers in turn help to shape equipment selection criteria for the whole of the Army.

Yet, paradoxically, while the Minimi clearly fits with an ethos that prizes action, the Army itself is having to pay even greater attention to force protection and minimising risks.[101] With regular numbers declining to their lowest levels since the early nineteenth century, it is clear that the infantry cannot afford to take casualties. Instead, soldiers are overburdened with a variety of protective measures, from osprey body armour to batteries for electronic countermeasures that prevent IED use. The result is that for every 5kg over 25kg being carried, soldiers can expect a decrease in the speed of movement by 0.1–0.2 km/h. Weight also undermines agility and limits the ability to sprint while producing cognitive effects in soldier's capacity to identify targets, fire small arms accurately and read maps.[102] Moreover, if soldiers are using different weapons with different ammunition, then the unit's commander can expect troops to fatigue at different rates.

The result of trying to relate a culture that values aggressive infantry tactics with a concern for force protection guarantees that only the very fittest of soldiers can be in the infantry. Closing with the enemy to engage targets below 300 metres demands a great deal from soldiers when they are carrying 30 kilos of gear. As a consequence, this has led to further demands for longer-ranged weapons and to the introduction of the L129A1 7.62mm Sharpshooter—recognised by soldiers to be a very Gucci piece of kit—which aims to provide soldiers with the capability to hit targets at medium ranges above 300 metres. From the perspective of soldier recruitment, it also has the effect of reducing the potential pool of prospective soldiers, and if taken to its logical extreme, can only have the effect of isolating and even alienating the elite regiments from wider civil society. Allowed to reach this extreme, the only means by which civil society might realistically understand the activities of these elite soldiers is through what one commentator describes as the 'militainment industry'.[103]

Paradoxically, then, while British soldiers talk about closing with the enemy, the Army's small arms choices may well just be reinforcing the Western tendency towards stand-off warfare.[104] Hyper-powers like the United States can afford to develop technologies that fill the half-kilometre gap created by poor manoeuvrability. By contrast, the British response typically has to be muscular in nature if the infantry's cultural ideal of closing with the enemy is to be achieved. One commentator argues that this reflects a shift in military temperament from heroic to post-heroic warfare.[105] According to this argument, whereas the mass armies of the twentieth century produced one or two highly effective soldiers per combat unit, in the wars of the twenty-first century professional armies train entire units to collectively orchestrate drills in an effort to increase effectiveness. Where this argument loses traction, however, is in the specificities of mapping military hardware to particular armies. The British Army, for instance, does not have the financial resources or the research capacity of the US military. As a result, the British Army has to either copy their American counterparts in the purchase and use of, for example, close support platforms like the Apache gunship helicopter, or place more stress on the combat soldier to make up for the technological gap.

In the first instance, this manifests itself in the British infantry section having to carry more and take a range of weapon systems with it to cover for the shortfall in capability. At the same time, in terms of military–technical change, the ambition to increase combat effectiveness by diversifying the range of small arms in the infantry section also has the effect of increasing the relative importance of the elite regiments in defining technology and tactics. This in turn attests to the concentration of power and changing status of the elite regiments within the Army and reflects the determination of the infantry to assert itself over engineers, scientists and bureaucrats.[106] Given the lack of trust in the engineer–soldier relationship and the way that expert advice is now substantially provided by private contractors, effective testing of elite regiment preferences by independently minded engineering and scientific staff is limited. Consequently, taxpayers, government and the rest of the Green Army become vulnerable to the marketing activities of manufacturers like Fabrique Nationale and Heckler & Koch, who find it easier to sell tricked out equipment to willing purchasers.

The manufacturers themselves have been very quick to identify new channels through which they can shape user preferences. In particular, manufacturers recognise that the best chance to influence future infantry needs is by direct selling to Special Forces. Both the American and British Special Forces communities have their own independent acquisition budgets, programmes and means of selection that in effect allow them to buy whatever they see fit. The result, as Peter Ratcliffe observes, is that in Britain:

> The SAS is the best equipped Regiment in the British Army. No other unit has better kit than we have. The system is brilliant; in effect, the Regiment has *carte blanche* on weapons purchase, and on all sorts of other equipment besides. Thus whatever the SAS wants, the SAS gets.[107]

This mirrors a pattern of weapon acquisition for US Special Forces. For example, in his description of the operation to kill/capture Osama Bin Laden, Mark Owen describes how US Navy SEAL Team Six were given free range to acquire the weapons that suited them personally.[108] This in turn is supported by an enormous industry of small arms trade fairs like the SHOT Show run every year by the US National Shooting Sports Foundation, where manufacturers can show off specialist devices to attract the attention of Special Forces.[109] Manufacturers and their sales teams go out of their way to give away small arms to potential buyers or take them on expensive days out and trips.[110] The result is that niche manufacturers can influence the most influential of communities who in turn frame the relative status and value of different equipment. Some in the United States would go further and argue that the approach leads to a stagnating innovation cycle within US small arms manufacturers and feeds the urge to gold-plate existing weapon systems rather than develop entirely new platforms.[111]

Moreover, because Special Forces 'coordinate and cooperate' with a range of agencies both domestic and foreign, it is clear that the equipment choices of one unit may well influence the preferences of another in a different country.[112] Thus when US Special Forces opted to replace the M-4 Carbine with Fabrique Nationale's Special Forces Combat Assault Rifle (SCAR) in both 7.62mm and 5.56mm in 2009, it did not take long before British forces started to argue for the same weapon.[113] Indeed, like their American counterparts, Britain's Royal Marines and Special Forces also started to argue for the SCAR. Conscious that user preferences can be shaped through these elite networks, manufacturers can now reach military consumers in ways that would previously have been impossible. The result may be that users get what they believe they need. However, they do so in a way that belies the interests of the manufacturers and not the views of a more considered acquisition process that also takes into account the interests of the taxpayer.

In this respect, the success of the modern arms industry lies in influencing the way elite user communities think about the weapons that they acquire. Recognising that Anglo-American Special Forces communities have their own acquisition processes and have a crucial role to play in defining what constitutes the best equipment within the wider Army, industry has identified another channel for creating user needs. At the same time, within the British Army at least, there has been a relative decline in the status of those engineers and scientists, operational researchers and civil servants who have over the past sixty years been instrumental in testing and substantiating the evidential basis for weapon selection. The result is that the democratic control over acquisition has declined relative to that of industry, which now uses its marketing power to assiduously shape the needs of the infantry.

Conclusion

Without a strong mediating influence on soldier preferences, manufacturers have ample opportunity to shape user needs. The result is that the only significant brake on the process is the government's willingness to pay. Inevitably, that leads to heated arguments geared around an imperative for soldiers to be armed with the very best equipment. This situation lends itself to arms manufacturers like Fabrique Nationale who have benefited from the relative changing status of the infantry compared with those expert professions who previously influenced weapon selection.

What might be considered the best equipment is nonetheless subject to considerable debate and interpretation among the user community itself. In this respect, it is not reasonable to characterise the effort to shape user preferences as the infantry being dominated by industry in a partial or one-sided manner.[114] A more precise description would observe that industry intentionally works within and finds ways to promote and sustain a framework in which elite regiments use their power to define what is best for the rest of the Green Army. This approach gives industry the opportunity to shape the terms of debate for the Army as a whole. In sociological terms, this 'concentration of military power' works as much in the domain of small arms as it does in relation to less obviously material factors like promotional opportunities.[115] The result is that weapons that might be appropriate for non-elite infantry regiments, weapons that might take into account the specificities of these units, their recruitment profiles and relative lack of expertise, tend to be overlooked in favour of equipment that benefits the interests of the elite units. Whether this is sound from the perspective of making the Army effective or more broadly ensures that the Army reflects the social make-up of civil society as a whole, is open to further discussion.

In an effort to illustrate how this state of affairs has come about in practice, this chapter explored a specific British Army case study and showed how between 1980 and 2010, soldiers' trust in engineering advice declined. This has been buttressed by the extensive use of private consulting engineers for the provision of technical advice. The knowledge that emerges from this process typically reflects the contractor's interest in getting repeated access to the Army customer rather than the considerations of a range of civil–military actors that have traditionally framed equipment choice. In this respect, an important enabler for the cultural changes that have shaped soldier preferences emerged out of the privatisation of Britain's defence manufactories in the mid-1980s.

In these circumstances, Britain's elite regiments have filled the vacuum produced by this relative decline in government expertise. Without strong analytical capability within the government, these units have used their privileged experience of the battlefield to shape soldier preferences. This has played a crucial role in reasserting the primacy of military judgement over those expert communities that quantify and analyse the battlefield.

Over the last twenty years, the driver of this process has been the Parachute Regiment—the archetypal light infantry unit. Not only have officers from this unit challenged the judgement of the engineer and scientist, but a number of highly influential officers have been instrumental in asserting the Regiment's status relative to those battalions that work in both a light and an armoured infantry role.[116] Of course, it would be wrong to suggest that the Parachute Regiment has been the sole arbiter of what constitutes military effectiveness in the British Army over the past twenty years. Nevertheless, the values of the elite regiments now dominate discussions of military effectiveness to such a great extent that it has become the cultural norm against which equipment choices are defined and new recruits selected.

In terms of military innovation, the declining importance of government engineers and scientists implies that military users are themselves the main drivers of change. This suggests that bottom-up innovation is indeed the order of the day. As we have seen, however, the preferences of soldiers can be manipulated through careful marketing by industry. By playing on the professionalism of the infantry, technological preferences can be shaped and fashions constructed. This can be particularly successful when technologies appeal to and fit within the military's existing markers of status. Given what we have learnt about the challenge of military–technical change over the last seven chapters, then, it remains an open question as to whether soldiers would be better served by having the support of more independently minded scientific and engineering professionals. For as it stands, there is little to stop industry taking advantage of the vacuum that has been created by the hollowing out of government expertise.

8

FROM THE MUNDANE TO THE SOPHISTICATED

MILITARY INNOVATION STUDIES AND THE QUESTION OF POWER

The dawn of the Atomic Age brought the scientist and the engineer to the heart of government.[1] As C. P. Snow astutely observed, the Ivy League-educated civil servant trained in the Classics now had to learn the language of the scientific advisors, the new boffins of the age.[2] Changes in personnel heralded significant changes in the management of the state. Operational research, mathematical calculation and scientific method replaced personal judgement. Interest groups could be managed through quantitative analysis. The best solution to a given problem could be established in an analysis of the numbers.

This left those who had previously exercised power through their organisational and personal status having to learn new ways to gain traction in bureaucratic debates. The result was typically an experiential gap between the 'facts' as established by the numbers and the preferences of those who had been in battle.[3] For the infantry, this proved particularly difficult. In Anglo-American armies, infantry officers were the least technical and the least likely to embrace the quantitative language of the new modes of discussion. The 'revolution in bureaucratic affairs' had the potential to leave the infantry with significantly less say than the more technical branches of the military over matters that affected their immediate professional status. With the arrival of the Atomic Age, the infantry had in effect reached the kind of horse and tank moment that the cavalry had faced during the inter-war period.

Thus the infantry have undergone a whole series of changes that have affected their professional status when compared with other actors in the small arms development and acquisition cycle. The First World War saw a perfection of fire and movement coordinated with artillery for suppression. This helped the infantry take and hold ground. Eclipsed in the Second World War by the combination and coordination of tanks, artillery and aircraft, the infantry's position relative to the other parts of the Army declined. Officer promotion in a Cold War army demanded an understanding of the technical details of war, something that officers from artillery and tank regiments could more readily offer. The Atomic Age had apparently left the infantry without a role in the defence of Europe other than to act as a trip wire for nuclear engagement.

Outside of Europe, the post-1945 experience of the British and American infantry was very different. In non-European environments, infantrymen contributed the mainstay of military capability in the defeat of post-colonial insurgencies and Communist-inspired insurrections, offering security as Britain withdrew from empire, and order as America sought to contain the Soviet threat. In effect, outside Europe, counterinsurgency ensured the ongoing relevance of the infantry even as other branches of the Army came to dominate tactical, operational and technological discussions inside the North Atlantic area.

Changes to the infantry's status within the Army were mirrored by its declining importance in weapon selection after the Second World War. Before 1914, a small circle of infantry officers and engineers were involved in defining small arms requirements. After the Second World War had ended, a new breed of interventionist engineers and scientists had inveigled their way into a process from which they had traditionally been marginalised. Engineers in particular started to assert a view of battle that sought to optimise technical choices as they might be framed in relation to battlefield datasets—datasets that the engineers themselves had gone out of their way to collect. The evidence that these engineers produced and the analysis that they undertook demonstrated that even more intervention in framing the needs of the infantry was required if war-winning technologies were to be given the opportunity to take their place in the inventory. They showed that soldiers were the weakest link in relation to weapon technologies that could be optimised for increased hit probability.

Scientists were recruited into this exercise so as to develop and deepen the evidence base that sustained the innovations of the engineers. Nourished by a broader culture change within Anglo-American bureaucracies that demanded quantitative evidence in support of weapons acquisition, scientists and engineers started to become powerful actors in the process of military–technical innovation. Anglo-American small arms communities may well have disagreed during the 1950s, but out of that disagreement it became clear that evidence was just one factor in the selection of equipment. If evidence was presented that did not fit within existing organisational preferences, engineers could either try to reframe the needs of the user community or assert their national perspective at the expense of argument for technological change. The NATO standardisation trial processes of the late 1970s show that the structural power of the United States could be used to shape technical outcomes at the expense of other countries. This in itself revealed the extent to which the scientific evidence was being affirmed through social processes.

In the face of this, we have seen that the infantry's response was to co-opt and shape the new approach to problem solving when the means for doing so presented itself. Engineers had identified that the infantry's shooting prowess was sub-optimal and therefore looked to reduce the importance of the solider in firing the weapon. Recognising this, the infantry's response was to select technologies that reaffirmed the importance of the individual soldier in the use of their weapon.

The small calibre, high velocity 5.56mm round and the M16 were particular instances of the American infantry defining its own vision of modernity and ignoring both the US Ordnance Corps and the work by the ORO. Once the Infantry Board had asserted its position on the tactical rationale for the M16, the extensive use of operational research provided by the ORO forced a change on the existing research and development processes that had been established by the Army chiefs and the US Ordnance Corps. However, the infantry ignored the ORO's unhelpful analysis that suggested automatic fire would not improve hit probability and selected the M16 anyway.

The result was a fudge whereby the infantry sought ways to protect their unique perspective on the battlefield by adopting a technology that might sustain the illusion that skilled riflemen were essential to increasing battlefield effectiveness. This has come back to haunt the US infantry who, without a general issue full-bore rifle like the M-1 or M-14, have had to create Squad Designated Marksmen. Intended to produce specialist infantrymen capable of hitting targets at longer range, doctrine revealed the difficulties of training soldiers to shoot out to 600 metres and thus exposed the limitations of the M16 and M-4 carbine.[4]

This kind of tactical challenge has played into the hands of arms manufacturers that can try to fill niche gaps in the military inventory. They have only managed to do this, however, because they have understood the tensions that emerged out of the relative change of status between the engineer, scientist and soldier. Over a number of chapters, I have described the approach adopted by Fabrique Nationale during the 1950s and 1970s. In the 1950s, FN was in the right place at the right time and was successful only after the British and Americans disagreed about ammunition calibre.

In the 1970s, FN's innovation strategy was to optimise an ammunition solution that had already emerged out of the research and development process in the 1960s. Consequently, they decided not to argue with the American approach to lethality, but to develop a round that would enhance their ongoing efforts to sell the FN Minimi to the US Army. With the end of the Cold War, however, a new FN strategy emerged. This involved more direct selling to the infantry community itself and represents yet another twist in the relationship between scientist, engineer and soldier; one that reflects the declining significance of government engineering expertise relative to that of the arms industry.

Since 2001, ten years of counterinsurgency have raised the prominence of the infantry as a profession within those NATO armies deployed to Iraq and Afghanistan. Professional drills, tactics and techniques are now the norm among regular units as much as they are for elite Special Forces. Under the guise of professionalism, this has fed the demand for niche weapon capabilities that further play into the marketing efforts of industry. The result is an increased interest among soldiers who believe a 'golf bag' approach, where different equipment is available for different types of operations, will ensure they can get the job done.

The military arguments that soldiers should be equipped with the same standard weapon type have thus been reversed. This mirrors an approach to small arms from non-Western armed forces. However, while the Kenyan Defence Forces, for example, are equipped with AK-47s and M16s, FN SCARs and FALs, H&K G3s, MP5s and MP7s for reasons to do with the availability of weapons, Western armed forces take the view that access to a wide range of small arms reflects their professional skill at arms. In both cases, the underlying reason for the propensity to buy different types of weapon is the infantryman's desire to look the part as much as it is to do the job. In this respect, weapon acquisition is as much about fashion as it is about effectiveness.

Yet, in the UK at least, the privatisation of government-owned defence industries has created the conditions for a fundamental breakdown of trust between the user and those state engineers who had previously provided the experienced analytical capacity to develop and evaluate equipment. The result has been to denude policymakers of the ability to appraise weapon choices in the light of a range of variables outside the immediate perceived military requirement. This has put the infantry in a much stronger position to dictate what equipment they will use in the future. Unfortunately, it also leaves the user community more vulnerable to the marketing efforts of the defence industry. Consequently, just as the Army itself feels most qualified to identify its own needs, the basis upon which those choices are being made has started to shift in favour of industry. In these circumstances, it is reasonable to conclude that the distribution of power in the military–industrial complex—certainly as far as the British are concerned—has now fundamentally shifted away from principles of democratic governance in favour of those framed by industry. Whether this represents a sensible posture from a grand strategic point of view is open to debate.

Military innovation studies and the question of power

So where does this detailed examination of small arms development leave us in relation to the original questions I posed about military innovation at the beginning of this book? Grint and Woolgar's anti-essentialist theory of technology may be counterintuitive for many who think of technologies having definite effects. Over the course of seven chapters, however, the approach has created the room to discuss military–technical change in ways that stretch well beyond the mainstream approaches to innovation I examined in Chapter 1. In particular, by taking the position that technology can be interpreted as a social construct, the kinds of reifications and bifurcations that I suggested typically creep into discussions of military–technical change, can be avoided. In the context of a number of communities looking to assert their professional status, weapon choice is contentious. It is clear that different actors in the innovation cycle work to unpick each other's perspectives in order to, among other things, assert their relative power. Acknowledging this and accounting for it in the organising principles for an investigation into the culture of innovation facilitates an analysis of power relations within the military–industrial complex.

By rights, however, the approach should also call into question the very categories I have used to examine small arms development. Indeed, although notions of marksmanship, firepower, willpower and stopping power are commonly recognised within shooter circles, as labels they are themselves reifications of complex socio-technical phenomena that in some ways mask the dynamic relations between weapon, engineer and soldier. While deconstructing the underpinning ideas that frame these terms, I have stuck to the recognised linguistic conventions for the sake of advancing an accessible and not overly theorised argument. For STS scholars, however, the approach might smack too greatly of treating the social and the technology as in some ways separate and that I am, therefore, reintroducing bifurcations or essentialist perspectives that do not do justice to the theory that has informed this study.

The specific application of the theory aside, as a heuristic approach for generating insights into the way that knowledge and power fold into sociotechnical change, Grint and Woolgar are considerably more appropriate to this investigation than alternative theoretical approaches in STS. It would be possible, for instance, to apply Actor Network Theory (ANT) to help us describe how various actors and technologies are enrolled into assemblages that align to produce circumstances which deliver socio-technical change.[5] In this respect, it would show how power was a product of those network arrangements. ANT would not, however, necessarily explain the relationships between actors in ways that showed how knowledge was produced for instrumental or, as I have described in Chapter 1, for professional purposes. As Grint and Woolgar observe, ANT relies on the possibility that networks are objectively describable and might therefore be considered neutral.[6] By contrast, this study has attempted to expose how knowledge about the capacities of artefacts is actively constructed in order to advance a particular perspective. In this respect, my goal has been to identify whose interpretation of weapon development we should believe and why.

Notwithstanding the technicalities of STS, the preceding chapters show that conventional approaches to military innovation studies fall short in their theorisation of military–technical change. By limiting their investigations to the top or the bottom of the military organisation, a whole series of social groups who have a part to play in the innovation cycle get left out of existing analyses. This stands in stark contrast to scholars of the military–industrial complex who have shown how change is not just a military preoccupation. Like David Edgerton, Tom McNaugher and Mary Kaldor, the preceding chapters have shown how civilian engineers, scientists, bureaucrats, analysts and industrialists are all involved in shaping socio-technical change. Compared to traditional approaches to military innovation, an investigation into military–technical change that applies an STS-type framework sets out to reveal the activities of these actors as a point of methodological principle.

There are similar limitations for those studies that invoke innovation culture. In these analyses, the goal has been to show how decisions are themselves framed by cultural values. This is a sensible ambition. As I outlined in Chapter 1, however, without a theoretical framework that avoids the twin philosophical challenge of technology as culture and culture as cause, these approaches struggle to explain the social processes that construct the value systems that frame weapon choice. In this respect, STS offers a toolset for thinking through the process and strategies by which one group or another gains autonomy and uses this for their professional advantage and social status.

A sociological enquiry into military innovation thus steps beyond a simple examination of military utility or effectiveness. It recognises that effectiveness is not fixed or predefined but is what different groups are arguing over. Instead, STS directs attention towards the way that power relationships between actors produce change through the fabrication of knowledge. The various narratives can then be mapped and the power relationships between actors identified. The artefact consequently becomes a metaphor for describing the changing balance of relationships between actors who apply all sorts of strategies for realising their professional objectives. Actors have a number of ways of framing outcomes. These range from the application of their structural power to refashioning choice through the careful manipulation of status anxiety. It is clear from an analysis of small arms development that, contrary to existing approaches to military innovation, change is not necessarily a bottom-up or top-down process. If anything, this book has shown that the source of military change comes from the middle-out. Engineers defined the future battlefield by developing an evidence base and building a viable technological solution. Users at the bottom of the organisation had little appreciation for the engineering possibilities, while generals at the top were focused on alternative ways for delivering victory. Whether all military–technical change follows a similar pattern would need to be shown empirically.

Nevertheless, in respect to this book, what we can say is that middle-out change did not emerge as a result of some recourse to scientific first principles. On the contrary, I show that science does not necessarily resolve socio-technical questions. Scientists found themselves enrolled into decision-making processes and used the opportunity to produce forms of knowledge that would contest existing analyses. Zuckerman claimed to have invented the field of wound ballistics. In the process, he unsettled existing evaluations and stirred up a scientific debate about wounding. None of this is properly accounted for in either Joanna Bourke's book on militarism and society, or Erik Prokosch's investigation into the evolution of anti-personnel weapons. As a consequence, they miss out key arguments in the history of wound ballistics, suggesting instead that the field has emerged along a single trajectory.[7]

When it comes to the technology of killing, then, the history of wound ballistics demonstrates that even an apparently binary phenomenon like life and death can produce multiple technological trajectories. For the fact of the matter is that the science was and remains contested. In these circumstances, the most fruitful way to interpret ballistic wounding is through an interdisciplinary prism that acknowledges the relevance of a number of sciences from medicine to international law, from physics to anatomy. Moreover, in the case of small arms ammunition, this prism must be further contextualised within national interpretations of these disciplines. By holding open all these possibilities, STS provides the methodological principles for critically thinking through a much wider range of perspectives on both the science and the technology of killing. In the process, it helps us to see how military innovation is itself considerably more problematic than most discussions concede.

From the mundane to the sophisticated

In light of my analysis of small arms, the question remains as to whether parallels can be drawn between mundane and sophisticated technology innovations. Advanced technologies now consume a vast proportion of the military budget. Some critics argue that this has now reached a point where, far from securing a country from attack, the expense and complexity of these technologies are themselves creating the conditions that potentially might lead to defeat in war.

Mark Urban, for instance, observes how the F-22 stealth fighter, at $377 million each, carries fewer air-to-air missiles than the planes it would replace. As the RAND Corporation observed in a 2008 study, the result is that in any confrontation with China, the F-22 would run out of missiles before it had destroyed a mass attack by conventional jets. Worse than this, Urban observes that, given the complexity of the F-22, the availability rate of these high-tech weapons might be in the region of 60 per cent of the total force in service.[8] With defence inflation reducing the affordability of high-tech systems, the result is fewer weapons to deter a potential enemy and a question mark over how to balance quantity and quality in procurement strategy.

By contrast, in the scheme of multi-billion dollar work programmes, small arms barely constitute a line item in the defence budget. Easily overlooked in favour of more expensive high-tech equipment that promises 'revolutionary' change to the battlefield, small arms typically only become the subject of politically contentious debate when they go wrong. Surprisingly, given the maturity of the technology, virtually every new Anglo-American infantry weapon that has come into service over the past 100 years has suffered from some kind of technical hiccup or controversy.

Bearing this in mind, one way of dodging this kind of controversy is to avoid developing new small arms. Advantageously, such a move also avoids unpicking existing socio-technical bargains between interested parties, bargains that at times may have been difficult to bring about. Thus, as of 2016 the US Army has once again decided not to replace the M-4 carbine and instead sought to bundle together a number of upgrade and improvement packages that would keep the weapon in service.[9] Wider organisational questions can be avoided, existing systems get gold-plated and incentives for developing totally new technologies are suppressed. When looked at in this way, there are clearly some asymmetries between mundane weapons like small arms and sophisticated technologies like the F-22. However, there also appear to be some echoes in the development trajectories that suggest it does make sense to use small arms innovation as a point of contrast with wider technology change.

Of course, part of the challenge of drawing analogies between mundane weapons like small arms and technologies like the F-22 stealth multirole fighter lies in the scale and complexity of these sophisticated systems of systems. The number of contractors and sub-contractors associated with large and complex weapons makes an analysis that takes into account the entire innovation cycle extremely hard. Nevertheless, an investigation into military innovation that does not take into account all these actors is unlikely to be complete. This is because weapon systems reflect and embed the values of those groups and constituencies who are engaged in their development.

Professional armed forces expect to have kit that maps to their sense of importance within civil–military relations. Utilitarian weapons may be cheap and reliable but they may also suggest that anyone can have them. Units with a strong military ethos will demand solutions that reflect their values. This applies as much to mundane as it does to sophisticated weapons. While this is well understood in procurement circles, changing the terms of debate to reflect strategic considerations beyond spreading around pork barrel spending takes considerable political sacrifice. In such circumstances, it is important to remain sensitive to the way technical knowledge is produced in order to advance the perspectives of powerful constituencies within the innovation cycle. Successful designs may well stabilise if they can conjoin values, doctrines or tactical preferences within user communities. Alternatively, a design might emerge that allows different user communities to continue working in ways that they prefer without dictating a particular battlefield solution on any one constituency. In both situations, the danger is that users don't understand the complexities of what they are asking for and thus requirements bloat in ways that engineers are asked to build something that defies the laws of physics. Unfortunately, this kind of solution works to the advantage of industry and the expense of the taxpayer and ultimately, should the system not work, the end user.

In the 1950s, President Eisenhower coined the term the military–industrial complex. At that time, democratically elected leaders with experience of warfare understood enough about simple technologies to more directly shape technical outcomes in ways that they believed reflected the strategic challenges facing their countries. In the UK, Winston Churchill asserted a democratic influence on the acquisition of small arms that has fashioned weapon choices right to the present day. Whether he was technically justified to overrule the experts is open to debate. As technology has become more complex, however, democratic decision-makers become more dependent on those that can interpret the implications of various technological choices. This clearly puts a lot of power in the hands of those responsible for developing these interpretations. Policymakers thus need to be attentive to the interests and concerns of commercial agencies beyond government, who are more committed to shareholder value than to the public interest. No doubt industry will continue to play an important role in providing the means to defend the state. However, if democratic principles and strategic sense are to prevail, then government needs to employ and empower more engineers to evaluate designs, educate users, model regulatory frameworks and shape policy formulation processes.

As it stands, however, private industry is much better placed to frame weapon choices. Indeed, an increasing reliance on the technical expertise of private industry corresponds with a decline in expertise within governments. Happy to exploit these advantages, industry itself is very aware of the benefits of upselling gold-plated, high-tech solutions to a user community that likes 'Gucci kit'. As a consequence, technological innovation, whether sophisticated or mundane, is as much subject to the whims of fashion as it is a mechanism for producing greater military effectiveness.

Table 5: Weapon Weights and Ammunition Types

Country: United Kingdom

Weapon	Rifle Weight	Ammunition	Bullet Weight
SMLE Mk3	4kg (8lbs 8oz)	.303 (7.7 x 56mm)	Mk7 = 11.27g
No.4 Rifle	4.1kg (9lbs)	.303 (7.7 x 56mm)	
Sten, MkII	3.kg (6lbs 6oz)	9 x 19mm	
Sterling Mk4, L2A3	2.72kg (6lbs)	9 x 19mm	
Bren Mk1	10.15kg (22lbs 3oz)	.303 (7.7 x 56mm)	
Bren Mk3	8.75kg (19lbs 3oz)	.303 (7.7 x 56mm)	
Bren L4	8.68kg (19lbs 1oz)	7.62 x 51mm	
FN MAG	11.79kg (26lbs)	7.62 x 51mm	Belgium SS77/1 = 9.3g (FN Herstal)
GPMG L7A2	10.9kg (24lbs)	7.62 x 51mm	UK L2A2 = 9.33g (BAE Systems RO Defence)
EM-2	3.3kg (7lbs 3oz)	.276 (aka .280) 7mm	Experimental = 9.09g
L1A1 SLR	4.3kg (9lbs 5oz)	7.62 x 51mm	
Enfield Weapon System	3.12kg (6lbs 9oz)	4.85 x 49mm	UK Experimental = 3.11g
SA80 IW L85	3.8kg (8lbs 4oz)	5.56 x 45mm	UK Ball L2A1 = 4g (BAE Systems RO Defence)
SA80 LSW L86	5.4kg (12lbs)	5.56 x 45mm	
LMG FN Minimi Para	7.14kg (15lbs 7oz)	5.56 x 45mm	

Country: United States

Weapon	Rifle Weight	Ammunition	Bullet Weight
Springfield M1903	3.9kg (8lbs 6oz)	.30'06 (7.62 x 63mm)	30–06 Springfield = 9.72g
Browning M1919	14kg (30lbs 9oz)	.30'06 (7.62 x 63mm)	
M1 Garand	2.36kg (5lbs 2oz)	.30'06 (7.62x63mm)	

M-14	5.1kg (11lbs 2oz)	.30 (7.62 x 51mm)	US T65 experimental = 7g US M80 Ball = 9.65g (Alliant Techsystems)
M16A1	2.9kg (6lbs 4oz)	5.56 x 45mm	US SS109/M855 = 4.02g (Alliant Techsystems) Swiss GP90 = 4.1g (RUAG Munition)
M16A2	3.4kg (7lbs 5oz)	5.56 x 45mm	
M4 Carbine	2.56kg (5lbs 6oz)	5.56 x 45mm	

Country: Germany

Weapon	*Rifle Weight*	*Ammunition*	*Bullet Weight*
H&K MG3	11.05kg (24lbs 3oz)	7.62 x 51mm	
H&K G3 fixed butt	4.4kg (9lbs 7oz)	7.62 x 51mm	
H&K G36	3.63kg (8lbs)	5.56 x 45mm	
H&K G11	3.8kg (8lbs 4oz)	4.75 x 33mm (caseless)	DM11—3.2g

Country: France

Weapon	*Rifle Weight*	*Ammunition*	*Bullet Weight*
FAMAS F1	3.61kg (7lbs 9oz)	5.56 x 45mm	
FUSIL MAS-49	4.7kg (10.4oz)	7.5 x 54mm	M1e 193 = 12.31g

Notes: It is not always possible to compare total ammunition size as it is reported differently in different sources. I have, therefore, chosen to quote bullet weight.

Also, in the final column I have only referenced bullet weight where there are obvious variations. Where easily identified, bullet weight is followed by ammunition manufacturer.

Sources:

Dugelby, T.B., *EM-2 Concept and Design*, Toronto: Collector Grade Publications, 1980.

Hogg, I.V., *The Greenhill Military Small Arms Data Book*, London: Greenhill Books, 1999.

Hogg, I.V. and J. Weeks, *Military Small Arms of the 20th Century*, London: Arms & Armour Press, 1991.

Hogg, I.V., *Jane's Directory of Military Small Arms Ammunition*, London: Jane's Publishing Co., 1985.

Jones, R. (ed.). *Jane's Infantry Weapons 2005–2006*. Coulsden: Jane's Information Group, 2005.

Jones, R. and A. White, *Jane's Guns Recognition Guide*, London: Collins, 2008.

Raw, S., *The Last Enfield: SA80; The Reluctant Rifle*, Cobourg: Collector Grade Publishing, 2003.

NOTES

INTRODUCTION: FROM MY COLD, DEAD HANDS

1. Abdul Hajji was the son of the former Kenyan defence minister; 'Terror in the Mall', *This World*, BBC documentary, first shown 21.00, 24 September 2014.
2. 'Terror in Westgate Mall: The Full Story of the Attacks That Devastated Kenya', *The Guardian*, 4 October 2013.
3. K. Jones, G. Macola and D. Welch (eds), *A Cultural History of Firearms in the Age of Empires*, Farnham: Ashgate, 2013; V. Farr, H. Myrttinen and A. Schnabel (eds), *Sexed Pistols: The Gendered Impacts of Small Arms and Light Weapons*, New York: United Nations University Press, 2009.
4. P.M. Barrett, *Glock: The Rise of America's Gun*, New York: Broadway Paperbacks, 2012.
5. J. Diamond, *Guns, Germs and Steel*, New York: Norton, 1997.
6. T. Diaz, *Making a Killing: The Business of Guns in America*, New York: The New Press, 2000; *The Last Gun: How Changes in the Gun Industry Are Killing Americans and What It Will Take to Stop It*, New York: The New Press, 2014.
7. For an excellent example of the social and technical challenges this presents in an early modern historical context, see K. Alder, *Engineering the Revolution: Arms and Enlightenment in France, 1763–1815*, Princeton: Princeton University Press, 1997.
8. D.F. Allsop and M.A. Toomey, *Small Arms: General Design*, Land Warfare, Brassey's New Battlefield Weapons Systems and Technology Series into the 21st Century, London: Brassey's, 1999.
9. C.J. Chivers, *The Gun*, New York: Simon & Schuster, 2011.
10. The most notable commentator on this is E. Ezell, *The Great Rifle Controversy: Search for the Ultimate Infantry Weapon from World War 2 through Vietnam and Beyond*, Harrisburg, PA: Stackpole Books, 1984.
11. S. Bidwell and D. Graham, *Fire-Power: British Army Weapons and Theories of War, 1904–1945*, London: George Allen & Unwin, 1982.

12. S. Biddle, *Military Power: Explaining Victory and Defeat in Modern Battle*, Princeton: Princeton University Press, 2004, pp. 28–51.

13. Ibid. p. 49.

14. R. Gilmore, '"The New Courage": Rifles and Soldier Individualism, 1876–1918', *Military Affairs*, 40, 3 (1976); A. Rose, *The American Rifle: A Biography*, New York: Delta, 2009.

15. M. Ward, 'Guns, Violence and Identity on the Trans-Appalachian American Frontier', in Jones, Macola, and Welch, *Cultural History of Firearms*.

16. Rose, *The American Rifle*, p. 286.

17. Chivers, *The Gun*.

18. S. Dyvik, '"Valhalla Rising": Gender, Embodiment and Experience in Military Memoirs', *Security Dialogue*, 47, 2 (2016).

19. 'The Gun That Killed Osama bin Laden Revealed', US News & World Report, 11 May 2011 (http://www.usnews.com/news/washington-whispers/articles/2011/05/11/the-gun-that-killed-osama-bin-laden-revealed; accessed 28 April 2014).

20. M. Shapiro, *Discourse, Culture, Violence*, Oxford: Routledge, 2012, p. 189.

21. C. Taylor, *Modern Social Imaginaries*, Durham, NC: Duke University Press, 2004, quoted in S. Lawson, 'Articulation, Antagonism, and Intercalation in Western Military Imaginaries', *Security Dialogue*, 42, 1 (2011), p. 41.

22. K. Grint and S. Woolgar, *The Machine at Work: Technology, Work, and Organization*, Cambridge: Polity Press, 1997, pp. 32–6.

23. Ibid. p. 36.

1. TECHNOLOGY AND CULTURE: GUNS AND INNOVATION

1. Carl Von Clausewitz, *On War*, trans. Michael Howard and Peter Paret, new edn, Everyman's Library, 121, London: Everyman, 1993, Book 4, Chapter XI.

2. The literatures on this are vast and will be explored in more detail in what follows. Some of the basic arguments, however, can be found in W. Murray, *Military Adaptation in War: With Fear of Change*, Cambridge: Cambridge University Press, 2011.

3. P. Porter, *The Global Village Myth: Distance, War and the Limits of Power*, London: Hurst, 2015, p. 167.

4. M.L.R. Smith and D. Martin Jones, *The Political Impossibility of Modern Counterinsurgency: Strategic Problems, Puzzles and Paradoxes*, New York: Columbia University Press, 2015.

5. James William Gibson, *The Perfect War: Technowar in Vietnam*, Boston: Atlantic Monthly Press, 2000.

6. T. McNaugher, *The M-16 Controversies: Military Organisations and Weapons Acquisition*, New York: Praeger, 1984.

7. M.C. Horowitz, *The Diffusion of Military Power: Causes and Consequences for International Politics*, Princeton: Princeton University Press, 2010.

8. A. Marshall, *Problems of Estimating Military Power*, Washington, DC: RAND, 1966.

9. Net Assessment, or versions of it, had been undertaken in US defense circles before. Robert McNamara, for instance, had used statistical analysis to establish the effectiveness of USAAF Bombing during the Second World War. After the war he had returned to business but upon his appointment as Secretary of Defense he encountered Alain Enthoven who had been in RAND in the 1950s. McNamara worked with Enthoven to bring more RAND analysts into the DoD so as to entrench the analytical study of military problems in defense circles.

10. W. Murray and A.R. Millett, *Calculations: Net Assessment and the Coming of World War II*, New York: Free Press, 1992, p. 1.

11. R. Martinage, *Toward a New Offset Strategy: Exploiting US Long-Term Advantages to Restore US Global Power Projection Capability*, Washington, DC: Center for Strategy and Budgetary Assessments, 2014, p. 13.

12. For more on the US military's attitude to technology, see T. Mahnken, *Technology and the American Way of Warfare since 1945*, New York: Columbia University Press, 2008.

13. A. Grissom, 'The Future of Military Innovation Studies', *Journal of Strategic Studies*, 29, 5 (2006), p. 907.

14. Marshall, *Problems of Estimating Military Power*.

15. Ibid. pp. 20–1.

16. A.R. Millett and W. Murray (eds), *Military Effectiveness, Volume 1: The First World War*, Boston: Allen & Unwin, 1988; *Military Effectiveness, Volume 2: The Interwar Period*, Boston: Allen & Unwin, 1988; *Military Effectiveness, Volume 3: The Second World War*, Boston: Allen & Unwin, 1988.

17. *Military Effectiveness, Volume 1*, p. 2.

18. Ibid. p. 27.

19. Grissom, 'The Future of Military Innovation Studies'.

20. The literatures on this are diverse and wide ranging and are not summarised here. In the footnotes below, I only outline the most significant contributions to the field. For a very good exposition of the range of literature in this field, see ibid.

21. B.R. Posen, *The Sources of Military Doctrine: France, Britain, and Germany between the World Wars*, Cornell Studies in Security Affairs, Ithaca: Cornell University Press, 1984. D. Avant, *Political Institutions and Military Change: Lessons from Peripheral Wars*, Cornell Studies in Security Affairs, Ithaca: Cornell University Press, 1994.

22. For example, H. Sapolsky, *Polaris System Development: Bureaucratic and Programmatic Success in Government*, Cambridge, MA: Harvard University Press, 1972. A. Bacevich, *The Pentomic Era: The US Army between Korea and Vietnam*, Washington, DC: National Defense University Press, 1986.

23. S. Rosen, *Winning the Next War: Innovation in the Modern Military*, Ithaca, NY: Cornell University Press, 1991.

24. Adam Grissom was the first to make this observation. See, Grissom, 'The Future of Military Innovation Studies'.

25. J.A. Russell, *Innovation, Transformation and War*, Stanford: Stanford University Press, 2011; T. Farrell, F.P.B. Osinga and J. Russell, *Military Adaptation in Afghanistan*, Stanford: Stanford University Press, 2013.

26. C. Serena, *A Revolution in Military Adaptation: The US Army in the Iraq War*, Washington, DC: Georgetown University Press, 2011.

27. T. Farrell and T. Terriff (eds), *The Sources of Military Change: Culture, Politics, Technology*, London: Lynne Rienner, 2002, p. 6.

28. Farrell, Osinga and Russell, *Military Adaptation in Afghanistan*, p. 7.

29. G. Gentile, 'A Strategy of Tactics: Population-Centric COIN and the Army', *Parameters*, XXXIX, 3 (2009); *A Wrong Turn: America's Deadly Embrace of Counterinsurgency*, New York: The New Press, 2013.

30. This is certainly the view of Lieutenant General H.R. McMaster Jr, deputy general/futures director, Army Capabilities Integration Center. See 'Army Must Stop Banking on "Leap Ahead" Technology', Military.com, 1 April 2015 (http://www.military.com/daily-news/2015/04/01/general-says-army-must-stop-banking-on-leap-ahead-technology.html; accessed 2 August 2015).

31. Murray, *Military Adaptation in War*, p. 3. There is a large literature that takes this idea as a cue for explaining why armed forces may resist socio-technical change.

32. D. Armstrong, *Bullets and Bureaucrats: The Machine Gun and the United States Army, 1861–1916*, London: Greenwood Press, 1982; John Ellis, *The Social History of the Machine Gun*, London: Pimlico, 1976.

33. T. Mahnken, *Uncovering Ways of War: US Intelligence and Foreign Military Innovation*, Ithaca, NY: Cornell University Press, 2002, pp. 101–9.

34. E. Kier, 'Culture and Military Doctrine: France between the Wars', *International Security*, 19, 4 (1995); *Imagining War: French and British Military Doctrine between the Wars*, Princeton: Princeton University Press, 1997.

35. Farrell and Terriff, *The Sources of Military Change*, p. 7.

36. A. Swidler, 'Culture in Action: Symbols and Strategies', *American Sociological Review*, 51, 2 (1986), p. 1.

37. Adamsky, *The Culture of Military Innovation*, p. 10.

38. Wiebe E. Bijker, 'Social Construction of Facts and Artefacts', in Wiebe E. Bijker, Thomas Hughes and T. Pinch (eds), *The Social Construction of Technological Systems*, Cambridge, MA: MIT Press, 1989; Wiebe E. Bijker and John Law (eds), *Shaping Technology/Building Society: Studies in Sociotechnical Change*, Inside Technology, Cambridge, MA: MIT Press, 1992; Donald A. MacKenzie and Judy Wajcman (eds), *The Social Shaping of Technology: How the Refrigerator Got Its Hum*, 2nd edn, Milton Keynes: Open University Press, 1999.

39. For examples of SST in a military setting, see D. MacKenzie, *Inventing Accuracy: A Historical Sociology of Nuclear Missile Guidance*, Cambridge, MA: MIT Press,

1990; D. Mackenzie and G. Spinardi, 'The Shaping of Nuclear-Weapon System Technology: United States Fleet Ballistic-Missile Guidance and Navigation, II: Going for Broke: The Path to Trident', *Social Studies of Science*, 18, 4 (1988); Timothy Moy, *War Machines: Transforming Technologies in the U.S. Military, 1920–1940*, College Station: Texas A & M University Press, 2001; J. Fallows, 'The American Army and the M16', in MacKenzie and Wajcman, *The Social Shaping of Technology.*

40. For more on relevant social groups, see Wiebe E. Bijker, *Of Bicycles, Bakelites, and Bulbs: Toward a Theory of Sociotechnical Change*, Inside Technology Series, Cambridge, MA: MIT Press, 1995.

41. This is derived from the empirical programme of relativism, see D. Bloor, *Knowledge and Social Imagery*, Chicago: University of Chicago Press, 1976.

42. Bijker, *Of Bicycles, Bakelites, and Bulbs*, pp. 26–8.

43. Lawson, 'Articulation, Antagonism, and Intercalation'.

44. N. Gilby, *Deception in High Places: A History of Bribery in Britain's Arms Trade*, London: Pluto Books, 2014.

45. For a good overview of the early debates on the Military Industrial Complex, see C.C. Moskos, 'The Concept of the Military-Industrial Complex: Radical Critique or Liberal Bogey?', *Social Problems*, 21, 4 (1974).

46. For example, see W.D. Hartung, *Prophets of War: Lockheed Martin and the Making of the Military-Industrial Complex*, New York: Nation Books, 2011; N. Turse, *The Complex*, London: Faber & Faber, 2008. P.W. Singer, 'Corporate Warriors: The Rise of the Privatized Military Industry and Its Ramifications for International Security', *International Security*, 26, 3 (2001); Eugenio Cusumano, 'Bridging the Gap: Mobilisation Constraints and Contractor Support to US and UK Military Operations', *Journal of Strategic Studies* (2015).

47. M. Kaldor, *The Baroque Arsenal*, London: Andre Deutsch, 1982.

48. T. McNaugher, 'Weapons Procurement: The Futility of Reform', *International Security*, 12, 2 (1987).

49. Ibid. p. 101.

50. Thomas L. McNaugher, *New Weapons, Old Politics: Americas Military Procurement Muddle*, Washington, DC: Brookings Institution, 1989, p. 6.

51. T. Farrell, 'Weapons Without a Cause: Buying Stealth Bombers the American Way', *Arms Control*, 14, 2 (1993); *Weapons Without Cause: The Politics of Weapons Acquisition in the United States*, New York: St. Martin's Press, 1997.

52. E. Prokosch, *The Technology of Killing: A Military and Political History of Anti-personnel Weapons*, London: Zed Books, 1995. David Edgerton, *Warfare State: Britain, 1920–1970*, Cambridge: Cambridge University Press, 2006.

53. M.E. O'Hanlon, *The Science of War: Defense Budgeting, Military Technology, Logistics and Combat Outcomes*, Princeton: Princeton University Press, 2009;

p. Dombrowski and E. Gholz, *Buying Military Transformation: Technology Innovation and the Defense Industry*, New York: Columbia University Press, 2003.

54. M.S. Larson, *The Rise of Professionalism: A Sociological Analysis*, Berkeley: University of California Press, 1979, p. xii.

55. Ibid. p. 181.

56. Grint and Woolgar, *The Machine at Work*, pp. 32–6.

57. The process by which this happens is fully explored in Chapter 7. See S. Lukes, *Power: A Radical View*, 2nd edn, Basingstoke: Palgrave Macmillan, 2005.

58. M. Hard, 'Beyond Harmony and Consensus: A Social-Conflict Approach to Technology', *Science Technology & Human Values*, 18, 4 (1993), pp. 408–32.

59. Michel Foucault, *Power/Knowledge: Selected Interviews and Other Writings, 1972–1977*, 1st American edn, New York: Pantheon Books, 1980, p. 131.

2. BATTLEFIELD DEMANDS: THE VIEWS OF THE INFANTRY

1. Sydney Jary, *18 Platoon*, 4th edn, Bristol: Sydney Jary, 1998, p. 31.

2. T. O'Brien, *If I Die in a Combat Zone*, London: Granada Publishing, 1973, p. 159.

3. See Joanna Bourke, *An Intimate History of Killing: Face-to-Face Killing in Twentieth-Century Warfare*, London: Granta, 1999, p. 1. Quote from J. Hockey, *Squaddies: A Portrait of a Subculture*, Exeter: Exeter University Press, 1986, p. 106.

4. Mutiny has affected virtually every armed force at some point, including the British, the French and the American. See, for instance, S. David, *Mutiny at Salerno: An Injustice Exposed*, London: Conway Maritime Press, 2005.

5. G. Lepre, *Fragging: Why US Soldiers Assaulted Their Officers in Vietnam*, Lubbock: Texas Tech University Press, 2011. Interview with Mr Henk Visser, Wassenaar, the Netherlands, 23 September 2004. Mr Visser was part of a team trying to sell mini-grenades to the US Marine Corps. The opportunity fell through in part because the Marines were concerned about the form factor of the grenade and the ease with which it might be concealed. See also 'Interview with Henk Visser: Part II', *Small Arms Review* (April 2006).

6. D. French, *Military Identities: The Regimental System, the British Army, and the British People, c.1870–2000*, Oxford: Oxford University Press, 2005.

7. M. Ford, 'Towards a Revolution in Firepower? Logistics, Lethality, and the Lee-Metford', *War in History*, 20, 3 (2013).

8. M. Asher, *Shoot to Kill: A Soldier's Journey through Violence*, London: Cassell Military, 2004, p. 30.

9. See, for example, R. Holmes, *Acts of War: The Behaviour of Men in Battle*, London: Weidenfeld & Nicolson, 2003, pp. 1–7. Ardant du Picq, *Battle Studies*, trans. Colonel John N. Greely and Major Robert C. Cotton, New York: Macmillan, 1921; D. Grossman, *On Killing: The Psychological Cost of Learning to Kill in War and Society*, A Black Bay Book, Boston: Little, Brown and Company, 1996; Clausewitz,

On War. The issue also raises ontological questions; see T. Barkawi and S. Brighton, 'Powers of War: Fighting, Knowledge, and Critique', *International Political Sociology*, 5, 2 (2011).

10. Holmes, *Acts of War*, p. 155.

11. E. Simpson, *War from the Ground up: 21st-Century Combat as Politics*, London: Hurst, 2013, p. 22.

12. A. King, *The Combat Soldier: Infantry Tactics and Cohesion in the Twentieth and Twenty-First Centuries*, Oxford: Oxford University Press, 2013, p. 19.

13. 'Summary: Status NATO Second Round Standard Ammunition', 3 September 1980, loose papers, Ezell Archive, Cranfield University, UK.

14. F. Fukuyama, *State-Building: Governance and World Order in the 21st Century*, London: Profile Books, 2005, p. 74.

15. A defensive formation in which soldiers fixed bayonets to create a wall of sharp objects that horses would be afraid of running into. By arranging themselves into square, soldiers could protect the backs of their comrades by preventing cavalry from reaching the middle. The classic example of this can be seen in the 1970 classic film, *Waterloo*, directed by Sergei Bondarchuk.

16. R. Holmes, *Redcoat: The British Soldier in the Age of Horse and Musket*, London: HarperCollins, 2002, pp. 43–4. J.F.C. Fuller, *Sir John Moore's System of Training*, London: Hutchinson & Co, 1925, pp. 221–2.

17. J.F.C. Fuller, *British Light Infantry in the Eighteenth Century (An Introduction to 'Sir John Moore's System of Training')*, London: Hutchinson, 1925, p. 232.

18. Hansard, HC (series 3), vol. 49, col. 212.

19. R. Challener, *The French Theory of the Nation in Arms, 1866–1939*, New York: Columbia University Press, 1955; p. Griffith, *Forward into Battle: Fighting Tactics from Waterloo to the Near Future*, revised and updated edn, Novato, CA: Presidio, 1991, pp. 59–67.

20. For example, the Admiralty noted that investigations into magazine arms had started with the French Navy. This prompted the Royal Navy to investigate these weapons in a way that the British Army had previously proven to be reluctant. See Committee on Machine Guns, War Office 1880, 2nd Progress Report, 1879 533 (200) AAA, RAA. See also 'Trial of Magazine Rifles in England', a Memorandum by Colonel C.G. Slade, Rifle Brigade, 7 February 1887, RAA. It should be noted that the Kropatschek Rifle introduced into France was initially a weapon given to the French Navy as *Le Fusil De Marine A Répétition Kropatschek Mle* 1878.

21. For example, in Britain the magazine arm was given its first proper hearing by a Small Arms Committee investigating machine guns for the Navy. Captain P.H. Colomb, RN, identified early on that the magazine arms might become useful to the Royal Navy and the Army and subsequently the British Army investigated the weapon. However, senior Army officers were cautious about the weapon. See Ford, 'Towards a Revolution in Firepower?', p. 282. Captain (later Vice-Admiral)

Colomb was a renowned innovator who pioneered new tactics and signals communications for the Royal Navy as it entered the steam age.

22. S. Jones, *From Boer War to World War: Tactical Reform of the British Army, 1902–1914*, Norman: Oklahoma University Press, 2012.

23. J. Boff, *Winning and Losing on the Western Front: The British Third Army and the Defeat of Germany in 1918*, Cambridge: Cambridge University Press, 2012.

24. P. Griffith, *Battle Tactics of the Western Front: The British Army's Art of Attack, 1916–1918*, London: Yale University Press, 1996, pp. 120–34. David Armstrong argues that institutional and organisational factors similarly undermined the American Army's willingness to introduce the machine gun before and during the First World War. See Armstrong, *Bullets and Bureaucrats*.

25. P. Cornish, *Machine Guns and the Great War*, Barnsley: Pen & Sword, 2009, pp. 78–85.

26. I am grateful to Dr Tim Gale for this insight.

27. See, for example, 'Final Report by the Committee on Automatic Rifles', 1914, 200 (200), Small Arms General Box 2, Royal Armouries Museum Archive (RAA) & WO 33/667, The National Archives (TNA), UK.

28. For the date on which the SMLE was accepted into service, see List of Changes, LC. 11947, RAA.

29. M. Ford, 'Marksmanship, Officer–Man Relations and the Short Magazine Lee-Enfield', *War in History*, 23, 3 (2016).

30. R. Johnson, *The Afghan Way of War: Culture and Pragmatism; A Critical History*, London: Hurst, 2011, pp. 149–74.

31. J. Lee, *A Soldier's Life: General Sir Ian Hamilton, 1853–1947*, London: Pan Books, 2000.

32. 'Musketry in India', *The Broad Arrow: A Paper for the Services*, 16 July 1892, Hamilton Papers, 17/3/2, Liddell Hart Centre for Military Archives (LHCMA).

33. Letter entitled 'Carbine in Lieu of the Rifle', from CISA to IGO, 20 December 1895, SUPP 6–651, TNA.

34. This was according to Sir Henry Brackenbury, then DGO and good friend to Wolseley. See Arnold Forster Papers, 50315, BL.

35. Ford, 'Marksmanship, Officer–Man Relations and the Short Magazine Lee-Enfield'.

36. For an excellent study of the Mounted Infantry, see A. Winrow, 'The British Regular Mounted Infantry, 1880–1913: Cavalry of Poverty or Victorian Paradigm?', PhD thesis, University of Buckingham, 2014.

37. Jones, *From Boer War to World War*, pp. 170–90. S. Badsey, 'The Boer War (1899–1902) and British Cavalry Doctrine: A Re-Evaluation', *Journal of Military History*, 71, 1 (2007); G. Phillips, 'Scapegoat Arm: Twentieth-Century Cavalry in Anglophone Historiography', *Journal of Military History*, 71, 1 (2007); J. Bou, 'Cavalry, Firepower, and Swords: The Australian Light Horse and the Tactical

Lessons of Cavalry Operations in Palestine, 1916–1918', *Journal of Military History*, 71, 1 (2007).

38. The literature on the attitude of the Cavalry to the firepower-intensive battle has grown significantly. See, for example, S. Badsey, *Doctrine and Reform in the British Cavalry, 1880–1918*, Aldershot: Ashgate, 2008; 'The Boer War (1899–1902) and British Cavalry Doctrine: A Re-Evaluation'; Bou, 'Cavalry, Firepower, and Swords'; G. Phillips, 'Scapegoat Arm: Twentieth-Century Cavalry in Anglophone Historiography'.

39. .30'06 ammunition is .30" calibre and first adopted in the United States in 1906.

40. McNaugher, *The M-16 Controversies*, p. 32.

41. Gilmore, '"The New Courage"'.

42. As an example of the changing attitude towards marksmanship in the French Army, French tank crews had abandoned aimed fire by 1918 and concentrated on area fire. I am indebted to Dr Tim Gale for this insight.

43. McNaugher, *The M-16 Controversies*, pp. 25, 27.

44. Ibid. pp. 25–9.

45. Ezell, *The Great Rifle Controversy*, p. 24.

46. McNaugher, *The M-16 Controversies*, p. 30.

47. Ezell, *The Great Rifle Controversy*, p. 29.

48. McNaugher, *The M-16 Controversies*, p. 31.

49. Ezell, *The Great Rifle Controversy*, pp. 29–32.

50. McNaugher, *The M-16 Controversies*, p. 31.

51. Ibid.

52. Ibid.

53. Ezell, *The Great Rifle Controversy*, p. 30.

54. Ibid. p. 33.

55. Compared to the SMLE, the No. 4 was designed for mass production. While the two weapons have very similar forms and share similar tactical ambitions, the SMLE shares no standard parts with the No. 4 Rifle. However, the weapon had the virtue of not opening up further discussion on small arms. Like the US Army, the British also carried out examinations of semiautomatic rifles in the early 1930s. In the British case, it was decided not to make the change. See Minute 1244, Small Arms Committee, 26 October 1932, RAA.

56. M.M. Postan, D. Hay and J.D. Scott, *Design and Development of Weapons: Studies in Government and Industrial Organisation*, History of the Second World War, United Kingdom Civil Series, London: H.M. Stationery Office, 1964, p. 357.

57. David Penn has a different perspective on the Stg44 and argues that 'the Stg44 was not so much a compromise as a niche weapon designed to outrange the PPSh41 SMG, and provide ease of use and firepower in extreme weather conditions'. David Penn, honorary historical consultant to the Royal Armouries, private email correspondence, 28 October 2015.

58. M. Van Creveld, *Fighting Power: German and US Army Performance, 1939–1945*, Westport, CT: Greenwood Press, 1982, p. 5.

59. Carlo D'Este, *Decision in Normandy*, Classic Military History, London: Penguin, 2001; M. Hastings, *Overlord: D-Day and the Battle for Normandy 1944*, London: Macmillan, 1993. This view has been subject to a great deal of criticism in J. Buckley, *Monty's Men: The British Army and the Liberation of Europe*, New Haven: Yale University Press, 2013.

60. See T.H. Place, 'Lionel Wigram, Battle Drill and the British Army in the Second World War', *War in History*, 7, 4 (2000); M. Ford, 'Operational Research, Military Judgement and the Politics of Technical Change in the British Infantry, 1943–1953', *Journal of Strategic Studies*, 32, 6 (2009).

61. D. French, *Raising Churchill's Army: The British Army and the War against Germany, 1919–1945*, Oxford: Oxford University Press, 2000, p. 71.

62. RAA, 120 Meetings—Conferences (Future Design of Weapons)—Box 2, Meeting of the Standing Committee on Infantry Weapon Development. Memo circulated by DInf on the objectives of the Standing Committee, 30 May 1943.

63. RAA, 120 Meetings—Conferences (Future Design of Weapons)—Box 2, Meeting of the Standing Committee on Infantry Weapon Development, 1 September 1943.

64. Wigram's experiences of Italy are described in very interesting detail in Denis Forman, *To Reason Why*, London: Abacus, 1993.

65. Details of the techniques taught can be found in L. Wigram, *(Infantry) Battle School (1941): A Detailed Description of the Evolution of Battle Drill Training in Its Early Stages*, Cambridge: John Bodsworth, 2005; T.H. Place, *Military Training in the British Army, 1940–1944: From Dunkirk to D-Day*, London: Frank Cass, 2000, p. 170.

66. T.N.F. Wilson, 'The Role of the Infantry', *J RUSI*, 89 (1944), p. 2.

67. Ibid.

68. The Sten was designed by Colonel Shepherd and Mr Turpin. As per tradition, the first two letters of the weapon's name were taken from the first letters of the surnames of those who had designed it, while the EN represented Enfield—the location of the RSAF. Similarly, the Bren LMG got its name from the factory in Czechoslovakia in Brno and the Small Arms factory at Enfield.

69. Indeed, in 1944 it was recognised that the main role of the infantry section in the attack had mainly been concerned with carrying the Bren gun ammunition. See TNA, WO 204/1895, 'Points Raised by Delegates, Infantry Training Conference', 23 April 1944.

70. See Laurier Centre for Military, Strategic and Disarmament Studies, Wilfrid Laurier University, Canada (LCMSDS), Shephard Papers Box 2—File 00028, Army Operational Research Group (AORG) memoranda 'The Fire-Power of the Infantry Section'; and TNA, WO 291/473, AORG Memo 125, interim report on performance of bullet weapons.

71. See, LCMDS, Shephard Papers Box 2—File 00028, AORG memoranda 'Infantry Battle' and 'The Fire-Power of the Infantry Section'.

72. A number of self-loading and automatic rifles were investigated. See Ford, 'Operational Research, Military Judgement and the Politics of Technical Change in the British Infantry'.

73. Report to Brigadier Kenchington, Directorate of Military Training, North African Forces (cc. Brigadier Cooney, deputy director military training, War Office) from Lieutenant Colonel Wigram, 17 August 1943, found in Forman, *To Reason Why*, p. 199.

74. Ibid.

75. Ibid. p. 72. Tragically, Wigram was later killed in action in Italy. I am grateful to William F. Owen for discussions on this point. Private email correspondence, 3 December 2015.

76. Ibid. p. 206.

77. The historiography on British command culture is contested and generally poorly researched. However, an excellent survey, which effectively challenges the received view of British command culture, can be found in Patrick Rose, 'Allies at War: British and US Army Command Culture in the Italian Campaign, 1943–1944', *Journal of Strategic Studies*, 36, 1 (2013).

78. Buckley, *Monty's Men*, p. 23.

79. S. Hart, *Montgomery and 'Colossal Cracks': The 21st Army Group in Northwest Europe, 1944–45*, Praeger Series in War Studies, Westport, CT: Praeger, 2000.

80. French, *Raising Churchill's Army*, p. 22.

81. Rose, 'Allies at War'. See also French, *Raising Churchill's Army*, pp. 212–73.

82. Buckley, *Monty's Men*, p. 38.

83. Michael D. Doubler, *Closing with the Enemy: How GIs Fought the War in Europe, 1944–1945*, Modern War Studies, Lawrence, KS: University Press of Kansas, 1994.

84. See F. Smoler, 'The Secrets of the Soldiers Who Didn't Shoot', *American Heritage*, 40, 2 (1989); R.J. Spiller, 'S.L.A. Marshall and the Ratio of Fire', *Journal of the Royal United Services Institute* (Winter 1988); J.W. Chambers, 'S.L.A. Marshall's Men against Fire: New Evidence Regarding Fire Ratios', *Parameters* (Autumn 2003). More recently, contemporary scholars have fundamentally disagreed on the value of Marshall's work. See Buckley, *Monty's Men*, p. 10. King, *The Combat Soldier*, p. 51.

85. S.L.A. Marshall, *Men Against Fire: The Problem of Battle Command*, revised 2nd edn, Norman: University of Oklahoma Press, 2000, p. 56.

86. Ibid. p. 78.

87. Ibid. p. 56.

88. Ibid. p. 60.

89. Jeremy Crang describes how this worked for the British Army in J. Crang, *The British Army and the People's War, 1939–1945*, Manchester: Manchester University

Press, 2000. In a similar vein, the American sociologist Sam Stouffer shaped approaches to training and maintenance of morale through extensive attitudinal surveys; see S.A. Stouffer, *The American Soldier*, Princeton: Princeton University Press, 1949.

90. See, for example, M. Janowitz and E.A. Shils, 'Cohesion and Disintegration in the Wehrmacht in World War II', *Public Opinion Quarterly*, 12 (1948).

91. McNaugher, *The M-16 Controversies*, p. 35.

92. B.P. Kneubuehl et al. (eds), *Wound Ballistics: Basics and Applications*, Berlin: Springer, 2008, p. 92.

93. McNaugher, *The M-16 Controversies*, p. 33.

94. Wound Ballistics Report, Bougainville Campaign, 1944, pp. 16–15, 69–82, Army Heritage and Education Center, Carlisle Barracks, United States.

95. Allsop and Toomey, *Small Arms*, p. 36.

96. 'Report on Comparative Trial of Enfield Martini and Rubini Rifles 1887', pp. 24–5.

97. S.M. Russell, *Soldier Perspectives on Small Arms in Combat*, Alexandria, VA: Center for Naval Analysis, 2006, p. 29.

98. N. Drummond and A. Williams, 'Time to Bite the Bullet over Under-Fire Ammo', *Jane's Defence Weekly* (2009); T.P. Ehrhart, *Increasing Small Arms Lethality in Afghanistan: Taking Back the Infantry Half-Kilometer*, Fort Leavenworth: School of Advanced Military Studies (SAMS), 2009; J.P. Avery, 'An Army Outgunned: Physics Demands a New Basic Combat Weapon', *Military Review*, XCII (July–August 2012).

99. W.F. Owen, 'True but Irrelevant: Small Arms Performance in Afghanistan', *RUSI Defence Systems*, 12, 3 (2010).

3. ENGINEERING THE BATTLEFIELD: DEFINING THE REQUIREMENT

1. C.P. Snow, *The Two Cultures: And a Second Look; An Expanded Version of the Two Cultures and the Scientific Revolution*, 2nd edn, Cambridge: Cambridge University Press, 1964, p. 32.

2. See 'Summary and Consolidated Report by WTSFF on Infantry Questionnaire and Answers from Units in First and Eighth Armies on Conclusion of N. African Campaign', May 1943, RAA, 200 Small Arms General Box 1.

3. Ibid.

4. 'Extracts from Reports by Officers Commanding Units in South Africa during 1899–1901', 200 Small Arms General Box 1, RAA.

5. 'Weapon Analysis of Patrols and Ambushes', Memorandum no. 4/53, 23 June 1953, Operational Research Section (Malaya), WO 291/1729, TNA.

6. 'Report of the M16 Rifle Review Panel: Appendix 7, M16 Surveys in the Republic of Vietnam', United States, 1 June 1968, pp. 7–28

7. 'Royal Small Arms Factory, Rifle Design Study Day', 20 January 1975, pp. 31–7, 121 Design of Weapons Box 1, RAA.

8. R.J. Smillie and T.E. Chitwood Jr, 'Literature Review: Army Training: M16A1 Rifle, TOW, and DRAGON Weapon Systems', US Army Research Institute for the Behavioral and Social Sciences, January 1986.

9. The British tabloid, *The Sun*, broke the story in June 2002. See, 'Army Gun Jam in Afghan Test', *The Sun*, 28 June 2002.

10. 'Marines Blamed for Rifle Failure', *The Telegraph*, 21 July 2002.

11. 'Gerald Howarth to Ask the Secretary of State for Defence', House of Commons, Hansard, Written Answers to Questions, vol. 389, part 183, 22 July 2002.

12. John Law and Michel Callon describe this process in relation to the development of military aircraft. See J. Law and M. Callon, 'Engineering and Sociology in a Military Aircraft Project: A Network Analysis of Technological Change', *Social Problems*, 35, 3 (1988).

13. J. Law, 'Technology and Heterogeneous Engineering', in Bijker, Hughes and Pinch, *The Social Construction of Technological Systems*.

14. K.H. Sorensen and N. Levold, 'Tacit Networks, Heterogeneous Engineers, and Embodied Technology', *Science, Technology, and Human Values*, 17, 1 (1992), p. 29.

15. S. Woolgar, 'Configuring the User: The Case of Usability Trials', in J. Law (ed.), *Sociology of Monsters: Essays on Power, Technology and Domination*, London: Routledge, 1991.

16. Although not directly concerned with battle, this idea of constructing the user is fully explored in N. Oudshoorn and T.J. Pinch (eds), *How Users Matter: The Co-construction of Users and Technologies*, Inside Technology, Cambridge, MA: MIT Press, 2003.

17. Before the war, the ADE was known as the Design Department. During the war, the Design Department was renamed the Armament Design Department. This name was retained until about 1947, when it was renamed the ADE. For the purposes of this book, the terms DD/ADD/ADE are, broadly speaking, referring to the same body of people responsible for designing small arms and ammunition.

18. For design process and organisation charts, see 121 Design of Weapons Box 4, RAA. It has not been possible to define precisely how many members of staff there were at any one time during the war. However, from a roll call list developed to make an ADD response to invasion easier, 170 members of staff are recorded; see 111 ROF Box 3, RAA.

19. Meeting of the Advisory Council on Scientific Research and Technical Development, 26 November 1946, 121 Design of Weapons Box 3, RAA.

20. G. Peden, 'The Treasury and Defence of Empire', in G. Kennedy (ed.), *Imperial Defence: The Old World Order, 1856–1956*, London: Routledge, 2008.

21. Historically, as wars ended, the Ordnance Departments were usually cut back to their pre-war levels; see T. Putnam and D. Weinbren, *A Short History of the Royal Small Arms Factory Enfield*, Enfield: Middlesex University, 1992, p. 112. In January

1947, the total R&D spend was £180.4 million, of which the minister of defence contended £66.1 million was for basic research that had a civil spin off. The chancellor, however, reckoned that the £66.1 million was 'excessive'. As it turned out, the Treasury was forced to increase R&D spending in the short term because the British government decided to develop a nuclear capability. C. Barnett, *The Lost Victory: British Dreams, British Realities, 1945–1950*, London: Pan Books, 1996, p. 73.

22. T.B. Dugelby, *EM-2 Concept and Design: A Rifle Ahead of Its Time*, Toronto: Collector Grade Publications, 1980, p. 15.

23. Unfortunately for the Army, re-armament was a slow process. Two examples demonstrate this point: (1) 1938 production of Bren LMGs amounted to 300 per week rising to 400 per week in September 1942. Before Dunkirk, the British Army had around 30,000 Bren guns. At Dunkirk, the British Army lost 8,000 Bren guns. After the fall of France, the total number of Brens in Britain amounted to only 2,300 weapons. By 1943, production reached 1,000 weapons per week. At the beginning of the war, however, production was centred at the Royal Small Arms Factory (RSAF) at Enfield Lock, north-east London. This was subject to regular air raids, which could severely disrupt output. At September 1939 production standards it would take around two years to replace all the lost Bren guns following the Dunkirk debacle. See A.J.R. Cormack, *Famous Rifles and Machine Guns*, London: Barrie and Jenkins, 1977, p. 27; and W. Churchill, *The Second World War, Vol. II: Their Finest Hour*, London: Cassell & Co., 1949, p. 125. (2) At a time when the number of men in uniform had risen from 224,000 in 1939 to 2,453,000 in 1942, the number of No.1 Short Magazine Lee-Enfield (SMLE) rifles that had been manufactured totalled only 177,491. For No.1 SMLE production figures, see, PREM 11/854, TNA. Data on the size of the wartime British Army can be found in Crang, *The British Army and the People's War*, pp. 144–5.

24. Meeting of the Organisation and Weapons Policy Committee, 4 January 1944, WO 32/105, TNA.

25. For the number of Stens made and the speed of their introduction, see Postan, Hay and Scott, *Design and Development of Weapons*, p. 357. For more detail on the Sten and for references to the number of Mk.Is and Mk.IIs that were withdrawn, see Peter Laidler, *The Sten Machine Carbine*, Cobourg, ON: Collector Grade Publications, 2000, pp. 299–302.

26. This was partly driven by the recognition that the ordnance factories had had some trouble delivering sufficient .303 ammunition during the first two years of the war and that there were a vast number of .30'06 weapons in Britain, see PREM 3/46/3, TNA. The staff policy on adopting US ammunition can be found in General Staff Policy Statement on Rimless Small Arms Ammunition, 20 March 1943, WO 32/10515, TNA.

27. Memo from the secretary of the Organisation and Weapons Policy Committee, 31 January 1944, WO32/105, TNA.

28. Ibid.

29. See 'The King's Prize at Bisley', *Ça Ira* (September 1938), p. 7, and the obituary entitled, 'Brigadier J. A. Barlow, CBE', *White Rose*, May 1975, p. 7. Barlow also wrote several books on rifle shooting, the most famous of which is J.A. Barlow, *The Elements of Rifle Shooting Dealing with the Service Rifle and Open Sight*, Aldershot: Gale & Polden, 1932. By 1961, this book had made it to a fifth edition.

30. See 'Special Meeting of the Small Arms Committee', 27 January 1937.

31. Meeting of the Committee on Infantry Weapon Development, 13 August 1943, 120 Meetings—Conferences (Future Design of Weapons)—Box 1, RAA.

32. 'Report on the Possibilities of Adopting American Weapons for Use in the British Service', 25 March 1946, CEAD, 200(200) Small Arms General Box 2, RAA.

33. Meeting of sub-committee appointed by the Standing Committee on Infantry Weapon Development, 8 February 1945, WO 32/10515, TNA.

34. 'The Choice of Standard Round for Small Arms', Armament Design Establishment, Technical Report, March 1947, DEFE 15/239, TNA.

35. 'The Ideal Small Arms Round', letter to DGofA from Richard Beeching, 30 August 1947, WO/242.

36. 'Directive for the Development of New Automatic Rifles', from A3, Brigadier Barlow to A/CEAD(SA), 18 September 1947, Ammo .280–3.280 (7mm) Ammunition, RAA.

37. Minutes of meeting held at War Office between DInf, DGofA and others, 22 June 1945, WO 32/10515, TNA.

38. General Staff policy statement no. 3, 27 November 1944, WO 32/10515, TNA.

39. The rounds had to be smoke- and flash-free and come in a variety of ammunition types including standard ball, incendiary, observing and armour piercing.

40. General Staff policy statement no. 3, 27 November 1944, WO 32/10515, TNA.

41. DofA (SA) directive on SA Weapon and Ammunition Development Programme for the future, 18 September 1947, letter from DofA (SA) to ADE, DGofA, and DOF, Ammo .280–3.280 (7mm) Ammunition, RAA.

42. These debates are described in much greater detail in M. Ford, 'The British Army and the Politics of Rifle Development, 1880 to 1986', PhD thesis: King's College London, 2008.

43. Minutes of meeting held on new SAA, 26 November 1948, Ammo .280–3.280 (7mm) Ammunition, RAA.

44. US War Department, 'War Department Equipment Board Report', 22 May 1946, quoted from McNaugher, *The M-16 Controversies*, p. 35.

45. Ezell, *The Great Rifle Controversy*, p. 41.

46. Meeting of the Organisation and Weapons Policy Committee, 18 April 1946, WO 32/10515, TNA.

47. Letter from BJSM to DWD, 'Future Small Arms Ammunition Policy', 31 July 1946, WO 32/10515, TNA.

48. Telegram from Brigadier Barlow to General Eldridge, 27 June 1947, Ammo .280–1.280(7mm) Ammunition 82 Series File, RAA.

49. Memo from Brigadier Barlow, 'Change of Nomenclature of .276″ Round', 29 October 1947, Ammo .280–1.280in (7mm) Ammunition 82 Series File, RAA.

50. Letter from DofA (SA) to DOF, 13 May 1949, Ammo .280–1.280in (7mm) Ammunition 82 Series File, RAA.

51. Meeting of the OWPC, 19 December 1946, WO 32/10515, TNA

52. General Staff policy statement no. 3, 27 November 1944, WO 32/10515, TNA

53. Report of meeting held on Monday, 20 May 1946 to discuss Rifle S.L. 7.92mm for MP43 Ammunition, 120 Meetings Conferences Box 1, RAA.

54. Meeting of the Advisory Council on Scientific Research and Technical Development, 26 November 1946, 121 Design of Weapons—Box 3, RAA.

55. 'Future Requirements of Small Arms for the Army', memorandum by the DMT, 19 April 1947, WO 32/10515, TNA.

56. Ibid.

57. 'Infantry Combat Weapon', 27 May 1947, 120 Meetings Conferences Box 1, RAA.

58. The concept of moving the trigger-housing mechanism forward of the magazine, however, was not new. Before the end of the Second World War, the ADE had been handed the designs for an automatic bullpup weapon by Major Hall who was leaving for his native Australia. The ADE had also built a prototype LMG called the Korsac and a sniper's rifle known as the Harris in the bullpup configuration. See Dugelby, *EM-2 Concept and Design*, pp. 7–24.

59. At the same time, the weapon designed by Major Hall (see footnote 42) was designated the EM-3 but no further development work was undertaken on this weapon, see ibid. p. 27. The lead designer for the EM-1 was called Mr Metcalfe, see 'Infantry Combat Weapon', 27 May 1947.

60. As will be shown in the next chapter, because the development schedule was so tight, work on the EM-1 was abandoned before the joint US–UK trials.

61. See Appendix 3 for diagram.

62. This was eventually demonstrated by the .280 ammunition, which had a recoil energy limited to 7.4ftlbs when fired from the EM-2, compared with 11ftlbs when using .303 ammunition in a No. 4 Rifle. As a result of the reduced recoil energies, it was possible to fire eighty aimed rounds per minute compared with the bolt action rifle's twenty. See Dugelby, *EM-2 Concept and Design*, p. 249.

63. In discussions during early 1947, it was also made clear that a rifle grenade might compromise the ability of the ADE to develop one rifle with two roles, as the additional stress of firing a rifle grenade could compromise the design of the IPW. For GS requirements, see 'Future Requirements of Small Arms for the Army', memorandum by the DMT, 19 April 1947, WO 32/10515, TNA.

64. 'Operation Niblick Stage III', memo from Brigadier Barlow DofA (SA), 25 May 1949, Ammo .280–3.280in (7mm) Ammunition, RAA.

65. Rose, *The American Rifle*, p. 329.

66. The T25 was a prototype weapon that fired the T65 .30 round. Correspondence between the BJSM and DGofA, 9, 11 and 17 November 1948, WO 185/242, TNA; letter from BJSM to DofA (SA), 17 May 1949, WO 185/242, TNA.

67. Ibid.

68. Ibid.

69. Letter from DGofA to CS(M), 'Comparative Tests of New US and UK Small Arms Ammunition and Rifles', 14 April 1949, WO 185/242, TNA.

70. Letter from DGofA to CEAD, 'Comparative Tests of New SAA and Light Rifles in USA', 5 January 1950, 340 (200) EM-2 S/L Rifles Box 1, RAA.

71. It was decided to drop the EM-1 because it was not at as an advanced a stage of development as the EM-2. This can partly be explained by the fact that there was only one designer working on the weapon. It was also decided at this stage to drop another rifle developed by BSA and only submit the FN .280 and EM-2 for trials in the United States. Regarding the Belgian company's weapon, see section on the FN later in this chapter. Letter from DGofA to CEAD, 'Comparative Tests of New SAA and Light Rifles in USA', 5 January 1950, and for references about the EM-1's under-staffing, see letter from DofA (SA) to A/CEAD (SA), 16 December 1949, 340 (200) EM-2 S/L Rifles Box 1, RAA.

72. A trial document had been signed in October 1949, called the Agreement on Comparative Tests of Light Rifles and Ammunition. See letter from BJSM to DInf, 18 September 1950, 340 (200) EM-2 S/L Rifles Box 1, RAA.

73. Ibid.

74. 'Report of US Army Equipment Board', 8 March 1950, letter from DofA (SA) to DGofA, 28 April 1950, WO 185/242, TNA.

75. Ibid.

76. Draft letter from DofA (SA) to DGofA titled, 'Report of US Army Equipment Board', 8 March 1950, WO 185/242, TNA.

77. Letter from A/CEAD to DofA (SA), 28 April 1950, 340 (200) EM-2 S/L Rifles Box 1, RAA.

4. THE SCIENCE OF KILLING

1. S. Zuckerman, *From Apes to Warlords: An Autobiography (1904–1946)*, London: Collins, 1988, p. 114.

2. Ibid. p. 125.

3. B. Rappert, 'Prohibitions, Weapons and Controversy: Managing the Problems of Ordering', *Social Studies of Science*, 35, 2 (2005).

4. Prokosch, *The Technology of Killing*; J. Bourke, *Wounding the World: How Military Violence and War-Play Invades Our Lives*, London: Virago, 2014.

5. P. Gummett and R. Bud (eds) *Cold War, Hot Science: Applied Research in Britain's Defence Laboratories, 1945–1990*, London: Routledge, 1998.

6. For more on the scientific method, see K. Popper, *The Logic of Scientific Discovery*, London: Hutchinson, 1959; *Conjectures and Refutations: The Growth of Scientific Knowledge*, 5th edn, London: Routledge, 1991.

7. The strongest proponents of the sociology of scientific knowledge included Bloor, *Knowledge and Social Imagery*; B. Latour and S. Woolgar, *Laboratory Life: The Social Construction of Scientific Facts*, London: Sage Publications, 1979.

8. Bijker, 'Social Construction of Facts and Artefacts', pp. 26–8.

9. G. Bowker and S. Leigh Star, *Sorting Things Out: Classification and Its Consequences*, Cambridge, MA: MIT Press, 1999.

10. J.C. Colonel Beyer Jr (ed.), *Wound Ballistics*, Washington, DC: Office of the Surgeon General, Department of the Army, 1962; Preface (http://history.amedd. army.mil/booksdocs/wwii/woundblstcs/preface.htm; accessed 11 June 2014).

11. Chivers, *The Gun*, p. 233.

12. Ibid. p. 235.

13. Zuckerman, *From Apes to Warlords*, p. 64.

14. Lt. Col. G.R. Callender and R.W. French, 'Wound Ballistics: Studies in the Mechanism of Wound Production by Rifle Bullets', *The Military Surgeon*, 77 (October 1935), p. 199.

15. G.R. Callender and R.W. French, 'Ballistic Characteristics of Wounding Agents', in Beyer Jr, *Wound Ballistics*, p. 93 (http://history.amedd.army.mil/booksdocs/ wwii/woundblstcs/chapter2.htm; accessed 11 June 2014).

16. Ibid. pp. 93–4. Dr Beat Kneubuehl believes that this can be traced back to the 1896 work of German ballistician Rhone. See Kneubuehl et al., *Wound Ballistics*, p. 180. The foot-pound is a unit of energy in imperial units. The corresponding SI unit is the joule (J). 1 ft-lb is approximately 1.36 J. Foot-pounds are still commonly used in the discussion of muzzle energy in the United States.

17. B. Delisle Burns and S. Zuckerman, 'The Wounding Power of Small Bomb and Shell Fragments', RC350, October 1942, Appendix II, HO 195/13/350, TNA, p. 4.

18. Ibid.

19. This calculation was made possible because two values in the equation for kinetic energy were known. Kinetic energy is defined as half mass multiplied by the square of velocity or $KE = \frac{1}{2}mv^2$. Rearranging the equation to determine the mass gives results in $m = 2KE/v^2$. Based on the assumption that it took 58ftlbs to incapacitate and that a fragment from a bomb blast struck the target at 2000fps, the mass of a projectile had to be greater than 0.014oz (i.e. 1/70th of an oz or 400mg). See, 'A Review of the Criteria of Wounding Power in Common Use', p. 4.

20. See Burns and Zuckerman, 'The Wounding Power of Small Bomb and Shell Fragments', RC350, p. 4.

21. Ibid. p. 6.

22. Ibid. p. 7.

23. Ibid. p. 2.
24. Momentum is defined, as kinetic energy is, by an equation involving mass and velocity. In contrast to the square relationship that we saw earlier, it is the simple product of the two values, i.e. momentum (p) = mv.
25. See 'Survey of Casualties in Combined Operations against Dieppe Carried Out on the 19th August 1942', report by Professor Solly Zuckerman to the chief of combined operations; found in SZ/OEMU/48/5, Zuckerman Papers, UEA.
26. Dr B. Delisle Burns and Dr p. L. Krohn, 'A Review of the Criteria of Wounding Power in Common Use', Ministry of Aircraft Production, Oxford Research Unit, Scientific and Technical Memoranda, 11 October 1945. SZ/OEMU/47/19/31, Zuckerman Papers, UEA.
27. Beyer Jr, *Wound Ballistics*. On his own initiative, Captain Dr James Hopkins undertook an additional survey on the Island of New Georgia in August 1943, before Colonel Callender put out a call for help.
28. R.W. Gurney, 'A New Casualty Criterion', Ballistic Research Laboratories Report no. 498, 31 October 1944. Ronald Wilfred Gurney was a British physicist who worked at Princeton during the 1930s until his death.
29. Prokosch, *The Technology of Killing*, p. 20.
30. See, 'Memorandum for Dr. J.F. Fulton on the Use of 58ftlbs as a Criterion of Incapacitation', 16 March 1945, SZ/OEMU/44/17/79, Zuckerman Papers, UEA.
31. Dr B Delisle Burns and Dr P.L. Krohn, 'A Review of the Criteria of Wounding Power in Common Use', Ministry of Aircraft Production, Oxford Research Unit, Scientific and Technical Memoranda, 11 October 1945. SZ/OEMU/47/19/31, Zuckerman Papers, UEA.
32. Letter from Zuckerman to Brigadier Leitch, 4 October 1946, SZ/OEMU/46/5/4, Zuckerman Papers, UEA.
33. See, 'Memorandum for Dr. J.F. Fulton on the Use of 58ftlbs as a Criterion of Incapacitation'.
34. Specifically, it had to be a .30′06 155 grain bullet. See DofA (SA) Directive on SA Weapon and Ammunition Development Programme for the Future, 18 September 1947, letter from DofA (SA) to ADE, DGofA, and DOF, Ammo .280–3.280in (7mm) Ammunition, RAA.
35. See 'History of the .280', ADE SAA Development Diary, entry from 5 November 1948, Ammo .280–3.280in (7mm) Ammunition, RAA. See Chapter 5, note 35.
36. The correspondence is incomplete. However, it is clear that the DofA (SA) believed this to be the case and was working to convince DInf likewise, 29 May 1949. Ammo .280–1.280 (7mm) Ammunition 82 Series File, RAA; see also DofA (SA) directive on SA Weapon and Ammunition Development Programme for the future, 18 September 1947, AMM 3–3.280 (7mm) Ammunition, RAA.
37. Dr C.M. Herget of the Edgewood Chemical Center and Dr H.P. Robertson of the US Weapons Systems Evaluation Group, '.280 inch SAA and .30 T65 Type', memo by Brigadier Barlow, 27 March 1951, WO 185/242, TNA.

38. Ibid.
39. Aberdeen Proving Ground test results concluded that .280 achieved an average velocity of 2211 fps at the beginning of the test and 2172 fps at its end. The T65, in contrast, achieved 2737 fps and 2754 fps respectively; see Dugelby, *EM-2 Concept and Design*, p. 119.
40. Ibid.
41. See Chapter 5, notes 33 and 34.
42. General Staff policy statement no. 3, 27 November 1944, WO 32/10515, TNA.
43. 'Future Requirements of Small Arms for the Army', memorandum by the DMT, 19 April 1947, WO 32/10515, TNA.
44. The point was explicitly conceded in 'A Report by the Military Committee on NATO Standardization', 16 January 1958, NATO Archive (http://archives.nato.int/uploads/r/null/1/0/105119/MC_0020_4_FINAL_ENG_PDP.pdf; accessed 1 August 2015).
45. Marshall, *Men against Fire*, pp. 27–35.
46. McNaugher, *The M-16 Controversies*, p. 53.
47. The US Air Force, the Marine Corps and the Military Assistance Command in Vietnam initially adopted the M16 in the period between 1962 and 1964. Only after it had been backed by these different commands did senior officers within the Army accept it into general service.
48. S.L.A. Marshall, *Commentary on Infantry Operations and Weapon Usage in Korea: Winter of 1950–51*, Chevy Chase, MD: Operations Research Office, Johns Hopkins University, 1951.
49. Ibid. p. 4.
50. N.A. Hitchman, *Operational Requirements for an Infantry Hand Weapon*, Chevy Chase, MD: Operations Research Office, Johns Hopkins University, 1952, p. 9.
51. Ibid. p. 15.
52. Ibid. p. 8.
53. Ibid. p. 16.
54. Ibid. p. 22.
55. Hitchman, *Operational Requirements for an Infantry Hand Weapon*, p. 25.
56. Ibid. p. 22.
57. Ibid. p. 6.
58. See, for example, the paper given by Colonel T.N. Dupuy, entitled 'Human Behavior in Combat: With a Focus on Suppression', found in 'The Fort Sill Fire Suppression Symposium Report, 24–25 July 1979', 14 January 1980 (http://www.dtic.mil/docs/citations/ADA081134; accessed 18 June 2014).
59. Kenneth R. Laughery and Robert W. Bauer, 'Platoon Weapons Preference: A Questionnaire Study; Psychological Weapons Study 1', US Army Human Engineering Laboratories, Aberdeen Proving Ground, Maryland, 1963.
60. Kneubuehl et al., *Wound Ballistics*, p. 163.

61. Hitchman, *Operational Requirements for an Infantry Hand Weapon*, p. 23.

62. Dr C.M. Herget of the Edgewood Chemical Center and Dr H.P. Robertson of the US Weapons Systems Evaluation Group, '.280 inch SAA and .30 T65 Type', memo by Brigadier Barlow, 27 March 1951, WO 185/242, TNA.

63. Callender and French, 'Ballistic Characteristics of Wounding Agents', p. 118.

5. THE BUREAUCRACY AS BATTLEFIELD

1. 'Note of the Meeting of the 20 Nov. with the Secretary of State for War and CIGS', 21 November 1951, PREM 11/854, TNA. Churchill and Slim quote taken from Ronald Lewin, *Slim: The Standardbearer; A Biography of Field-Marshal the Viscount Slim*, London: Pan Books, 1978, pp. 272–3.

2. Anon., *Wanat: Combat Action in Afghanistan 2008*, Fort Leavenworth, KS: Combat Studies Institute Press, 2010; R. Steeb et al., *Perspectives on the Battle of Wanat: Challenges Facing Small Unit Operations in Afghanistan*, Washington, DC: RAND, 2011.

3. 'The Battle of Wanat: Inside the Wire', *The Washington Post*, 4 October 2009 (http://www.washingtonpost.com/wp-dyn/content/article/2009/10/03/AR2009100303048.html; accessed 7 July 2014).

4. 'Cover-up? Army Historian Says Report on Deadly Afghan Battle Was Altered to Absolve Faulty Gun: Survivors of Bloody Battle Report M4 Jams', *Washington Times*, 20 February 2014 (http://www.washingtontimes.com/news/2014/feb/20/cover-up-army-historian-says-report-on-deadly-afgh/; accessed 7 July 2014).

5. This story has been discussed extensively. The best author on the subject is McNaugher, *The M-16 Controversies*, pp. 135–70. See also Fallows, 'The American Army and the M16'.

6. For some insightful discussions of these problems see Bill Kincaid, *A Dinosaur in Whitehall: The True Cost of Defence Procurement Bureaucracy*, 1st edn, London: Brassey's, 1997; McNaugher, 'Weapons Procurement'; M. Urban, *The Edge: Is the Military Dominance of the West Coming to an End?*, London: Little, Brown, 2015.

7. This prompted the British government to establish an inquiry under Sir James Stephen, see 'Report of the Royal Commission Appointed to Inquire in the System Under Which Patterns of Warlike Stores are Adopted and the Stores Obtained and Passed for Her Majesty's Service', C. 5062 (1887), RAA.

8. 'The SA80 Rifle and Light Support Weapon, Report together with the Proceedings of the Committee relating to the Report, Minutes of Evidence and Memoranda', London: HMSO, 1993.

9. 'SAS to Use Bigger Bullets to Kill Enemy Outright after Claiming "Shoot-to-Wound" Policy Put Their Lives at Risk', *Daily Mail*, 17 March 2013 (http://www.dailymail.co.uk/news/article-2294631/SAS-use-bigger-bullets-kill-enemy-outright-claiming-shoot-wound-policy-lives-risk.html; accessed 7 July 2014).

10. The initial purchase of 5,000 weapons was ostensibly for troop trials. The weapon was adopted fully in 1957. For the initial decision, see 'Conclusions of a Meeting of the Cabinet', Tuesday, 1 December 1953, CAB 128/26, TNA. See List of Changes LC. C8288 EA. W/321 and LC. C8387, EA. W/151, RAA.

11. G. Allison and M.H. Halperin, 'Bureaucratic Politics: A Paradigm and Some Policy Implications', *World Politics*, 24, Supplement: Theory and Policy in International Relations (1972), p. 43.

12. Before the Second World War, there had been a Small Arms Committee to establish the inefficiencies of Britain's research, design and manufacturing capability. In April 1945, conscious of this possibility occurring again, the chief engineer in armament design wrote a report making a case for sustaining R&D in the UK after the war had ended. See 'Proceedings of a Special Meeting of the Small Arms Committee', 27 January 1937, RAA and 'The Future of Armament Development with Special Reference to the Armaments Research Department and the Armaments Design Department', CEAD, April 1948, DEFE 15/86, TNA.

13. There had been a standardisation conference between Britain and the Dominions in February 1946, where the matter was discussed. See WO 32/11606, TNA.

14. Letter from Brigadier Barlow to Colonel Galbraith, 16 December 1951; and letter from Colonel Galbraith to Brigadier Barlow, 9 January 1951, both found in RG24 Box 3502, Library and Archives Canada (LAC).

15. 'Summary of Discussion Concerning Standardisation of Infantry Weapons', 11 and 12 October 1949, RG24 Box 3502, LAC.

16. H. MacKenzie, 'The ABCs of Canada's International Economic Relations, 1945–1951', in G. Donaghy (ed.), *Canada and the Early Cold War, 1943–1957*, Ottawa: Department of Foreign Affairs and International Trade, 1998, p. 217.

17. Letter from Canadian minister of defence, Mr Brooke Claxton, to UK secretary of state for war, Mr Emanuel Shinwell, 22 June 1951, CAB 21/3465, TNA.

18. Ibid.

19. '.280 SAA and .30 T65 Type', Brigadier Barlow, 27 March 1951, WO 185/242, TNA.

20. Letter from BJSM to DCIGS, 22 January 1951, Ammo .280–1 .280in (7mm) Ammunition 82 Series File, RAA.

21. Letter from BJSM to DofA (SA), 9 February 1951, WO 185/244, TTNA.

22. 'The Adoption of the New Small Arms Ammunition and Weapon into the British Armed Forces', note by the chiefs of staff to the Cabinet Defence Committee, 16 March 1951, WO 185/244, TNA.

23. Parliamentary Debates (Hansard), House of Commons, Oral Answers, 25 April 1951, col. 378.

24. Ibid.

25. 'Conference of Defence Ministers, United Kingdom, France, Canada, United States: On Small Arms Standardisation', 2–3 August 1951, Ezell Archive, Cranfield University, UK.

26. Ministry of Defence to BJSM, 5 July 1951, CAB 21/3465, TNA.

27. Telegram from BJSM to Ministry of Defence, 23 June 1951, CAB 21/3465, TNA.

28. Memorandum for General Ely, Air Chief Marshal Sir William Ellliot, Admiral Wright from C.H. Donnelly 'Small Arms Standardization: The Secretary of Defense Washington', 22 August 1951, NATO Archive (http://archives.nato.int/uploads/r/null/1/2/120543/SGM-1364–51_ENG_PDP.pdf; accessed 16 July 2015).

29. Ibid.

30. 'Précis of the Defence Ministers' Conference in Washington, 2 to 3 August 1951', CAB 21/3465, TNA.

31. Ibid. Soldiers in the Canadian Army fighting in Korea who had been provided with a variety of kit from Canada, the United States and the UK, were experiencing problems with unsuitable equipment and standardised logistics on a day-to-day basis. See B. Watson, 'Far Eastern Tour: The Experiences of the Canadian Infantry in Korea, 1950–53', PhD thesis, University of Victoria, 1999, pp. 96–129.

32. Report on the Small Arms Conference held in the United States on 2 and 3 August 1951, CAB 21/3465, TNA.

33. Ibid.

34. Ibid.

35. Text of communiqué following conference on the standardisation of weapons, 3 August 1951, found in 'Adoption of the New Small Arms Ammunition and Weapons by the British Armed Forces', memorandum by the minister of defence, Cabinet Defence Committee, 12 September 1951, CAB 21/3465, TNA.

36. 'Précis of the Defence Ministers' Conference in Washington'.

37. The rifle question surfaced in the House of Commons a further five times after 25 April and before the general election of October 1951; see Hansard Parliamentary Debates, 1951.

38. 'Appendix: Standardisation of Small Arms Ammunition; A Report by a Working Party to the Standing Group North Atlantic Military Committee', 5 October 1951, CAB 21/3465, TNA.

39. Ibid.

40. Parliamentary Debates (Hansard), House of Commons, Oral Answers, 25 April 1951, col. 378.

41. Note by the prime minister, 12 November 1951, PREM 11/854, TNA.

42. The DCIGS had asked for intelligence information on Russian small arms in July 1951. This had been provided by the British small arms community who, it seems, used it as an opportunity to make the point that the .280 round was far superior to the equivalent weapons available to the Red Army; see 'Russian Equipment: Comparison of British and Russian Rifles and Ammunition', 18 July 1951, WO 185/244, TNA. Letter from Anthony Head to Winston Churchill, 19 June 1951, Churchill College Archives, CHUR 2/34.

43. Letter from Emanuel Shinwell to Sir Alfred Herbert K.B.E, 25 June 1951, CAB 21/3465, TNA.

44. A clear indication of the prime minister's distrust of the firepower argument is illustrated by the following story. Churchill met with Brigadier Barlow, Noel Kent Lemon and the deputy director of infantry, Brigadier Gordon, at Chequers to fire the EM-2 and T25 on 24 November 1951. When it was pointed out that the British infantryman had been expected to use .303 ammunition for fifty years and that it was time for it to be replaced, 'Mr Churchill replied, with a smile, that we had used the long bow for very much longer than 50 years.' See 'Brief Record of Demonstration of the .280 and EM-2 at Kimble Range near Chequers to the Prime Minister on Saturday 24th November', 29 November 1951, WO 185/320, TNA.

45. 'Some Logistics Problems Affecting the U.S. Calibre .30 t104 and UK Calibre .280 Ammunition', Ammo .280–.280in (7mm) Ammunition SAA 82 & D2 Series, RAA

46. '.280 SAA and .30 T65 Type', Brigadier Barlow, 27 March 1951, WO 185/242, TNA.

47. Letter from unknown (possibly Brigadier Barlow) to Winston Churchill, July 1951, Churchill College Archives, CHUR 2/34.

48. Ibid.

49. Lewin, *Slim: The Standardbearer*, pp. 272–3; see also 'Note of the Meeting of the 20th November with the Secretary of State for War and CIGS', 21 November 1951, PREM 11/854, TNA.

50. See 'Note by the Prime Minister', 12 November 1951.

51. Bringing back the Home Guard was some of the first legislation passed by the new government. See A. Seldon, *Churchill's Indian Summer: The Conservative Government, 1951–55*, London: Hodder & Stoughton, 1981, p. 311; for revised requirement and production figures, see letter from secretary of state for war to prime minister, 'The .280 Rifle', 16 November 1951, PREM 11/854, TNA.

52. '.280 Rifle Memorandum by the War Office and Ministry of Supply, Note by the Joint Secretary', Joint Weapons Policy Committee, 23 July 1951, CAB 21/3465, TNA.

53. Shinwell taunted Brigadier Head by saying that 'His attempt to enrol the Home Guard in face of advice given him has proved a complete flop', quoted from Seldon, *Churchill's Indian Summer*, p. 311.

54. Letter from secretary of state for war to CIGS, 25 July 1951, CAB 21/3465, TNA.

55. 'The Prime Minister's Visit to Washington and Ottawa', January 1952, pp. 7–8, CAB 21/3057, TNA.

56. Letter from A.P. Wickens to Duncan Sandys, MP, minister of supply, 26 January 1954, 340 (200) EM-2 SL Rifles Box 1, RAA.

57. Letter from DofA (SA) to CS(M), 7 November 1947, WO 185/242; and letter from ACS(M) to DWD, 29 October 1947, WO 185/242, TNA.

58. See minute sheet notes of correspondence between DofA (SA), CS(M), DWD and FN. References include notes from 15 to 17, 20 to 27, 30, 40 to 50 located at front of file WO 185/242, TNA.

59. Ibid. References include notes from: 15 to 17, 20 to 27, 30, 40 to 50 located at front of file.

60. Letter from DWD to ACS(M), 'Development of British Self-Loading Rifle', 4 November 1947, WO 185/242, TNA.

61. Letter from DofA (SA) to CS(M), 7 November 1947, WO 185/242, TNA.

62. 'Operation Niblick Stage III, Preliminary View of New Auto Rifles at Enfield Lock', 3 March 1949, 340 (200) EM-2 S/L Rifles Box 1, RAA.

63. Letter from DofA (SA) to CEAD, '.280 SAA', 30 January 1951, Ammo .280–1 .280in (7mm) Ammunition 82 Series File, RAA.

64. Letter from superintendent Royal Ordnance Factories Radway Green to 'anonymous', 10 June 1948; see also letter from A/CEAD to CEAD, 9 April 1951; and letter from A/CEAD to DofA (SA), 21 March 1951, all in Ammo .280–1.280in (7mm) Ammunition 82 Series File, RAA.

65. Letter from DGofA to CS(M), 8 August 1949, WO 185/242, TNA. As a result of US intransigence in organising the initial comparative trials, Britain's engineers had been forced to abandon the EM-1. However, a number of other designs were also abandoned at this point. These included the FN bullpup and a weapon made by the Birmingham Small Arms Company (BSA) called the 28P. The BSA weapon is not central to the story of the EM-2 and FN. The Ministry of Supply almost certainly asked the BSA to develop a weapon mainly for political reasons so that they could show they wanted to work with the UK as well as foreign companies. Most of the files related to the 28P do not seem to have survived, although it does appear that the weapon failed its proof tests. Technical information about the weapon can be found in Major Hobart's article: F.W.A. Hobart, 'The BSA 28p .280 Rifle', *Guns Review*, 12, 5 (1972), pp. 185–7.

66. Letter from DWD to ACS(M), 'Development of British Self-Loading Rifle', 4 November 1947, WO 185/242, TNA.

67. Letter from CEAD to DGofA, '7mm Ammunition: Conditions for Demonstration etc. vis-à-vis FN', 12 September 1951, letter from Brigadier Barlow DofA (SA) to Fabrique Nationale d'Armes de Guerre, 15 August 1951, WO 185/244, TNA.

68. Operational Research Section, Korea, memorandum no. 1, 'Belgian FN .30 Automatic Rifle, Model M.2', WO 291/1890, TNA.

69. Letter from DofA (SA) to BJSM, 20 April 1951, WO 185/244, TNA.

70. 'Rifles Automatic: .280inch Check Tests of FN and EM-2', 5 June 1951, 340 (200) EM-2 SL Rifles Box 3, RAA.

71. Letter from director of infantry to DofA (SA), 3 December 1951, 340 (200) EM-2 SL Rifles Box 2, RAA.

72. Letter from secretary of state for war to prime minister, 4 June 1952, WO 216/374,

TNA. Work on this round continued throughout 1952 and into 1953; see 'Military Report by the Military Representatives Committee to the North Atlantic Military Committee on Standardisation of Small Arms Ammunition', 12 November 1952, RG24, Box 3502, LAC.

73. Letter entitled 'Compromise Small Arms Round' from Brigadier A.E. Wrinch to Major-general S.F. Clark, 8 February 1952, RG24 Box 3502, LAC. See also Dugelby, *EM-2 Concept and Design*, p. 166.

74. Letter from secretary of state for war to prime minister, 4 June 1952, WO 216/374, TNA; 'New SAA and the New Light Rifle', note by the CS(M) for the secretary of state at the Ministry of Supply, 21 April 1953, WO 185/320, TNA.

75. The decision to set up this committee was first taken by General Guy Simonds, the Canadian CGS and General Sir John Whiteley, the DCIGS, at a War Office meeting in May 1952. See 'Directorate of Armament Development Canadian Participation in Tripartite Small Arms Standardisation Programme', Development Report no. 6, 12 May 1952, RG 24 Box 3502, LAC. The official title of the committee was the Small Arms Development Committee and it first met in the summer of 1952; see 'Minutes of Informal Meeting of Technical Representatives of the Small Arms Development Committee', 25 June 1952, 120 Meetings—Conferences (Future Design of Weapons)—Box 2, RAA.

76. 'Minutes of Informal Meeting of Technical Representatives of the Small Arms Development Committee', 25 June 1952, 120 Meetings—Conferences (Future Design of Weapons)—Box 2, RAA.

77. Letter from CEAD to DofA (SA), 3 June 1952, 120 Meetings—Conferences (Future Design of Weapons)—Box 2, RAA.

78. 'Minutes of the Meeting of the Technical Representatives of the Small Arms Development Committee', 24 September 1952, 120 Meetings—Conferences (Future Design of Weapons)—Box 2, RAA.

79. Recommendation of the BBC committee from 24 September 1952; see ibid.

80. 'Minute of Meeting Held in War Office between Canada, FN, Ministry of Supply and Director of Infantry', 3 October 1952, 120 Meetings—Conferences (Future Design of Weapons)—Box 2, RAA.

81. Letter from Lt Gen. Ward (DCIGS) to Gen. Crawford (CS(M)), 17 April 1953, WO 185/320, TNA.

82. 'Adoption of the New Rifle', paper by the DCIGS for the Army Council, 17 April 1953, WO 185/320, TNA.

83. Letter from DGofA to CS(M), 23 April 1953, WO 185/320, TNA.

84. Letter from DofA (SA) to DGofA, regarding paper by the DCIGS, 22 April 1953, WO 185/320, TNA.

85. E. Ezell, 'Cracks in the Post-War Anglo-American Alliance: The Great Rifle Controversy, 1947–1957', *Military Affairs*, 38, 4 (1974), p. 141.

86. J. Huon, *Military Rifle and Machine Gun Cartridges*, London: Arms & Armor

Press, 1989, p. 100; interview with Mr Henk Visser, Wassennaar, the Netherlands, 23 September 2004.

87. The decision was ratified by a full meeting of the Cabinet on 1 December 1953, PREM 11/854, TNA.

6. ALLIANCE POLITICS AND NATO STANDARDISATION: INTERESTS, POWER, RATIONALITY

1. The Center for Strategic and International Studies, Transatlantic Policy Panel, Allied Interdependence Newsletter no. 9, March 1979, DEFE 13/1167

2. The US public announcement was made on 1 May 1957. Letter from Duncan Sandys to Sir Richard Powell, PUS, 15 May 1957, DEFE 70/80, TNA.

3. 'Programme for Presentation of SA for the 1980s', 11 July 1974, RSAF Enfield. GM000064215. See also 'Review of Small Arms Capacity in the United Kingdom', paper by the MGO, 16 July 1965, WO 32/20838, TNA.

4. McNaugher, *The M-16 Controversies*, p. 127.

5. From an examination of the 'Extracts for Approval' (the index that replaced the List of Changes from about 1965), it is not possible to establish the exact date on which the SA80 entered into service. The main reason for this is the extensive modifications and improvements that were made to the weapon. The L85A1 designation for the weapon suggests it was formally adopted in 1985. Certainly, large-scale orders for the weapon were placed with the RSAF in July 1985. See 'Handover Programme SO2 INF WPNS(a)', December 1990.

6. The weapon also 'borrowed' a number of design features from the Armalite A-18, see 'A Historical Review of the Armalite', 4 January 2010 (http://www.ammo-land.com/2011/10/historical-review-of-armalite/#axzz47xOlSM14).

7. Interview with Lt. Col. Tony Thornburn, former Commandant ITDU, Shrivenham, UK, 6 March 2012.

8. 'Point Paper: Impact of US Army Adoption of 5.56mm Second Standard NATO Ammunition', 9 March 1980, loose papers, Ezell Archive. No doubt among others, Colt Industries undertook a major programme of research into caseless ammunition.

9. 'NATO Standardization, Interoperability and Readiness: Report of the Special Subcommittee on NATO RSI of the Committee on Armed Services House of Representative with Additional Views', 95th Congress, Second Session. DEFE 13/1167, TNA.

10. Keith Hartley, 'Nato, Standardisation and Nationalism: An Economist's View', *RUSI: Royal United Services Institute for Defence Studies Journal*, 123, 3 (1978).

11. Lukes, *Power: A Radical View*, p. 16.

12. Satisficing is a decision-making strategy that produces decisions that satisfy the minimum necessary requirements of all those involved.

13. 'Anglo-German Steering Committee: Sub-Group for Small Arms and Ammunition', 23 January 1961, DEFE 7/1325, TNA.

14. 'Points for Future Consideration by the Tactical Doctrine Committee', 7 March 1958, WO 32/15874, TNA.

15. NATO Basic Military Requirements are put into historical context in 'Aspects of NATO, Armaments Cooperation, Planning and Support. Series 1, Issue 9', 1 January 1982, NATO Archive (http://archives.nato.int/uploads/r/null/1/3/ 137751/0193_Aspects_of_NATO-Armaments_Cooperation__Planning_and_ Support_ENG.pdf; accessed 15 August 2015).

16. Other NATO powers like West Germany preferred to use a heavier belt-fed machine gun like the MG42 re-chambered to fire NATO 7.62mm ammunition. This weapon (eventually renamed the MG3), which is suitable for troops who could rely on motorised transport, was appropriate for troops that did not need to fight out of theatre. See J. Weller, 'The West German MG42–59 and Its Influence on Tactics', *British Army Review*, 27 (1967), pp. 18–19.

17. Report of a visit to FRG MOD, Bonn on 2 January 1969 by Lt. Col. R.M. Porter, 5 February 1969, DEFE 13/1167, TNA.

18. W. Blair Haworth Jr, *The Bradley and How It Got That Way: Technology, Institutions, and the Problem of Mechanized Infantry in the United States Army*, London: Greenwood Press, 1999, p. 39.

19. Ibid.

20. Ibid.

21. 'Standardisation on 5.56mm', draft reply to Lt Gen. George Lea's letter to CDS, 17 April 1969, WO 32/21452, TNA.

22. McNaugher, *The M-16 Controversies*.

23. 'Development and Cost of the Army's Special Purpose Individual Weapon System', the comptroller general of the United States, 7 May 1970, Ezell Archive.

24. For the AR15's weight, and more importantly, the distribution of weight across the platoon, see 'Distribution of the Weights of the Various Small Arms Combinations', found in G (Operational Requirements and Analysis) memorandum no. 2/65, 'A Summary of the Evidence from the FARELF Trial of the AR15 Rifle ("Armalite")', March 1965, WO 291/2346, NA; See also 'Trial Report, Armalite Rifle AR15 .223inch', 22 April 1964, Box 340(870), RAA.

25. See List of Changes Rifle M16, 5.56mm Colt Model 604, RAA; and 'Brief Prepared for DCGS on Purchase of Lightweight Rifles for FARELF', 3 March 1965, DEFE 24/644, TNA.

26. See F.E. Sturtevant, 'England Trip Report', Colt Industries Inc., Colt's Firearms Division, 7 April 1965, Ezell Archive.

27. Letter from assistant secretary, ES1 to AEP, 12 March 1965, WO 32/20815, NA.

28. 'Lightweight Personal Weapon System: Study of Replacements for Existing Rifle and SMG, US Standardisation on 5.56mm, UK Views', WO 32/21452, TNA.

29. Lt. Col. D.S. Haynes (ret'd), 'The Light Machine Gun: A Survey', Royal Armament Research and Design Establishment, May 1967, DEFE 15/2032, TNA.

30. Ibid.

31. T.B. Dugelby, *Modern Military Rifles: The EM-2 Concept Comes of Age*, Toronto: Collector Grade Publications, 1984, p. 29.

32. See C. Taylor, 'A Brief Guide to Previous British Defence Reviews', House of Commons Library, SN/IA/5714, 19 October 2010.

33. C. McInnes, *Hot War, Cold War: The British Army's Way in Warfare, 1945–1995*, London: Brassey's, 1996, p. 55.

34. J. Strachey, *On the Prevention of War*, London: Macmillan, 1962, pp. 106–7.

35. D. French, *Army, Empire & Cold War: The British Army and Military Policy, 1945–1971*, Oxford: Oxford University Press, 2012.

36. See S.J. Moody, 'Deterrence or Defence? The British Army and the Changing Strategic Environment, 1945–1952' (http://www.academia.edu/1564725/Deterrence_or_Defence_The_British_Army_and_the_Changing_Strategic_Environment_1945–1952; accessed 9 July 2014).

37. McInnes, *Hot War, Cold War*, p. 56.

38. 'UK Design and Experimental Work', 16 September 1970, GEN000006484

39. Blair Haworth Jr, *The Bradley and How It Got That Way*, pp. 41–64.

40. It should be noted that, during the military trials at Hammelburg, 20,000 litres of 'good Bavarian beer' were consumed! The total cost to the NATO taxpayer was around $10 million. See 'A History of the 1977–1979 NATO Small Arms Test and Evaluation Programme', NATO Small Arms Test Control Commission, Ezell Archive.

41. Lukes, *Power: A Radical View*, p. 29.

42. Letter from Paul Lever, Defence Department, to Mr Wilberforce, 'Rationalisation, Standardisation and Specialisation', 6 November 1975, FCO 41/1674, TNA.

43. Summary SAW Status, 2 February 1980, SAW (Squad Automatic Weapon) M249, 5.56mm MINIMI, Ezell Archive.

44. S.G. Madden, 'Criteria for Wounding', July 1972, WO 189–1515, TNA.

45. 'Contribution by CDE to the Feasibility Study of Small Arms for the 1980s, (GST 3518)', Chemical Defence Establishment, Porton Down, Wilts. Loose Minutes Wounding Capacity, 1974.

46. 'Note from PUS to Minister on Standardisation', 3 July 1957, DEFE 7/1613, TNA.

47. This was certainly underlining much of the British Army's thinking during the early 1970s but was not quite made explicit by Britain's foremost theorist of low-intensity operations, Frank Kitson. See F. Kitson, *Bunch of Five*, London: Faber & Faber, 2010.

48. A.C. Elcomb, 'Training the Battle Shot', *British Army Review*, 34 (1970), p. 24.

49. Ibid. p. 31. The shooting skill of the Army had not significantly improved by the

late 1970s either. See A.E. Stockley, 'Recruit Shooting Standards', *British Army Review*, 62 (1979), pp. 70–1.

50. See paper entitled 'Future Tactical Doctrine and Equipment Requirements for Operations in Support of the Civil Power', 31 July 1970, HO 325–132, TNA.

51. 'Report of Task No.13a: Test of Armalite Rifle, AR-15(U), Research and Development Field Unit, Advance Research Project Agency, Office of the Secretary of Defense, August 20, 1962' (http://www.dtic.mil/dtic/tr/fulltext/u2/343778.pdf; accessed 23 July 2014).

52. See 'Armalite Post Action Report on 23 Feb 65', DEFE 24/644, TNA.

53. Quoted from Fallows, 'The American Army and the M16', p. 383.

54. 'Letter from Assistant Treasury Solicitor to Assistant Secretary Armament Design', 2 March 1964, DEFE 24/644, TNA.

55. 'Letter from C Davenport to PS Mr Alison', 'Armalite Rifles', 10 July 1979, CJ 4/2351, TNA.

56. After the British Army adoption of NATO SS109 5.56mm SAA, and in direct response to the concern over its apparent lethality when used in a Northern Ireland context, the MOD decided to make changes to the jacket thickness of the ammunition so as to prevent fragmentation. This led to the modification of the SS109 round and the eventual selection of L2A2 ammunition.

57. Kneubuehl et al., *Wound Ballistics*, p. 184.

58. Ibid. p. 185.

59. See, for example, 'Contribution by CDE to the Feasibility Study of Small Arms for the 1980s, (GST 3518)', Chemical Defence Establishment, Porton Down, Wilts. Loose Minutes Wounding Capacity, 1974.

60. Kneubuehl et al., *Wound Ballistics*, p. 185.

61. Ezell, *The Great Rifle Controversy*, p. 270. The agreement was publicised in 1976. See 'Alliance Moves Towards Further Standardization', NATO Press Release, 3 November 1976. NATO archive (http://archives.nato.int/uploads/r/null/1/3/139420/PRESS_RELEASE__76_12_BIL.pdf; accessed 1 July 2015).

62. Point Paper, 'Impact of US Army Adoption of 5.56 Second Standard NATO Ammunition', Ezell Archive.

63. See 'A History of the 1977–1979 NATO Small Arms Test and Evaluation Programme', NATO Small Arms Test Control Commission, Ezell Archive.

64. Point Paper, 'Impact of US Army Adoption of 5.56 Second Standard NATO Ammunition', Ezell Archive.

65. Thomas Glakas, 'Firing the New M16 Variant', *Defense & Foreign Affairs* (January/February 1982).

66. Don Walsh, 'Faster than a Speeding Bullet', *Defense & Foreign Affairs* (December 1982).

67. Henry Stanhope, 'The Germans Invent the Wonder Rifle', *The Times*, 24 July 1981.

68. Point Paper, 'Impact of US Army Adoption of 5.56mm Second Standard NATO Ammunition', 9 March 1980, loose papers, Ezell Archive

69. Don Walsh, 'Infantry Weapons: The Year in Review', *Defense & Foreign Affairs* (April 1988).

70. 'British Aerospace Sets Accord to Purchase German Rifle Maker', *Wall Street Journal*, 17 January 1991.

71. Walsh, 'Faster than a Speeding Bullet'.

72. M. Fackler, *What's Wrong with the Wound Ballistics Literature and Why: Institute Report No. 239*, Presidio, San Francisco: Letterman Army Institute of Research, 1987, p. 44.

73. W. Walker and p. Gummett, *Nationalism, Internationalism and the European Defence Market*, Paris: Institute for Security Studies, 1993.

74. E.B. Kapstein, 'Allies and Armaments', *Survival*, 44, 2 (2002).

75. J.S. Corum, 'Building a New Luftwaffe: The United States Air Force and Bundeswehr Planning for Rearmament, 1950–60', *Journal of Strategic Studies*, 27, 1 (2004).

76. 'NATO Standardization, Interoperability and Readiness: Report of the Special Subcommittee on NATO RSI of the Committee on Armed Services, House of Representatives with Additional Views, 95th Congress, Second Session', found in DEFE 13/1167, TNA.

7. IS IT GUCCI? INDUSTRY, STATUS ANXIETY AND THE FN MINIMI

1. 'Gucci Kit', ARRSEPEdia, 31 December 2007 (http://www.arrse.co.uk/wiki/Gucci; accessed 30 May 2016).

2. R. Mason, *Chickenhawk*, London: Corgi Books, 1983, p. 350.

3. W. Fowler, *Operation Barras: The SAS Rescue Mission; Sierra Leone*, London: Cassell, 2004, p. 142.

4. Interview with Major X, Portsdown West, UK, 30 November 2009.

5. Y.N. Harari, *The Ultimate Experience: Battlefield Revelations and the Making of Modern War Culture, 1450–2000*, Basingstoke: Palgrave MacMillan, 2008, pp. 231–40.

6. Hockey, *Squaddies*, pp. 75–7.

7. A. King, 'Understanding the Helmand Campaign: British Military Operations in Afghanistan', *International Affairs*, 86, 2 (2010).

8. S. Lukes, 'Further Thoughts on Power', *Political Studies Review*, 4, 2 (2006), p. 169.

9. See *Power: A Radical View*, pp. 144–151.

10. I. Shapiro, 'On the Second Edition of Lukes' *Third Face*', *Political Studies Review*, 4, 2 (2006), p. 148.

11. A more theoretical explanation of this can be found in Woolgar, 'Configuring the User: The Case of Usability Trials'.

12. 'Infantry Trials & Development Unit', September 1988, Loose Minutes, RAA.

13. Interview with Colonel David Benest, former CO 2nd Battalion, Parachute Regiment, London, UK, 2 August 2012.

14. 'Interview: Jonathan Lyle, DSTL', Civil Service World, 4 October 2014 (http://www.civilserviceworld.com/interview-jonathan-lyle; accessed 19 October 2014).

15. J. Sweetman, *War and Administration: The Significance of the Crimean War for the British Army*, Edinburgh: Scottish Academic Press, 1984; James H. Lewis, 'The Development of the Royal Small Arms Factory (Enfield Lock) and Its Influence Upon Mass Production and Product Design *c*.1820–1880', PhD thesis, Middlesex University, 1996.

16. See 'Author Interview with Frank Vowles, RSAF Apprentice 1939–1967', Enfield, UK, 9 August 2006, RAA.

17. See 'Note from MGO Sec to AUS ORD', 7 May 1987.

18. This is also clear in the response to tender documentation from each of the engineering companies that put in bids for the Tranche 2 contract. See boxes named, 'Britain Rifles 5.56mm SA80 Second Tranche BTR/SERCK' and 'Britain Rifles 5.56mm SA80 Second Tranche Ferranti/Ketlon/Pylon Group/Royal Ordnance/Chiltern'.

19. J. Edmiston, *The Sterling Years: Small Arms and the Men*, Barnsley: Pen & Sword, 2011, p. 143.

20. Quote from Geoff Ellis, assistant factory manager, RSAF *c*.1987. See 'Author Interview with Geoff Ellis, Enfield, UK', 9 June 2006, transcript in the RAA. Other Enfield employees, like Paul Ellis, Ken Wilkes and Malcolm Slater, expressed similar views. This is also illustrated in the 'Poo Files', a satirical cartoon series produced by an anonymous Enfield worker. Copies found in the RAA.

21. For a better idea of the apprenticeship scheme, see Graham Birchmore, Roy Burges and Association of Royal Small Arms Factory Apprentices, *The Lads of Enfield Lock: 172 Years of Apprentice Training at the Royal Small Arms Factory, Enfield, Middlesex, England, 1816–1988*, [England]: Royal Small Arms Factory, Apprentices Association, 2005.

22. Discussions with John Henshaw (member) and Ray Tuthill (honorary treasurer and membership secretary), RSAF Enfield Apprentices Association, Enfield, held at various times between 2004 and 2007, and former Enfield and later H&K employees, Dick Moyle and Barry Watkins, held at various times between 2011 and 2013.

23. 'MGO's Project Review of the INF WPNs', meeting held 6 June 1989. Document found in Britain Rifles SA80 5.56mm SA80 MOD Papers and MOD Steering Committee.

24. 'Section Small Arms post 1980 (GSR3518) for Consideration by Operational Requirements Committee', Army Department, 25 November 1974.

25. This was certainly the opinion of Paul Ellis, RSAF apprentice (1979–83) and member of the factory tool shop working with the SA80 design team. See 'Author Interview with Paul Ellis, Enfield, UK', 9 June 2006, transcript in the RAA.

26. 'Small Arms for the 1980s (SA80), Ordnance Board Proceeding', 42580, 21 March 1989.

27. 'Implications for SA80 for Adopting Ball Powder Propellants', Small Arms Tactical Support Unit, Royal College of Military Science, Shrivenham, August 1989.

28. For evidence of these discussions, see 'Royal Ordnance plc (Agreement)', HC Deb, 28 June 1988, vol. 136, cc225–6W (http://hansard.millbanksystems.com/written_answers/1988/jun/28/royal-ordnance-plc-agreement#S6CV0136P0_19880628_CWA_546; accessed 11 August 2014).

29. See 'Explosives and Propellants', HC Deb, 10 July 1995, vol. 263, c466W (http://hansard.millbanksystems.com/written_answers/1995/jul/10/explosives-and-propellants#S6CV0263P2_19950710_CWA_527; accessed 11 August 2014).

30. 'Revealed: MoD Told in 1985 New Rifle Was a Dud', *The Observer*, 23 August 1992.

31. 'The SA80 Rifle and Light Support Weapon, Report together with the Proceedings of the Committee relating to the Report, Minutes of Evidence and Memoranda', London: HMSO, 1993. S. Raw, *The Last Enfield: SA80; The Reluctant Rifle*, A Collector Grade Book, Cobourg, ON: Collector Grade Publications, 2003.

32. 'Revealed: MoD Told in 1985 New Rifle Was a Dud', *The Observer*, 23 August 1992.

33. 'OP GRANBY, Summary of Major Lessons Learned (C31 & LAND OPS), Interview with Lt. Col. David Parker, Sparsholt, UK', 6 March 2015.

34. Interview with Lt. Col. Tony Thornburn, Shrivenham, UK, 6 March 2012.

35. Specifically, within the Programme Directorate Engineering and Light Weapons (PD ELWS) team at DE&S. D/ELWS/19/10/5/3, October 1997.

36. See 'Evaluation Procedures for Future NATO Small Arms Weapon Systems', NATO document number: AC/225(LG/3-SG/1)D14, NATO archives, Brussels.

37. The specific group was the NATO Armaments Advisory Group (NAAG)/Land Group 3/Sub Group 1.

38. Interview with Lt. Col. Tony Thornburn, Shrivenham, UK, 6 March 2012.

39. Twenty-four changes of components in the IW and twenty-five in LSW.

40. Kincaid, *A Dinosaur in Whitehall*.

41. And 'Crows belong in the Depot'. Asher, *Shoot to Kill*, p. 100.

42. S. Ball, 'The Unchanging Lessons of Battle: The British Army and the Falklands War, 1982', in H. Strachan (ed.), *Big Wars and Small Wars: The British Army and the Lessons of War in the Twentieth Century*, London: Routledge, 2006, p. 149.

43. French, *Military Identities*.

44. Phone interview with Officer X, 20 April 2013

45. P. Bury, *Callsign Hades*, London: Simon & Schuster, 2010, p. 195.

46. King, *The Combat Soldier*, pp. 315–37.

47. See 'Summary and Consolidated Report by WTSFF on Infantry Questionnaire and Answers from Units in First and Eighth Armies on Conclusion of N. African Campaign May 1943', RAA, 200 Small Arms, General Box 1.

48. Ball, 'The Unchanging Lessons of Battle', p. 149.

49. 'Effectiveness of Rifle and LMG Fire Against Moving Targets', Trial Report TD/LMG/5B, ITDU, 10 July 1969, RAA. Lt. Col. D.S. Haynes (ret'd.) 'The Light Machine Gun: A Survey', Royal Armament Research and Design Establishment, May 1967, DEFE 15/2032, TNA.

50. Letter from J.R. McGregor, War Office, to D.R. Serpell, HM Treasury, 15 September 1958, DEFE 7–1325, TNA.

51. 'Memo for Ministry of Defence from Director of Infantry', 20 May 1957, DEFE 7–1613, TNA.

52. See List of Changes LC. C9773, LC. C9723, LC. C9860 and LC D121, EA. W/678, RAA.

53. See 'Record of Meeting Held in West Brigade Kuching on Monday, 15 February 1965 to Discuss the Armalite Rifle', DEFE 24/644, TNA.

54. Ibid. p. 230.

55. S. McMichael, *A Historical Perspective on Light Infantry*, Fort Leavenworth, KS: Combat Studies Institute, 1987, pp. 115–16.

56. D. Marston, 'Lost and Found in the Jungle: The Indian and British Army Jungle Warfare Doctrines for Burma, 1943–1945, and the Malayan Emergency, 1948–1960', in Strachan, *Big Wars and Small Wars*, pp. 92–3, 101–3. McMichael, *A Historical Perspective on Light Infantry*, pp. 107–14.

57. In the jungles of Borneo, it can take up to an hour to travel just 200 metres. See M. Kelly, *The Last Conflict: The Durham Light Infantry, Borneo 1966*, Bristol: Broadcast Books, 2004, p. 78.

58. 'Weapon Analysis of Patrols and Ambushes', memorandum no. 4/53, 23 June 1953, Operational Research Section (Malaya), WO 291/1729, TNA

59. For the AR15's weight and more importantly the distribution of weight across the platoon, see 'Distribution of the Weights of the Various Small Arms Combinations' found in G(Operational Requirements and Analysis) memorandum no. 2/65, 'A Summary of the Evidence from the FARELF Trial of the AR15 Rifle ("Armalite")', March 1965, WO 291/2346, TNA.

60. This was certainly the experience of Colin Shortis, the future director of infantry; interview with Major-general Colin Shortis, Topsham, UK, 7 January 2008.

61. 'A Report on a Light Support Weapon Comparative Trial', ITDU, 10 August 1984.

62. Ibid.

63. Interview with Major-general Colin Shortis, Topsham, UK, 7 January 2008.

64. Ibid. This team is not to be confused with the Northern Ireland Training and Advisory Team that provided cover for the Special Reconnaissance Unit (sometimes known as 14 Intelligence Company) which ran close surveillance of and undertook clandestine operations against the IRA.

65. Ibid.

66. Ibid.; A. Bain, 'The Infantry Section: Lifting Its Capability', *RUSI Defence Systems*, 10, 1 (2007), p. 87.

67. Interview with Major-general Colin Shortis, Topsham, UK, 7 January 2008.

68. Bain, 'The Infantry Section', p. 87.

69. Interview with Major-general Colin Shortis, Topsham, UK, 7 January 2008; interview with Lt. Col. Tony Briard, Warminster, UK, 24 May 2007.

70. 'SA80's Enfield Weapon System, Report and Submission for Acceptance and Approval of the Light Support Weapon', RSAF, September 1984.

71. 'A Report on a Light Support Weapon Comparative Trial', ITDU, 10 August 1984, RAA.

72. Interview with Major-general Colin Shortis, Topsham, UK, 7 January 2008.

73. Ibid.

74. Ibid. According to Lt. Col. Thornburn, the LSW was never formally accepted into service—partly because it could not pass the 'cook-off' test, with a round up a hot chamber. H&K subsequently corrected this in a later mid-life upgrade by introducing a heavier barrel. Private correspondence with author, 28 November 2014.

75. Reference withheld.

76. 'A Report on a Light Support Weapon Comparative Trial', ITDU, 10 August 1984, RAA.

77. J. Storr, 'The Real Role of Small Arms in Combat', *RUSI Defence Systems* (June 2009).

78. See 'A History of the 1977–1979 NATO Small Arms Test and Evaluation Programme', NATO Small Arms Test Control Commission, Ezell Archive.

79. Interview with Lt. Col. Tony Thornburn, Shrivenham UK, 6 March 2012.

80. Interview with Colonel David Benest, former CO 2nd Battalion, Parachute Regiment, London, UK, 2 August 2012.

81. For Jary's views on the Bren versus the MG34/42, see Jary, *18 Platoon*, p. 51.

82. For more detail on the engagement, see H. Bicheno, *Razor's Edge: The Unofficial History of the Falklands War*, London: Weidenfeld & Nicolson, 2006; M. Adkin, *Goose Green: The Crucial Battle of the Falklands*, London: Cassell, 1992.

83. Colonel David Benest, '2 PARA Falklands: 30 Years On', lecture given at the War Studies Seminars, University of Birmingham, 2 October 2012. Bicheno, *Razor's Edge*.

84. M. Ford and J. Levett, 'Confrontation or Culture? Marksmanship, the M16 and the Transatlantic Relationship', *British Journal for Military History* (forthcoming).

85. Minutes of meeting held by VCIGS in Hotel Metropole at 3 p.m., 20 July, to discuss 'The steps to be taken to improve small arms shooting in the Army and further support for the Army Rifle Association', 20 July 1949, p. 2, WO 216/324, TNA.

86. Interview with Colonel David Benest, former CO 2nd Battalion, Parachute Regiment, London, UK, 2 August 2012.

87. Ibid.

88. Interview with Lt. Col. Tony Thornburn, Shrivenham, UK, 6 March 2012.

89. Storr, 'The Real Role of Small Arms in Combat', pp. 45–6.

90. S. Junger, *War*, London: Fourth Estate, 2011, pp. 150–1.

91. W.F. Owen, 'UK Platoon Weapons and the Weight Capability Myth', *RUSI Defence Systems*, 10, 90–3 (2007), p. 90.

92. A. King, 'The Digital Revolution: Camouflage in the Twenty-First Century', *Millennium: Journal of International Studies*, 42, 2 (2014).

93. 'The Basics of Army Life', ARRSEPEdia, 6 March 2014 (http://www.arrse.co.uk/wiki/The_Basics; accessed 2 August 2014).

94. King, 'The Digital Revolution'.

95. David Benest, who, as SO2b, LSOR 10b in MOD, endorsed the Operational Requirement for M16A2 and Minimi in 1988 for UK SOF. Private correspondence, 10 December 2014.

96. 'An Historical Analysis of the Suppressive Effects of Infantry Small Arms/Direct Fire Support Weapons', October 1995.

97. See, for example, J. Fergusson, *A Million Bullets: The Real Story of the British Army in Afghanistan*, London: Bantam Press, 2008.

98. 'British Forces Fired 10,000 Rounds Every Day during Eight Year Conflict with Taliban', Daily Mail Online, 8 April 2015 (http://www.dailymail.co.uk/news/article-3029794/British-forces-fired-46-MILLION-bullets-Taliban-10–000-rounds-shot-day-eight-year-conflict-cost-200million-taxpayer.html; accessed 25 July 2015).

99. Private correspondence with Lt. Col. Tony Thornburn, 28 November 2011.

100. P. Higate, '"Cowboys and Professionals": The Politics of Identity Work in the Private and Military Security Company', *Millennium: Journal of International Studies*, 40, 2 (2012), p. 332.

101. Mark Clegg, 'Force Protection and Society', *Defense & Security Analysis*, 28, 2 (2012).

102. W.F. Owen, 'Alice in Warminster: Capability Gain or Increased Performance?', *RUSI Defence Systems*, 12, 1 (2009).

103. R. Stahl, *Militainment, Inc.: War, Media, and Popular Culture*, New York: Routledge, 2010.

104. A.J. Echevarria, 'Redefining Stand-Off Warfare: Modern Efforts and Implications', in S. Scheipers (ed.), *Heroism & the Changing Character of War: Toward Post-Heroic Warfare?*, Basingstoke: Palgrave MacMillan, 2014.

105. A. King, 'Cohesion: Heroic and Post-Heroic Combat', in ibid.

106. 'The Special Air Service and the Concentration of Military Power', *Armed Forces & Society*, 35, 4 (2009).

107. P. Ratcliffe, *Eye of the Storm*, London: Michael O'Mara, 2001, p. 90.

108. M. Owen, *No Easy Day: The Navy Seal Mission That Killed Osama Bin Laden*, London: Penguin, 2013, p. 48.

109. For more information on the SHOT Show, see 'How Big Is the SHOT Show?' (http://visual.ly/how-big-shot-show; accessed 10 November 2014).

110. A similar pattern can be observed in the way the Glock was sold to US police forces. See Barrett, *Glock*.

111. J. Schatz, 'US Military Losing Edge in Small Arms', National Defense, November 2015 (http://www.nationaldefensemagazine.org/archive/2015/November/Pages/USMilitaryLosingEdgeinSmallArms.aspx; accessed 9 November 2015).

112. King, 'The Special Air Service', p. 661.

113. Rose, *The American Rifle*, p. 399; A. Feickert, *CRS Report for Congress: The Army's M-4 Carbine; Background and Issues for Congress*, Washington, DC: Congressional Research Service, 2010, p. 5. 'UK Royal Marines Call for Rifle Improvements', PR Newsire, 25 July 2013 (http://www.prnewswire.co.uk/news-releases/uk-royal-marines-call-for-rifle-improvements-216882531.html; accessed 30 May 2016).

114. K. Dowding, 'Three-Dimensional Power: A Discussion of Steven Lukes' *Power: A Radical View*', *Political Studies Review*, 4, 2 (2006), p. 137.

115. King, 'The Special Air Service'.

116. Of course, similar sentiments could be asserted for the Royal Marines Commando, but as a branch of the Royal Navy this unit has not had as direct an impact on the rest of the Green Army as the Parachute Regiment.

8. FROM THE MUNDANE TO THE SOPHISTICATED: MILITARY INNOVATION STUDIES AND THE QUESTION OF POWER

1. I. Welsh, *Mobilising Modernity: The Nuclear Moment*, London: Routledge, 2000.

2. Snow, *The Two Cultures*.

3. This topic is thoroughly explored in A. Bousquet, *The Scientific Way of Warfare*, London: Hurst, 2009.

4. The Squad Designated Marksman concept is outlined in detail in Headquarters Department of the Army, *FM 3–21.8: The Infantry Rifle Platoon and Squad*, Washington, DC: US Army, 2007. The main critic is Ehrhart, *Increasing Small Arms Lethality in Afghanistan*, p. 47.

5. John Law gives a good summary of ANT in J. Law, 'Actor Network Theory and Material Semiotics', in B.S. Turner (ed.), *The New Blackwell Companion to Social Theory*, Oxford: Blackwell, 2008.

6. Grint and Woolgar, *The Machine at Work*, p. 30.

7. Prokosch, *The Technology of Killing*; Bourke, *Wounding the World*.

8. Urban, *The Edge*, pp. 19–24.

9. 'Army aims for positive improvements with M4A1+', 7 July 2015 (http://www.armytimes.com/story/military/tech/2015/07/04/m4a1plus-army-carbine-industry/28161275/; accessed 30 May 2016).

BIBLIOGRAPHY

Adamsky, D., *The Culture of Military Innovation: The Impact of Cultural Factors on the Revolution in Military Affairs in Russia, the US and Israel*, Stanford: Stanford University Press, 2010.

Adkin, M., *Goose Green: The Crucial Battle of the Falklands*, London: Cassell, 1992.

Alder, K., *Engineering the Revolution: Arms and Enlightenment in France, 1763–1815*, Princeton: Princeton University Press, 1997.

Allison, G. and M.H. Halperin, 'Bureaucratic Politics: A Paradigm and Some Policy Implications', *World Politics*, 24, Supplement: Theory and Policy in International Relations (1972), pp. 40–79.

Allsop, D.F. and M.A. Toomey, *Small Arms: General Design*, Land Warfare, Brassey's New Battlefield Weapons Systems and Technology Series into the 21st Century, London: Brassey's, 1999.

Anon., *Wanat: Combat Action in Afghanistan 2008*, Fort Leavenworth, KS: Combat Studies Institute Press, 2010.

Armstrong, D. *Bullets and Bureaucrats: The Machine Gun and the United States Army, 1861–1916*, London: Greenwood Press, 1982.

Army, Headquarters Department of the, *FM 3–21.8: The Infantry Rifle Platoon and Squad*, Washington, DC: US Army, 2007.

Asher, M., *Shoot to Kill: A Soldier's Journey through Violence*, London: Cassell Military, 2004.

Avant, D., *Political Institutions and Military Change: Lessons from Peripheral Wars*, Cornell Studies in Security Affairs, Ithaca: Cornell University Press, 1994.

Avery, J.P., 'An Army Outgunned: Physics Demands a New Basic Combat Weapon', *Military Review*, XCII (July–August 2012), pp. 2–8.

Bacevich, A., *The Pentomic Era: The US Army Between Korea and Vietnam*, Washington, DC: National Defense University Press, 1986.

Badsey, S., 'The Boer War (1899–1902) and British Cavalry Doctrine: A Re-evaluation', *Journal of Military History*, 71, 1 (2007), pp. 75–97.

—— *Doctrine and Reform in the British Cavalry, 1880–1918*, Aldershot: Ashgate, 2008.

Bain, A., 'The Infantry Section: Lifting Its Capability', *RUSI Defence Systems*, 10, 1 (2007), pp. 86–8.

Ball, S., 'The Unchanging Lessons of Battle: The British Army and the Falklands War, 1982', in H. Strachan (ed.), *Big Wars and Small Wars: The British Army and the Lessons of War in the Twentieth Century*, pp. 145–61, London: Routledge, 2006.

Barkawi, T. and S. Brighton, 'Powers of War: Fighting, Knowledge, and Critique', *International Political Sociology*, 5, 2 (June 2011), pp. 126–43.

Barrett, P.M., *Glock: The Rise of America's Gun*, New York: Broadway Paperbacks, 2012.

Bicheno, H., *Razor's Edge: The Unofficial History of the Falklands War*, London: Weidenfeld & Nicolson, 2006.

Biddle, S., *Military Power: Explaining Victory and Defeat in Modern Battle*, Princeton: Princeton University Press, 2004.

Bidwell, S. and D. Graham, *Fire-Power: British Army Weapons and Theories of War 1904–1945*, London: George Allen & Unwin, 1982.

Bijker, Wiebe E., *Of Bicycles, Bakelites, and Bulbs: Toward a Theory of Sociotechnical Change*, Inside Technology Series, Cambridge, MA; London: MIT Press, 1995.

—— 'Social Construction of Facts and Artefacts', in Wiebe E. Bijker, Thomas Hughes and T. Pinch (eds), *The Social Construction of Technological Systems*, Cambridge, MA: MIT Press, 1989.

Bijker, Wiebe E. and John Law (eds), *Shaping Technology/Building Society: Studies in Sociotechnical Change*, Inside Technology, Cambridge, MA: MIT Press, 1992.

Birchmore, Graham, Roy Burges and Association Royal Small Arms Factory Apprentices, *The Lads of Enfield Lock: 172 Years of Apprentice Training at the Royal Small Arms Factory, Enfield, Middlesex, England, 1816–1988*, [England]: Royal Small Arms Factory, Enfield, Apprentices Association, 2005.

Blair Haworth Jr, W., *The Bradley and How It Got That Way: Technology, Institutions, and the Problem of Mechanized Infantry in the United States Army*, London: Greenwood Press, 1999.

Bloor, D., *Knowledge and Social Imagery*, Chicago: University of Chicago Press, 1976.

Bou, J., 'Cavalry, Firepower, and Swords: The Australian Light Horse and the Tactical Lessons of Cavalry Operations in Palestine, 1916–1918', *Journal of Military History*, 71, 1 (2007), pp. 99–125.

Bourke, J., *Wounding the World: How Military Violence and War-Play Invade Our Lives*, London: Virago, 2014.

Bourke, Joanna, *An Intimate History of Killing: Face-to-Face Killing in Twentieth-Century Warfare*, London: Granta, 1999.

Bousquet, A., *The Scientific Way of Warfare*, London: Hurst, 2009.

Bowker, G. and S. Leigh Star, *Sorting Things Out: Classification and Its Consequences*, Cambridge, MA: MIT Press, 1999.

Buckley, J., *Monty's Men: The British Army and the Liberation of Europe*, New Haven: Yale University Press, 2013.

Bury, P., *Callsign Hades*, London: Simon & Schuster, 2010.

Callender, G.R. and R.W. French, 'Ballistic Characteristics of Wounding Agents', in J.C. Colonel Beyer Jr (ed.), *Wound Ballistics*, Washington, DC: Office of the Surgeon General, Department of the Army, 1962.

——— 'Wound Ballistics: Studies in the Mechanism of Wound Production by Rifle Bullets', *The Military Surgeon*, 77 (October 1935), pp. 177–201.

Challener, R., *The French Theory of the Nation in Arms, 1866–1939*, New York: Columbia University Press, 1955.

Chambers, J.W., 'S.L.A. Marshall's Men against Fire: New Evidence Regarding Fire Ratios', *Parameters* (Autumn 2003), pp. 113–21.

Chivers, C.J., *The Gun*, New York: Simon & Schuster, 2011.

Churchill, W., *The Second World War, Vol. II: Their Finest Hour*, London: Cassell & Co., 1949.

Clausewitz, Carl Von, *On War*, trans. Michael Howard and Peter Paret, Everyman's Library 121, new edn, London: Everyman, 1993.

Clegg, Mark, 'Force Protection and Society', *Defense & Security Analysis*, 28, 2 (June 2012), pp. 131–9.

Colonel Beyer Jr, J.C. (ed.), *Wound Ballistics*, Washington, DC: Office of the Surgeon General, Department of the Army, 1962.

Cormack, A.J.R., *Famous Rifles and Machine Guns*, London: Barrie and Jenkins, 1977.

Cornish, P., *Machine Guns and the Great War*, Barnsley: Pen & Sword, 2009.

Corum, J.S., 'Building a New Luftwaffe: The United States Air Force and Bundeswehr Planning for Rearmament, 1950–60', *Journal of Strategic Studies*, 27, 1 (March 2004), pp. 89–113.

Crang, J., *The British Army and the People's War, 1939–1945*, Manchester: Manchester University Press, 2000.

Cusumano, Eugenio, 'Bridging the Gap: Mobilisation Constraints and Contractor Support to US and UK Military Operations', *Journal of Strategic Studies* (2015), pp. 1–29.

D'Este, Carlo, *Decision in Normandy*, Classic Military History, London: Penguin, 2001.

David, S., *Mutiny at Salerno: An Injustice Exposed*, London: Conway Maritime Press, 2005.

Diamond, J., *Guns, Germs and Steel*, New York: Norton, 1997.

Diaz, T., *The Last Gun: How Changes in the Gun Industry Are Killing Americans and What It Will Take to Stop It*, New York: The New Press, 2014.

——— *Making a Killing: The Business of Guns in America*, New York: The New Press, 2000.

Dombrowski, P. and E Gholz, *Buying Military Transformation: Technology Innovation and the Defense Industry*, New York: Columbia University Press, 2003.

Doubler, Michael D., *Closing with the Enemy: How GIs Fought the War in Europe, 1944–1945*, Modern War Studies, Lawrence, KS: University Press of Kansas, 1994.

Dowding, K., 'Three-Dimensional Power: A Discussion of Steven Lukes' *Power; A Radical View*', *Political Studies Review*, 4, 2 (2006), pp. 136–45.

Drummond, N. and A. Williams, 'Time to Bite the Bullet over Under-Fire Ammo', *Jane's Defence Weekly* (2009).

Dugelby, T.B., *EM-2 Concept and Design: A Rifle Ahead of Its Time*, Toronto: Collector Grade Publications, 1980.

——— *Modern Military Rifles: The EM-2 Concept Comes of Age*, Toronto: Collector Grade Publications, 1984.

Dyvik, S., '"Valhalla Rising": Gender, Embodiment and Experience in Military Memoirs', *Security Dialogue*, 47, 2 (2016), pp. 133–50.

Echevarria, A.J., 'Redefining Stand-Off Warfare: Modern Efforts and Implications', in S. Scheipers (ed.), *Heroism & the Changing Character of War: Toward Post-Heroic Warfare?*, pp. 203–20. Basingstoke: Palgrave MacMillan, 2014.

Edgerton, David, *Warfare State: Britain, 1920–1970*, Cambridge: Cambridge University Press, 2006.

Edmiston, J., *The Sterling Years: Small Arms and the Men*, Barnsley: Pen & Sword, 2011.

Ehrhart, T.P., *Increasing Small Arms Lethality in Afghanistan: Taking Back the Infantry Half-Kilometer*, Fort Leavenworth: School of Advanced Military Studies (SAMS), 2009.

Elcomb, A.C., 'Training the Battle Shot', *British Army Review*, 34 (1970), pp. 22–5.

Ellis, John, *The Social History of the Machine Gun*, London: Pimlico, 1976.

Ezell, E., 'Cracks in the Post-War Anglo-American alliance: The Great Rifle Controversy, 1947–1957', *Military Affairs*, 38, 4 (1974), pp. 138–41.

——— *The Great Rifle Controversy: Search for the Ultimate Infantry Weapon from World War 2 through Vietnam and Beyond*, Harrisburg, PA: Stackpole Books, 1984.

Fackler, M., *What's Wrong with the Wound Ballistics Literature and Why: Institute Report No. 239*, Presidio, San Francisco: Letterman Army Institute of Research, 1987.

Fallows, J., 'The American Army and the M16', in D. MacKenzie and J. Wajcman (eds), *The Social Shaping of Technology*, pp. 382–94, Maidenhead: Open University Press, 1999.

Farr, V., H. Myrttinen and A. Schnabel (eds), *Sexed Pistols: The Gendered Impacts of Small Arms and Light Weapons*, New York: United Nations University Press, 2009.

Farrell, T., 'Weapons without a Cause: Buying Stealth Bombers the American Way', *Arms Control*, 14, 2 (1993), pp. 115–50.

——— *Weapons without Cause: The Politics of Weapons Acquisition in the United States*, New York: St. Martin's Press, 1997.

Farrell, T., F.P.B. Osinga and J. Russell (eds), *Military Adaptation in Afghanistan*, Stanford: Stanford University Press, 2013.

Farrell, T. and T. Terriff (eds), *The Sources of Military Change: Culture, Politics, Technology*, London: Lynne Rienner, 2002.

Feickert, A., *CRS Report for Congress: The Army's M-4 Carbine; Background and Issues for Congress*, Washington, DC: Congressional Research Service, 2010.

Fergusson, J., *A Million Bullets: The Real Story of the British Army in Afghanistan*, London: Bantam Press, 2008.

Ford, M., 'The British Army and the Politics of Rifle Development, 1880 to 1986', PhD thesis, King's College, London, 2008.

——— 'Marksmanship, Officer–Man Relations and the Short Magazine Lee-Enfield', *War in History*, 23, 3 (2016).

——— 'Operational Research, Military Judgement and the Politics of Technical Change in the British Infantry, 1943–1953', *Journal of Strategic Studies*, 32, 6 (2009), pp. 871–97.

——— 'Towards a Revolution in Firepower? Logistics, Lethality, and the Lee-Metford', *War in History*, 20, 3 (2013), pp. 273–99.

Ford, M. and J. Levett, 'Confrontation or Culture? Marksmanship, the M16 and the Transatlantic Relationship', *British Journal for Military History* (forthcoming).

Forman, Denis, *To Reason Why*, London: Abacus, 1993.

Foucault, Michel, *Power/Knowledge: Selected Interviews and Other Writings, 1972–1977*, 1st American edn, New York: Pantheon Books, 1980.

Fowler, W., *Operation Barras: The SAS Rescue Mission: Sierra Leone*, London: Cassell, 2004.

French, D., *Army, Empire & Cold War: The British Army and Military Policy, 1945–1971*, Oxford: Oxford University Press, 2012.

——— *Military Identities: The Regimental System, the British Army, and the British People, c.1870–2000*, Oxford: Oxford University Press, 2005.

——— *Raising Churchill's Army: The British Army and the War against Germany, 1919–1945*, Oxford: Oxford University Press, 2000.

Fukuyama, F., *State-Building: Governance and World Order in the 21st Century*, London: Profile Books, 2005.

Fuller, J.F.C., *British Light Infantry in the Eighteenth Century (An Introduction to 'Sir John Moore's System of Training')*, London: Hutchinson & Co., 1925.

——— *Sir John Moore's System of Training*, London: Hutchinson & Co., 1925.

Gentile, G., 'A Strategy of Tactics: Population-Centric COIN and the Army', *Parameters*, XXXIX, 3 (2009), pp. 5–17.

——— *A Wrong Turn: America's Deadly Embrace of Counterinsurgency*, New York: The New Press, 2013.

Gibson, James William, *The Perfect War: Technowar in Vietnam*, Boston: Atlantic Monthly Press, 2000.

Gilby, N., *Deception in High Places: A History of Bribery in Britain's Arms Trade*, London: Pluto Books, 2014.

Gilmore, R., '"The New Courage": Rifles and Soldier Individualism, 1876–1918', *Military Affairs*, 40, 3 (October 1976), pp. 97–102.

Griffith, P., *Battle Tactics of the Western Front: The British Army's Art of Attack, 1916–1918*, London: Yale University Press, 1996.

——— *Forward into Battle: Fighting Tactics from Waterloo to the Near Future*, revised and updated edn, Novato, CA: Presidio, 1991.

Grint, K. and S. Woolgar, *The Machine at Work: Technology, Work, and Organization*, Cambridge: Polity Press, 1997.

Grissom, A., 'The Future of Military Innovation Studies', *Journal of Strategic Studies*, 29, 5 (2006), pp. 905–34.

Grossman, D., *On Killing: The Psychological Cost of Learning to Kill in War and Society*, A Black Bay Book, Boston: Little, Brown and Company, 1996.

Gummett, P. and Bud, R., *Cold War, Hot Science: Applied Research in Britain's Defence Laboratories, 1945–1990*, London: Routledge, 1998.

Harari, Y.N., *The Ultimate Experience: Battlefield Revelations and the Making of Modern War Culture, 1450–2000*, Basingstoke: Palgrave MacMillan, 2008.

Hard, M., 'Beyond Harmony and Consensus: A Social-Conflict Approach to Technology', *Science, Technology & Human Values*, 18, 4 (Fall 1993), pp. 408–32.

Hart, S., *Montgomery and 'Colossal Cracks': The 21st Army Group in Northwest Europe, 1944–45*, Praeger Series in War Studies, Westport, CT; London: Praeger, 2000.

Hartley, Keith, 'Nato, Standardisation and Nationalism: An Economist's View', *RUSI: Royal United Services Institute for Defence Studies Journal*, 123, 3 (1978), p. 57.

Hartung, W.D., *Prophets of War: Lockheed Martin and the Making of the Military-Industrial Complex*, New York: Nation Books, 2011.

Hastings, M., *Overlord: D-Day and the Battle for Normandy 1944*, London: Macmillan, 1993.

Higate, P., '"Cowboys and Professionals": The Politics of Identity Work in the Private and Military Security Company', *Millennium: Journal of International Studies*, 40, 2 (2012), pp. 321–41.

Hitchman, N.A., *Operational Requirements for an Infantry Hand Weapon*, Chevy Chase, MD: Operations Research Office, Johns Hopkins University, 1952.

Hobart, F.W.A., 'The BSA 28p. 280 Rifle', *Guns Review*, 12, 5 (May 1972), pp. 185–7.

Hockey, J., *Squaddies: A Portrait of a Subculture*, Exeter: Exeter University Press, 1986.

Holmes, R., *Acts of War: The Behaviour of Men in Battle*, London: Weidenfeld & Nicolson, 2003.

——— *Redcoat: The British Soldier in the Age of Horse and Musket*, London: HarperCollins, 2002.

Horowitz, M.C., *The Diffusion of Military Power: Causes and Consequences for International Politics*, Princeton: Princeton University Press, 2010.

Huon, J., *Military Rifle and Machine Gun Cartridges*, London: Arms & Armor Press, 1989.

Janowitz, M. and E.A. Shils, 'Cohesion and Disintegration in the Wehrmacht in World War II', *Public Opinion Quarterly*, 12 (1948), pp. 280–315.

Jary, Sydney, *18 Platoon*, 5th edn, Winchester, Hants: The Light Infantry Regimental Headquarters, 2003.

Johnson, R., *The Afghan Way of War: Culture and Pragmatism; A Critical History*, London: Hurst, 2011.

Jones, K., G. Macola and D. Welch (eds), *A Cultural History of Firearms in the Age of Empires*, Farnham: Ashgate, 2013.

Jones, S., *From Boer War to World War: Tactical Reform of the British Army 1902– 1914*, Norman: Oklahoma University Press, 2012.

Junger, S., *War*, London: Fourth Estate, 2011.

Kaldor, M., *The Baroque Arsenal*, London: Andre Deutsch, 1982.

Kapstein, E.B., 'Allies and Armaments', *Survival*, 44, 2 (Summer 2002), pp. 141–55.

Kelly, M., *The Last Conflict: The Durham Light Infantry, Borneo 1966*, Bristol: Broadcast Books, 2004.

Kier, E., 'Culture and Military Doctrine: France between the Wars', *International Security*, 19, 4 (1995), pp. 65–93.

——— *Imagining War: French and British Military Doctrine between the Wars*, Princeton: Princeton University Press, 1997.

Kincaid, Bill, *A Dinosaur in Whitehall: The True Cost of Defence Procurement Bureaucracy*, 1st edn, London: Brassey's, 1997.

King, A., 'Cohesion: Heroic and Post-Heroic Combat', in S. Scheipers (ed.), *Heroism & the Changing Character of War: Toward Post-Heroic Warfare?*, pp. 221–36, Basingstoke: Palgrave MacMillan, 2014.

——— *The Combat Soldier: Infantry Tactics and Cohesion in the Twentieth and Twenty-First Centuries*, Oxford: Oxford University Press, 2013.

——– 'The Digital Revolution: Camouflage in the Twenty-First Century', *Millennium: Journal of International Studies*, 42, 2 (2014), pp. 397–424.

——— 'The Special Air Service and the Concentration of Military Power', *Armed Forces & Society*, 35, 4 (July 2009), pp. 646–66.

——— 'Understanding the Helmand Campaign: British Military Operations in Afghanistan', *International Affairs*, 86, 2 (March 2010), pp. 311–33.

Kitson, F., *Bunch of Five*, London: Faber & Faber, 2010.

Kneubuehl, B.P., R.M. Coupland, M.A. Rothschild and M.J. Thali (eds), *Wound Ballistics: Basics and Applications*, Berlin: Springer, 2008.

Laidler, Peter, *The Sten Machine Carbine*, A Collector Grade Book, Cobourg, ON: Collector Grade Publications, 2000.

Larson, M.S., *The Rise of Professionalism: A Sociological Analysis*, Berkeley: University of California Press, 1979.

Latour, B. and S. Woolgar, *Laboratory Life: The Social Construction of Scientific Facts*, London: Sage Publications, 1979.

Law, J., 'Actor Network Theory and Material Semiotics', in B.S. Turner (ed.), *The New Blackwell Companion to Social Theory*, pp. 141–58, Oxford: Blackwell, 2008.

——— 'Technology and Heterogeneous Engineering', in W. E. Bijker, T. P. Hughes and T. Pinch (eds), *The Social Construction of Technological Systems*, pp. 113–34, Cambridge, MA: MIT Press, 1987.

Law, J. and M. Callon, 'Engineering and Sociology in a Military Aircraft Project: A Network Analysis of Technological Change', *Social Problems*, 35, 3 (1988), pp. 284–97.

Lawson, S., 'Articulation, Antagonism, and Intercalation in Western Military Imaginaries', *Security Dialogue*, 42, 1 (2011), pp. 39–56.

Lee, J., *A Soldier's Life: General Sir Ian Hamilton, 1853–1947*, London: Pan Books, 2000.

Lepre, G., *Fragging: Why US Soldiers Assaulted Their Officers in Vietnam*, Lubbock: Texas Tech University Press, 2011.

Lewin, Ronald, *Slim: The Standardbearer; A Biography of Field-Marshal the Viscount Slim*, London: Pan Books, 1978.

Lewis, James H., 'The Development of the Royal Small Arms Factory (Enfield Lock) and Its Influence Upon Mass Production and Product Design *c.*1820–1880', PhD thesis, Middlesex University, 1996.

Lukes, S., 'Further Thoughts on Power', *Political Studies Review*, 4, 2 (2006), pp. 164–73.

——— *Power: A Radical View*, 2nd edn, Basingstoke: Palgrave Macmillan, 2005.

MacKenzie, D., *Inventing Accuracy: A Historical Sociology of Nuclear Missile Guidance*, Cambridge, MA: MIT Press, 1990.

Mackenzie, D. and G. Spinardi, 'The Shaping of Nuclear-Weapon System Technology: United-States Fleet Ballistic-Missile Guidance and Navigation 2. Going for Broke; The Path to Trident', *Social Studies of Science*, 18, 4 (November 1988), pp. 581–624.

MacKenzie, Donald A. and Judy Wajcman (eds), *The Social Shaping of Technology: How the Refrigerator Got Its Hum*, 2nd edn, Milton Keynes: Open University Press, 1999.

MacKenzie, H., 'The ABCs of Canada's International Economic Relations, 1945–1951', in G. Donaghy (ed.), *Canada and the Early Cold War, 1943–1957*, Ottawa: Department of Foreign Affairs and International Trade, 1998.

Mahnken, T., *Technology and the American Way of Warfare since 1945*, New York: Columbia University Press, 2008.

——— *Uncovering Ways of War: US Intelligence and Foreign Military Innovation*, Ithaca, NY: Cornell University Press, 2002.

Marshall, A., *Problems of Estimating Military Power*, Washington, DC: RAND, 1966.

Marshall, S.L.A., *Commentary on Infantry Operations and Weapon Usage in Korea: Winter of 1950–51*, Chevy Chase, MD: Operations Research Office, Johns Hopkins University, 1951.

—— *Men Against Fire: The Problem of Battle Command*, revised 2nd edn, Norman: University of Oklahoma Press, 2000 [1947].

Marston, D., 'Lost and Found in the Jungle: The Indian and British Army Jungle Warfare Doctrines for Burma, 1943–1945, and the Malayan Emergency, 1948–1960', in H. Strachan (ed.), *Big Wars and Small Wars: The British Army and the Lessons of War in the Twentieth Century*, pp. 54–83, London: Routledge, 2006.

Martinage, R., *Toward a New Offset Strategy: Exploiting US Long-Term Advantages to Restore US Global Power Projection Capability*, Washington, DC: Center for Strategy and Budgetary Assessments, 2014.

Mason, R., *Chickenhawk*, London: Corgi Books, 1983.

McInnes, C., *Hot War, Cold War: The British Army's Way in Warfare, 1945–1995*, London: Brassey's, 1996.

McMichael, S., *A Historical Perspective on Light Infantry*, Fort Leavenworth, KS: Combat Studies Institute, 1987.

McNaugher, T., *The M-16 Controversies: Military Organisations and Weapons Acquisition*, New York: Praeger, 1984.

—— *New Weapons, Old Politics: America's Military Procurement Muddles*, Washington, DC: Brookings Institution, 1989.

—— 'Weapons Procurement: The Futility of Reform', *International Security*, 12, 2 (Autumn 1987), pp. 63–104.

Millett, A.R. and W. Murray (eds), *Military Effectiveness, Volume 1: The First World War*, Boston: Allen & Unwin, 1988.

—— (eds), *Military Effectiveness, Volume 2: The Interwar Period*, Boston: Allen & Unwin, 1988.

—— (eds), *Military Effectiveness, Volume 3: The Second World War*, Boston: Allen & Unwin, 1988.

Moskos, C.C., 'The Concept of the Military-Industrial Complex: Radical Critique or Liberal Bogey?', *Social Problems*, 21, 4 (1974), pp. 498–512.

Moy, Timothy, *War Machines: Transforming Technologies in the U.S. Military, 1920–1940*, College Station: Texas A & M University Press, 2001.

Murray, W., *Military Adaptation in War: With Fear of Change*, Cambridge: Cambridge University Press, 2011.

Murray, W. and A.R. Millett, *Calculations: Net Assessment and the Coming of World War II*, New York: Free Press, 1992.

O'Brien, T., *If I Die in a Combat Zone*, London: Granada Publishing, 1973.

O'Hanlon, M.E., *The Science of War: Defense Budgeting, Military Technology, Logistics and Combat Outcomes*, Princeton: Princeton University Press, 2009.

Oudshoorn, N. and T.J. Pinch (eds), *How Users Matter: The Co-Construction of Users and Technologies*, Inside Technology, Cambridge, MA; London: MIT Press, 2003.

Owen, M., *No Easy Day: The Navy Seal Mission That Killed Osama Bin Laden*, London: Penguin Books, 2013.

Owen, W.F., 'Alice in Warminster: Capability Gain or Increased Performance?', *RUSI Defence Systems*, 12, 1 (2009), pp. 40–3.

Owen, W.F., 'UK Platoon Weapons and the Weight Capability Myth', *RUSI Defence Systems*, 10, 90–3 (2007).

Peden, G., 'The Treasury and Defence of Empire', in G. Kennedy (ed.), *Imperial Defence: The Old World Order 1856–1956*, pp. 71–90, London: Routledge, 2008.

Phillips, G., 'Scapegoat Arm: Twentieth-Century Cavalry in Anglophone Historiography', *Journal of Military History*, 71, 1 (2007), pp. 37–74.

Picq, Ardant du, *Battle Studies*, trans. Colonel John N. Greely and Major Robert C. Cotton, New York: Macmillan, 1921.

Place, T.H., 'Lionel Wigram, Battle Drill and the British Army in the Second World War', *War in History*, 7, 4 (November 2000), pp. 442–62.

——— *Military Training in the British Army, 1940–1944: From Dunkirk to D-Day*, London: Frank Cass, 2000.

Popper, K., *Conjectures and Refutations: The Growth of Scientific Knowledge*, 5th edn, London: Routledge, 1991.

——— *The Logic of Scientific Discovery*, London: Hutchinson, 1959.

Porter, P., *The Global Village Myth: Distance, War and the Limits of Power*, London: Hurst, 2015.

Posen, B.R., *The Sources of Military Doctrine: France, Britain, and Germany between the World Wars*, Cornell Studies in Security Affairs, Ithaca: Cornell University Press, 1984.

Postan, M.M., D. Hay and J.D. Scott, *Design and Development of Weapons: Studies in Government and Industrial Organisation*, History of the Second World War, United Kingdom Civil Series, London: H.M. Stationery Office, 1964.

Prokosch, E., *The Technology of Killing: A Military and Political History of Anti-Personnel Weapons*, London: Zed Books, 1995.

Rappert, B., 'Prohibitions, Weapons and Controversy: Managing the Problems of Ordering', *Social Studies of Science*, 35, 2 (April 2005), pp. 211–40.

Ratcliffe, P., *Eye of the Storm*, London: Michael O'Mara, 2001.

Raw, S., *The Last Enfield: SA80; The Reluctant Rifle*, A Collector Grade Book, Cobourg, ON: Collector Grade Publications, 2003.

Rose, A., *The American Rifle: A Biography*, New York: Delta, 2009.

Rosen, S., *Winning the Next War: Innovation in the Modern Military*, Ithaca, NY: Cornell University Press, 1991.

Russell, J.A., *Innovation, Transformation and War*, Stanford: Stanford Universty Press, 2011.

Russell, S.M., *Soldier Perspectives on Small Arms in Combat*, Alexandria, VA: Center for Naval Analysis, 2006.

Sapolsky, H., *Polaris System Development: Bureaucratic and Programmatic Success in Government*, Cambridge, MA: Harvard University Press, 1972.

Seldon, A., *Churchill's Indian Summer: The Conservative Government, 1951–55*, London: Hodder & Stoughton, 1981.

Serena, C., *A Revolution in Military Adaptation: The US Army in the Iraq War*, Washington, DC: Georgetown University Press, 2011.

Shapiro, I., 'On the Second Edition of Lukes' *Third Face*', *Political Studies Review*, 4, 2 (2006), pp. 146–55.

Shapiro, M., *Discourse, Culture, Violence*, Abingdon: Routledge, 2012.

Simpson, E., *War from the Ground Up: 21st-Century Combat as Politics*, London: Hurst, 2013.

Singer, P.W., 'Corporate Warriors: The Rise of the Privatized Military Industry and Its Ramifications for International Security', *International Security*, 26, 3 (2001), pp. 186–220.

Smith, M.L.R. and D. Martin Jones, *The Political Impossibility of Modern Counterinsurgency: Strategic Problems, Puzzles and Paradoxes*, New York: Columbia University Press, 2015.

Smoler, F., 'The Secrets of the Soldiers Who Didn't Shoot', *American Heritage*, 40, 2 (1989), pp. 37–45.

Snow, C.P., *The Two Cultures: And a Second Look; An Expanded Version of the Two Cultures and the Scientific Revolution*, 2nd edn, Cambridge: Cambridge University Press, 1964.

Sorensen, K.H. and N. Levold, 'Tacit Networks, Heterogeneous Engineers, and Embodied Technology', *Science, Technology, and Human Values*, 17, 1 (1992), pp. 13–35.

Spiller, R.J., 'S.L.A. Marshall and the Ratio of Fire', *Journal of the Royal United Services Institute* (Winter 1988), pp. 63–71.

Stahl, R., *Militainment, Inc.: War, Media, and Popular Culture*, New York: Routledge, 2010.

Steeb, R., J. Matsumura, T.J. Herbert, J. Gordon IV and W.H. Horn, *Perspectives on the Battle of Wanat: Challenges Facing Small Unit Operations in Afghanistan*, Washington, DC: RAND, 2011.

Stockley, A.E., 'Recruit Shooting Standards', *British Army Review*, 62 (August 1979), pp. 70–1.

Storr, J., 'The Real Role of Small Arms in Combat', *RUSI Defence Systems* (June 2009), pp. 44–6.

Stouffer, S.A., *The American Soldier*, Princeton: Princeton University Press, 1949.

Strachey, J., *On the Prevention of War*, London: Macmillan, 1962.

Sweetman, J., *War and Administration: The Significance of the Crimean War for the British Army*, Edinburgh: Scottish Academic Press, 1984.

Swidler, A., 'Culture in Action: Symbols and Strategies', *American Sociological Review*, 51, 2 (April 1986), pp. 273–86.

Taylor, C., *Modern Social Imaginaries*, Durham, NC: Duke University Press, 2004.

Turse, N., *The Complex*, London: Faber & Faber, 2008.

Urban, M., *The Edge: Is the Military Dominance of the West Coming to an End?*, London: Little, Brown, 2015.

Van Creveld, M., *Fighting Power: German and US Army Performance, 1939–1945*, Westport, CT: Greenwood Press, 1982.

Walker, W. and P. Gummett, *Nationalism, Internationalism and the European Defence Market*, Paris: Institute for Security Studies, 1993.

Ward, M., 'Guns, Violence and Identity on the Trans-Appalachian American Frontier', in K. Jones, G. Macola and D. Welch (eds), *A Cultural History of Firearms in the Age of Empires*, pp. 17–37, Farnham: Ashgate, 2013.

Watson, B., 'Far Eastern Tour: The Experiences of the Canadian Infantry in Korea, 1950–53', PhD thesis, University of Victoria, 1999.

Welsh, I., *Mobilising Modernity: The Nuclear Moment*, London: Routledge, 2000.

Wigram, L., *(Infantry) Battle School (1941): A Detailed Description of the Evolution of Battle Drill Training in Its Early Stages*, Cambridge: John Bodsworth, 2005.

Wilson, T.N.F., 'The Role of the Infantry', *Journal of the Royal United Services Institute*, 89 (February 1944), pp. 1–9.

Winrow, A., 'The British Regular Mounted Infantry, 1880–1913: Cavalry of Poverty or Victorian Paradigm?', PhD thesis, University of Buckingham, 2014.

Woolgar, S., 'Configuring the User: The Case of Usability Trials', in J. Law (ed.), *Sociology of Monsters: Essays on Power, Technology and Domination*, London: Routledge, 1991.

Zuckerman, S., *From Apes to Warlords: An Autobiography (1904–1946)*, London: Collins, 1988.

INDEX

Netherlands: 126

Newton Harvey, E.: 86; definition of wounding power, 95

non-commissioned officer (NCOs): targeting of, 29

North American Regional Test and Evaluation Centre (NARTEC): 153

North Atlantic Treaty Organization (NATO): 2, 9, 12, 58, 104, 113, 130, 136, 153; Agency for Standardisation, 130; ammunition types used by, 28, 63, 78, 94, 115, 127, 150, 158; Archives, 8; Conference of National Armament Directors, 128–9; defence-industrial policy of, 3; establishment of (1949), 105; member states of, 7, 119–21, 124, 126, 128–9, 133, 156; Nominated Weapons List, 153; Standardisation Agreement (STANAG), 28, 56, 117–20, 126–8, 134, 136, 149; Standardisation Trials (1979–80), 128, 133, 136, 138, 140, 148, 161, 175; Standing Group on Standardisation, 105–6, 113; weaponry used by, 90, 115

Northern Ireland: Troubles, The (c. 1961–98), 131, 159

Norway: 129

O'Hanlon, Michael: 20–1; *Science of War, The*, 21

Oman: 54

Operation Enduring Freedom (2001–14), 11–12, 15, 56, 176; Battle of Wanat (2008), 99–100; casualties of, 99; Urgent Operational Requirement process, 155; weaponry used during, 166–7

Operation Iraqi Freedom (2003–11): 11, 56, 176; Urgent Operational

Requirement process, 155; weaponry used during, 48

Operations Research Office (ORO): 91–2, 175; concept of Pattern SALVO Weapon, 93; definition of wounding power, 95; Hitchman Report, 157; range characteristics identified by, 93; study of US infantry performance during Korean War (1950–1)(1952), 92

Owen, Mark: 169

Oxford University: Nuffield College, 7

Paget, General Sir Bernard: 40

Pakistan: North West Frontier, 32

Patton, General George S.: 34

Pederson, John: designer of .276" round, 35–6

Pederson .276" (ammunition): lethality of, 36

Pershing, General: view of effective use of rifles, 35

Persian Gulf War (1990–1): 20, 151; Operation Desert Storm (1991), 151; weaponry used during, 100, 118, 150

personal defence weapons (PDW): 176

pistols: 2, 28, 52, 80; automatic, 80

Popper, Karl: 78

Portugal: ammunition types used by, 28

Princeton Group: 86

Princeton University: faculty of, 85

private military contractors (PMCs): personnel, 167

Prokosch, Eric: criticisms of, 77, 179; observations of military weapon R&D activities, 20

Provisional Irish Republican Army (PIRA): 132, 159–60